PRINCIPLES
OF SURVEYING

Fourth Edition

PRINCIPLES
OF SURVEYING

CHARLES A. HERUBIN, PE
Hudson Valley Community College

PRENTICE HALL, Englewood Cliffs, New Jersey, 07632

Library of Congress Cataloging-in-Publication Data

Herubin, Charles A., (date)
  Principles of surveying/Charles A. Herubin.—4th ed.
    p. cm.
  Includes index.
  ISBN 0-13-717695-3
  1. Surveying. I. Title.
TA545.H47 1991
526.9—dc20

Editorial/production supervision and
  interior design: Maria McColligan
Cover design: Bruce Kenselaar
Manufacturing buyer: Paula Massenaro

The Publisher offers discounts on this book when ordered in bulk
quantities. For more information write:
Special Sales/College Marketing
Prentice-Hall, Inc.
College Technical and Reference Division
Englewood Cliffs, New Jersey 07632

Printed in the United States of America
10 9 8 7 6 5 4 3 2 1

ISBN 0-13-717695-3

Prentice-Hall International (UK) Limited, *London*
Prentice-Hall of Australia Pty. Limited, *Sydney*
Prentice-Hall Canada Inc., *Toronto*
Prentice-Hall Hispanoamericana, S.A., *Mexico*
Prentice-Hall of India Private Limited, *New Delhi*
Prentice-Hall of Japan, Inc., *Tokyo*
Simon & Schuster Asia Pte. Ltd., *Singapore*
Editora Prentice-Hall do Brasil, Ltda., *Rio de Janeiro*

CONTENTS

4 VERTICAL DISTANCES   **65**

5 MEASURING ANGLES   **95**

PREFACE

This book is intended for colleges and technical schools.

I believe that the purpose of a surveying course should be to impart basic knowledge plus training in the use of traditional surveying equipment— tape, transit, and level. The use of this equipment requires thorough understanding and much practice for success, while the use of more sophisticated equipment requires less understanding and less practice. Since the surveyor may be called on to use any type of equipment, it seems advisable that he or she be well versed in the use of traditional equipment and have sufficient knowledge of basic principles to learn quickly the use of more modern equipment. This fourth edition is written in accordance with this philosophy, as were the previous editions.

Nevertheless, discussions of laser, theodolites, electronic distance measuring, and total station are now included. In addition, the number and variety of problems at the ends of chapters have been increased. These are the most noticeable additions in the fourth edition. Also, because a surveying course provides so many opportunities to teach logical thinking and space visualization, I have again attempted to take advantage of such opportunities in the way I have worded my book.

The following procedures are employed throughout the book to enhance its clarity to the student reader:

1. Logical progression from easier topics to more difficult ones. The book is designed to be studied in order from start to finish.
2. Consistent use of terms as defined in this text.

3. Complete explanation of each operation as it is introduced, without trying to relate it to other operations not yet understood by the student.

4. Avoidance of reference to historical methods, involved theory, or lengthy introductions that, while providing smoothness of transition, I believe often hide from the student what it is he or she should master.

5. Explanation with words and diagrams of the way work is actually performed in the field, so that the reader with no previous experience can duplicate the operations.

6. Inclusion of enough theory so that understanding it will enable the student to reconstruct proper procedures rather than memorize them.

The book includes enough material for two semesters of instruction, including several lectures and one field period per week. It is not intended primarily as a reference book, but I think the sample field notes and descriptions of certain methods of operation will be valuable as references.

Charles A. Herubin, P.E.

PRINCIPLES
OF SURVEYING

1

INTRODUCTION

INSTRUCTIONAL OBJECTIVES

1. *Given several bearings and azimuths, the student should be able to convert bearings to azimuths and azimuths to bearings.*
2. *Given coordinates of a point in the first quadrant, the student should be able to compute bearing and distance from the origin to the point.*
3. *Given coordinates of two points in the first quadrant, the student should be able to compute bearing and distance of one from another.*
4. *Given the bearing and distance of a point from the origin, the student should be able to compute the coordinates of the point.*
5. *Given the bearing and distance of a second point from a point of known coordinates, the student should be able to determine the coordinates of the second point.*
6. *Given station and offset of a point, the student should be able to demonstrate by sketch that station and offset positions are actually coordinate positions.*
7. *Given stations and elevations of two points, the student should be able to determine the slope between them.*
8. *Given elevation of a point, and slope and distance to a second point, the student should be able to determine the elevation of the second point.*

No one can work long in the fields of civil engineering, architecture, or construction without becoming involved with surveying. Planning and design are based on the results of surveys, and construction is controlled by surveying. The persons employed in these fields will work with plots made from surveys and will build in accordance with surveyors' marked stakes. In addition, a high percentage of these employees will find themselves surveying occasionally, even though they are not primarily surveyors.

1.1 DEFINITIONS

Surveying. Surveying is the art of determining and establishing large measurements of the required accuracy in an economical way. Determining the positions of existing objects is called **preliminary surveying** since it is done as a first step so that a design may be prepared based on the existing situation. Establishing positions so that construction will conform to design drawings is called **construction stakeout** since it is done by positioning stakes at key points to control construction.

Plane Surveying. Plane surveying is that type of surveying in which the curvature of the earth is not considered. This book deals with plane surveying.

Geodetic Surveying. Geodetic surveying is that type of surveying in which the curvature of the earth is considered. This consideration is not necessary except for surveys of great length requiring a high degree of accuracy.

1.2 REASONS FOR SURVEYING

Surveying is the first step (except for early planning) in all but the smallest engineering or architectural projects and is often the last step before the finished construction is accepted by the owner.

A typical case follows to illustrate reasons for surveying. Notice that, in addition to the large number of persons involved in the surveying work, many more are involved to the extent that they must understand and depend on the surveying results.

1. A large company decides to build a new manufacturing plant. Its development department locates suitable land, and a purchase price per acre is agreed upon with the present owner.
2. A surveyor hired by the company determines the location of the property's boundaries and the area of the property. The surveyor prepares a map of the property boundary and a written legal description of the property boundary, which includes the area in acres. An agreement is

made to transfer ownership of the property, as defined by the legal description, from its present owner to the company, and the total price is computed according to the area determined by the surveyor.

3. A designer is selected by the company to prepare construction plans for the new plant. The designer hires a surveyor who obtains locations of all existing objects of importance to the designer, such as ground surface elevations; nearby roads, railroads, water lines, gas lines, electric lines, and sewers; streams, swamps, or ponds; and adjacent buildings. The surveyor then prepares a map called a *plot plan,* which the designer uses to situate the plant for economy of construction and efficiency of operation.

4. During the preliminary stages of design, a soil investigation is made to determine suitability of the soil to carry the weight of the plant buildings. Borings are made in the soil to extract samples of soil for examination and testing. Holes must be bored at the points where building weight on the soil is critical. A surveyor hired by the designer sets stakes at the points where the holes are to be bored.

5. When the design drawings are completed, an agreement is made between the company and a builder to construct the plant in accordance with the design drawings and specifications for a certain price. The designer inspects the work of the builder as it proceeds and must approve the work before the owner pays the builder.

    The builder must construct each building or other improvement in the proper location as shown on the plot plan on which the designer has superimposed the buildings and other improvements. A surveyor hired by the builder provides construction stakeout for the builder. The stakeout involves setting stakes and other controls on a continuing basis as various portions of the construction require them. A surveyor hired by the designer checks the stakeout before the builder uses it.

6. As a portion of the work is completed, the builder applies for payment for that portion. In many cases, such as construction of earth embankment or excavation, a surveyor hired by the designer measures the quantity of work completed, and the builder is paid for this quantity. A surveyor hired by the builder checks the measurements of the designer's surveyor.

7. Some variations from the original plans are usually required as the construction proceeds. As a result, the finished work does not agree exactly with the original drawings. A surveyor hired by the designer measures the final construction in the field, and the original drawings are then revised to show the construction "as built."

The surveyors referred to in this hypothetical case may be independent contractors specializing in surveying who are engaged for any one of the surveying projects; they may be surveyors who are full-time employees of the company, designer, or builder; or they may be employees who perform surveys in addition to other technical duties.

The group doing the field work is called a *survey party*, and the person in charge is called the *party chief.* Other members are named according to the equipment each one uses.

1.3 SURVEYING REFERENCE

Horizontal and Vertical

Surveying dimensions are vertical and horizontal distances, using the earth as a framework. The *vertical* direction is toward the center of the earth and is the direction of the pull of gravity. A string with a weight on it hangs in a vertical line because it is pulled toward the center of the earth by gravity. The horizontal direction is perpendicular to the vertical direction. Points on a vertical line have no horizontal displacement from each other. They are at different *elevations,* meaning at different distances from the center of the earth.

This system allows the relationship between points to be determined in the field or be described mathematically on the framework of vertical and horizontal directions. Geodetic computations are required in addition to field measurements to relate points a great distance apart.

A vertical line is called *plumb*, and a horizontal line is called *level.* Lines from two points on the earth's surface that intersect at the center of the earth (vertical lines) are not parallel. However, because of the great distance to the center of the earth compared with the relatively short distances involved in plane surveying, they are so nearly parallel that they are assumed to be so with no significant error. In addition, the perpendicular (horizontal line) to one vertical line is not perpendicular to any other vertical line; but, in plane surveying, a horizontal line is assumed to be perpendicular to all vertical lines. Again, no significant error is introduced by this assumption.

The *plumb bob* (shown in Fig. 1.1) is used to establish a vertical line, specifically to transfer a point from one elevation to a higher or lower elevation with no horizontal displacement. The weight of the bob on the string holds it plumb, and all points on the string are on a plumb line through the point of the bob.

The *hand level* (shown in Fig. 1.1) is used to establish a horizontal line of sight. It contains a glass vial in the shape of a circular arc that contains fluid. An air bubble in the fluid stays at the high point of the arc because of gravity no matter how the vial is moved. The vial is marked and the line of sight is arranged to be parallel with a line tangent to the circular vial at the mark. When the mark is at the center of the bubble, it is at the highest point of the arc. A tangent line at that point is horizontal, and a radius line

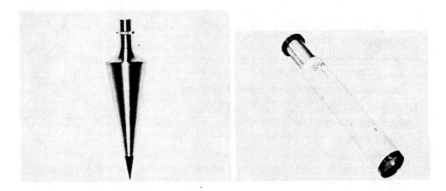

Figure 1.1   Plumb bob and hand level (*Courtesy of Keuffel and Esser Company*)

through the mark is vertical.   The line of sight is then horizontal.   See Fig. 1.2.

A flat curve of the vial (large circle) makes it difficult to center the mark in the bubble because a slight movement causes the bubble to move.   A sharper curve (smaller circle) has the opposite effect.   Therefore, the flatter the curve, that is the larger the radius, of the vial, the greater the leveling accuracy.

The hand level is held up to the eye by hand and is used for approximate work.   Other equipment of far greater accuracy is also aligned with level vials constructed according to the same principle.

Relationship Between Survey Sites

Measurements within one project must often be related to another project by a more extensive framework than that considered in the previous section.   Some examples follow:

1. A water supply project must be accurately related in elevation to the source of water that may be miles away.

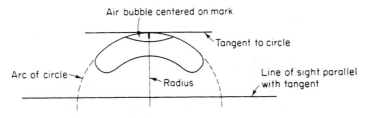

Figure 1.2   Level vial and line of sight

2. A rocket launching pad must be oriented with great accuracy in the proper direction to project a rocket to a particular location a great distance away.

3. A conveyor belt leading from one building to another must be manufactured at a distant plant to fit accurately between the buildings. The position of the buildings relative to each other must be known.

4. A new section of highway must be designed to run from one existing highway to another many miles away and must join each existing highway at the proper location.

Each example points out two or more objects whose locations must be known with reference to each other. If both are located with reference to a common system, their locations with respect to each other can be determined.

Sea Level and Elevation

Mean sea level is used as a reference, called a *datum*, for elevations. The mean or average sea level is designated as zero, and the elevation of any other point can then be designated by a number of feet vertically above sea level or vertically below sea level. The sea level datum is a curved surface parallel with the average surface of the earth. It is horizontal; therefore its use as a reference is consistent with the vertical and horizontal reference system.

A *bench mark* is a permanent or semipermanent point of known elevation that can be used to establish other elevations. Bench marks with elevations referred to mean sea level have been established throughout the United States by the *National Geodetic Survey*. This organization is a branch of the U.S. Department of Commerce and is responsible for establishing and maintaining survey control networks in the United States.

Some areas, such as cities or industrial plants, have all their elevations referenced to an assumed datum assigned to a bench mark in the immediate area. Therefore, all elevations in the area are referenced to the same datum and to each other, but not to elevations outside the area.

A small survey may be made from a datum assumed for that one project and unrelated to any other.

Elevations are often called *grades*, especially in the construction industry.

North Pole and Directions

The direction to the North Pole is used as a reference for horizontal directions from one point to another. True north determined by astronomical observation or magnetic north determined with a compass may be used. Any direction may be indicated as an azimuth or bearing.

An *azimuth* is the angle clockwise from the north direction to another direction. It varies from zero to 360°. The hands of a clock produce azimuths. A hand turning from 12 (north) to three has rotated 90°. The number three has an azimuth of 90° from the center, six has an azimuth of 180°, and nine has an azimuth of 270°.

The *bearing* to a point is based on the smallest angle that can be obtained by starting from a north or south direction and turning east or west to the direction of the point. A bearing angle cannot exceed 90°. A direction indicated by bearing consists of three parts including a starting direction, either north or south, followed by the angle from the starting direction and by the direction of that angle, either east or west.

In Fig. 1.3 the numbers adjacent to lines are the azimuths of those lines from the center, point A. The direction from A to B may be designated as Az 045° or a bearing of N45°E; the direction from A to C may be designated as Az 210° or a bearing of S30°W; and the direction from A to D may be designated as Az 330° or a bearing of N30°W.

An assumed north is often used as a reference when true directions are not needed. However, separate projects cannot be related to each other unless the north direction is the same for each.

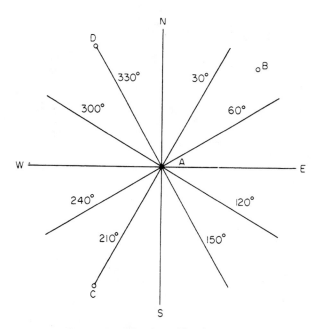

Figure 1.3   Azimuths and bearings

Coordinates

A *coordinate system* is used to locate points on a horizontal plane with reference to one point called the *origin*. Two axes, called x and y, are established through the origin. The y axis runs north and south. The x axis runs east and west. The previous discussion under North Pole and Directions applies to the location of these axes. Distances up (north) or to the right (east) are positive, and distances in the opposite directions are negative. All distances are horizontal.

A complete coordinate system is shown in Fig. 1.4. Usually only the first quadrant is used for surveying. The surveyor establishes the origin so that all points fall within the first quadrant. The y axis runs north from the origin and the x axis runs east from the origin. The use of negative directions is thus avoided.

Coordinate locations are given by two numbers, the first being the distance from the origin in the north direction (y coordinate) and the second being the distance from the origin in the east direction (x coordinate). In

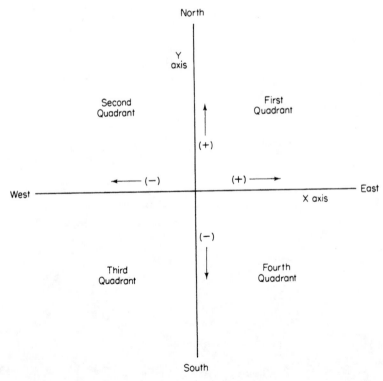

Figure 1.4 Coordinate system

Fig. 1.5, point A has coordinates (10, 20) and point B has coordinates (50, 45).

The coordinates describe a way of traveling from the origin to the point. If you start at the origin and travel the distance of the y coordinate in the north direction, then turn 90° to the right and travel the distance of the x coordinate in the east direction, you reach the desired point.

Within a coordinate system, any distance in a north-south direction is a *latitude* and any distance in an east-west direction is a *departure*. See Figs. 1.6 and 1.7. A line in any direction, whether or not it starts at the origin, may be considered to be made up of two components—its latitude and its departure. The latitude and departure may be considered as a way of traveling from one point to the other, as projections on the y axis and x axis, or as components of the line.

The bearing and distance to a point from the origin can be determine from the coordinates of the point. The direction of A from the origin can be found by using the triangle whose three sides are the line from the origin to the point, the north axis, and an east-west line. This triangle includes the unknown bearing angle. See Fig. 1.6.

The bearing angle can be found by trigonometry as follows:

$$\text{Bearing angle} = \arctan \frac{\text{departure}}{\text{latitude}}$$

$$\beta = \arctan \frac{20}{10}$$

$$\beta = 63°26'06''$$

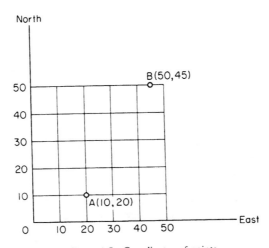

Figure 1.5 Coordinates of points

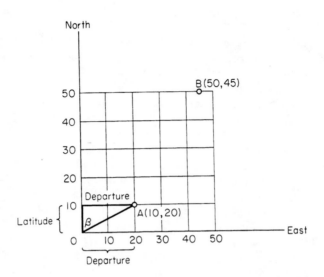

Figure 1.6   Method of determining bearing and distance to a point

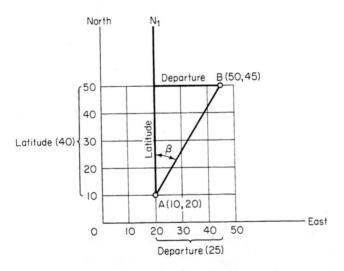

Figure 1.7   Relationship between coordinate points

The compass points can be determined by inspection: The bearing from origin to A is N 63°-26'-06" E.

The distance can also be found by trigonometry using the bearing angle and either the latitude or departure. In the triangle of Fig. 1.6 the side adjacent to the bearing angle is the latitude and the side opposite the bearing angle is the departure.

Therefore:

$$\text{Cos bearing angle} = \frac{\text{latitude (adjacent side)}}{\text{distance (hypotenuse)}}$$

and

$$\text{Sin bearing angle} = \frac{\text{departure (opposite side)}}{\text{distance (hypotenuse)}}$$

Therefore, the distance from the origin to a point is:

$$\text{Distance} = \frac{\text{latitude}}{\cos \beta}$$

or

$$\text{Distance} = \frac{\text{departure}}{\sin \beta}$$

The distance from the origin to point A is:

$$\text{Distance} = \frac{10}{0.4472135} = 22.36 \text{ ft}$$

or

$$\text{Distance} = \frac{20}{0.8944271} = 22.36 \text{ ft}$$

Distance can also be found by the Pythagorean theorem, which is that the square of the hypotenuse of a triangle is equal to the sum of the squares of the other two sides.   The distance from the origin to the point is the hypotenuse of the triangle with latitude and departure as the lengths of the other two sides.

Therefore:

$$\text{Distance}^2 = \text{latitude}^2 + \text{departure}^2$$

or

$$\text{Distance} = \sqrt{\text{lat}^2 + \text{dep}^2}$$

The distance from the origin to point A is:

$$\text{Distance} = \sqrt{10^2 + 20^2} = 22.36 \text{ ft}$$

The direction and distance between points A and B can be found once their coordinates are known using the methods that were used to find bearing and distance to a point from the origin.   The projection of the line $\overline{AB}$ on the y axis is the latitude of $\overline{AB}$, and the projection on the x axis is the departure. See Fig. 1.7. The two points are related to each other the same as they would be if the origin were moved to A. Direction and distance are determined as if the origin is at A.

The direction of $\overline{AB}$ can be found by trigonometry as follows:

$$\text{Angle } N_1AB \text{ (bearing angle)} = \arctan \frac{\text{departure}}{\text{latitude}}$$

The latitude of $\overline{AB}$ equals the difference between the north coordinate of B and the north coordinate of A, and the departure of $\overline{AB}$ equals the difference between their east coordinates. Therefore:

$$\beta = \arctan \frac{25}{40} = \arctan 0.625$$

$$\beta = 32°\text{-}00'\text{-}19''$$

The bearing from A to B is N32°-00'-19" E and from B to A it is S32°-00'-19"W. The second one is called the *back bearing* of the first. The back bearing of any bearing is the opposite direction and consists of the same bearing angle and opposite compass points. Therefore, each one is the back bearing of the other.

The distance can also be found by trigonometry using the bearing angle and either the latitude or departure. In the triangle of Fig. 1.7, the hypotenuse is $\overline{AB}$, the side adjacent to the bearing angle is the latitude of $\overline{AB}$, and the side opposite the bearing angle is the departure of $\overline{AB}$.

$$\text{Cos bearing angle} = \frac{\text{latitude (adjacent side)}}{\overline{AB} \text{ (hypotenuse)}}$$

and

$$\text{Sin bearing angle} = \frac{\text{departure (opposite side)}}{\overline{AB} \text{ (hypotenuse)}}$$

Therefore, $\overline{AB}$ equals latitude divided by the cos of the bearing angle or departure divided by the sin of the bearing angle.

$$\overline{AB} \text{ or } \frac{\text{lat}}{\cos \beta}$$

or

$$\overline{AB} = \frac{\text{dep}}{\sin \beta}$$

For Fig. 1.7:

$$\overline{AB} = \frac{40}{0.8479983} = 47.17 \text{ ft}$$

or

$$\overline{AB} = \frac{25}{0.5299989} = 47.17 \text{ ft}$$

The distance $\overline{AB}$ can be found by the Pythagorean theorem

$$\overline{AB}^2 = x^2 + y^2$$

$$\overline{AB}^2 = \text{latitude}^2 + \text{departure}^2$$

$$\overline{AB}^2 = (50\text{-}10)^2 + (45\text{-}20)^2$$

$$\overline{AB} = \sqrt{40^2 + 25^2}$$

$$\overline{AB} = 47.17 \text{ ft}$$

Coordinates can be computed for a point if the bearing and distance from the origin to the point are known. The same sine and cosine formulas are used with the latitude and departure being the unknown quantities. The latitude and departure are numerically equal to the coordinates when the line starts at the origin. Therefore, as indicated in Fig. 1.8:

$$\text{Latitude (N coordinate)} = \text{distance} \times \cos \beta$$

and

$$\text{Departure (E coordinate)} = \text{distance} \times \sin \beta$$

Therefore,

$$\text{N coordinate} = 207.93 \cos 52°13'00''$$

$$= 207.93 \times 0.6126771 = 127.39$$

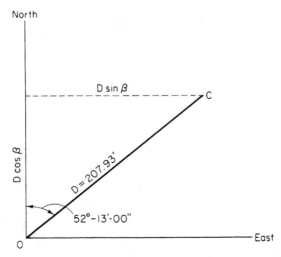

Figure 1.8 Computation of coordinates

and

$$\text{E coordinate} = 207.93 \sin 52°13'00''$$

$$= 207.93 \times 0.7903332 = 164.33$$

The coordinates of a point can also be computed when its bearing and distance are known from a point having coordinates other than (0,0). The bearing and distance are converted to latitude and departure, which are added algebraically to the known coordinates to get the new coordinates. See Fig. 1.9 for application.

For point E:

$$\text{North coordinate} = \text{north coordinate of } D + \text{distance} \times \cos \beta$$

and

$$\text{East coordinate} = \text{east coordinate of } D + \text{distance} \times \sin \beta$$

Therefore:

$$\text{N coordinate} = 108.35 + 59.24 \times \cos 18°11'00''$$

$$= 108.35 + 59.24 \times 0.9500628 = 164.63$$

and

$$\text{E coordinate} = 136.84 + 59.24 \times \sin 18°11'00''$$

$$= 136.84 + 59.24 \times 0.3120585 = 155.33$$

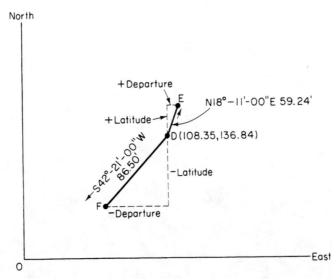

Figure 1.9 Finding coordinates of points E and F when coordinates of point D and bearing and distance from D are given

For point *F*:

North coordinate = north coordinate of *D* − distance × cos β

and

East coordinate = east coordinate of *D* − distance × sin β

Therefore,

N coordinate = 108.35 − 86.50 × cos 42°21′00″

= 108.35 − 86.50 × 0.7390435 = 44.42

and

E coordinate = 136.84 − 86.50 × sin 42°21′00″

= 136.84 − 86.50 × 0.6736577 = 78.57

Stationing

Stationing is a variation of the coordinate method used for long narrow projects such as pipelines and highways. A line that may be straight or have angles or curves in it is established from an origin of zero designated as station 0 + 00. Points on the line are designated by stations 100-ft apart horizontally as measured along the line whether straight or not. Station 1 + 00 is 100 ft from the origin, station 2 + 00 is 200 ft from the origin, and so on. Points on the line between stations are called *plus stations* or *plusses* and are designated to the hundredth of a foot; e.g., station 1 + 20.00 or station 2 + 55.29. Points not on the line are designated by station and plus and by offset distance in a direction perpendicular to the line right or left when looking forward or "up station." Examples are shown in Fig. 1.10.

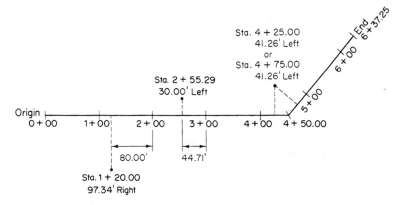

Figure 1.10   Locations by station and offset

The key to calculating with stations is to line up the decimal points. The calculation of distance between two stations and the adding or subtracting of a distance to or from a station are performed as follows:

Distance between Sta. 79 + 17.42 and 132 + 68.93:

$$\begin{array}{r} 132 + 68.93 \\ -79 + 17.42 \\ \hline 53 + 51.51 \end{array} = 5,351.51 \text{ ft} \qquad \text{or} \qquad \begin{array}{r} 13,268.93 \text{ ft} \\ -7,917.42 \text{ ft} \\ \hline 5,351.51 \text{ ft} \end{array}$$

Station of a point 6490.36 ft up station from Sta. 3 + 42.16:

$$\begin{array}{r} 3 + 42.16 \\ +64 + 90.36 \\ \hline \text{Sta.} \qquad 68 + 32.52 \end{array}$$

Station of a point 37.28 ft down station from Sta. 84 + 17.22:

$$\begin{array}{r} 84 + 17.22 \\ - \qquad\quad 37.28 \\ \hline 83 + 79.94 \end{array}$$

Slopes

Slope is a measure of how much a line varies from a horizontal line. It is the tangent of the angle between the sloping line and a horizontal line, expressed as a decimal or percent.   The slope between two points of known location is found by dividing the vertical distance between the points by the horizontal distance between them.   A line sloping up has a plus slope, and one sloping down has a minus slope.   If the line is stationed, the direction of slope is toward the higher numbered stations.   See Fig. 1.11.

Slope may be considered a rate of change in grade (elevation) because it describes how much the grade or elevation changes in any horizontal distance.   It is a ratio of change in elevation per unit length.   Although it is

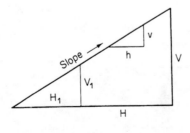

$$\text{Slope} = \frac{V}{H} = \frac{v}{h} = \frac{V_1}{H_1}$$

Figure 1.11   Horizontal, vertical, and sloping lines

written without units, it has units of foot change in elevation per horizontal foot, yard change per horizontal yard, meter per meter, or any other unit of linear measurement divided by the same unit. Accordingly, slope is often called *rate of grade*, or simply *grade*, in which case it may be confused with grade meaning "elevation."

If a point at station 0 + 50 has an elevation of 784.36 and a point at station 4 + 00 has an elevation of 801.68, the slope is determined this way:

$$\text{Slope} = \frac{\text{vertical distance}}{\text{horizontal distance}}$$

$$\text{Vertical distance} = 801.68 - 784.36 = 17.32 \text{ ft}$$

$$\text{Horizontal distance} = 400 - 50 = 350 \text{ ft}$$

$$\text{Slope} = \frac{17.32}{350} = +0.0495 \text{ or } + 4.95\%$$

The slope is positive because the line rises in the direction of the stationing. If the surface does not rise in a straight line (the case with natural ground), the answer is the average slope between the two points.

If a line slopes -0.0013 or -0.13 percent from station 6 + 17.39 to station 8 + 29.76, the difference in elevation between the two points is determined this way.

$$\text{Slope} = \frac{\text{vertical distance}}{\text{horizontal distance}}$$

Therefore:

$$\text{Vertical distance} = \text{horizontal distance} \times \text{slope}$$

$$\text{Horizontal distance} = 829.76 - 617.39 = 212.37$$

$$\text{Vertical distance} = 212.37 \times 0.0013 = 0.28 \text{ ft}$$

The elevation at station 8 + 29.76 is below that at station 6 + 17.39 because the slope is negative. If the elevation at either location is known, the elevation at the other location can be determined by adding or subtracting the vertical distance from the known elevation. If the elevation at station 6 + 17.39 is 1856.35, the elevation at 8 + 29.76 is 1856.35 − 0.28 = 1856.07.

1.4 NOTEKEEPING

Measurements and sketches are entered in pencil or ink that will not run in the rain in a field notebook as the work progresses. Measurements should be entered as soon as they are made in order to lessen the chance of making a mistake.   The notebook is a field record, and ordinarily no change or addition should be made after the party has left the field.   A field entry that must be changed in the office should be changed in such a way that the original can still be read and there is a clear indication that the change is an office change.   Colored pencil may be used for an office change or addition; otherwise, a note should be added stating that the correction was made in the office.

For routine field work the party chief is often responsible to a supervisor who spends very little or no time at the field site but reviews the field notes. Notes must therefore indicate to the supervisor that the field work was properly performed.

Notes must be complete, legible, self-explanatory, logically arranged, and in many cases, arranged according to recognized practice.   The reasons are that the notes may be used by another surveyor years later; they may be used by office personnel who have not seen the field site; and they may be used as proof of field conditions in negotiations, in arbitration, or in a court of law.   In any of these cases, if members of the field crew are unavailable, the notes must speak for them.

Because of the possibility that field notes may become court evidence, many surveyors do not allow erasing in the field book.   An erasure could cause suspicion that the field record was altered after the field work was finished.   Instead, mistakes are crossed out in the field in such a manner that they can still be read, and the correct entry is made while still in the field.

The following information must be included in the field book for each day:

1. Name of project (often the owner's name) and location.
2. Type of surveying (e.g., leveling or building stakeout).
3. Date.
4. Weather conditions, with special attention to conditions that can affect the accuracy of the type of work being done.
5. Names or initials of party members and their positions in the party.
6. Identification of equipment used.

This information is helpful when a mistake is made in the field and is not discovered until field work is finished.   Often, the mistake can be traced to weather conditions or faulty equipment, and a correction can be made without redoing all the field work.

An index should be kept at the front of each book showing the name of each project and its page number.   Each page, consisting of the two facing sheets, should be numbered, and a new page should be used for a new date. The note keeper should use a straightedge for sketches and should not crowd notes.

PROBLEMS

1. Convert the following bearings to azimuths:

    (a) N 24° E   (g) N 23°15'07" W
    (b) S 34° E   (h) N 29°07'22" E
    (c) S 19° W   (i) N 78°18'46" W
    (d) S 27°31'20" E   (j) S 52°59'11" E
    (e) S 84°17'30" E   (k) S 39°06'02" W
    (f) S 18°56'15" E   (l) S 88°11'28" W

2. Convert the following azimuths to bearings:

    (a) 073°   (g) 181°19'00"
    (b) 136°   (h) 312°27'40"
    (c) 201°   (i) 008°17'52"
    (d) 277°18'30"   (j) 197°08'17"
    (e) 294°10'02"   (k) 064°58'09"
    (f) 099°42'13"   (l) 172°11'24"

3. Determine coordinates of points described here:

	Bearing from origin	*Distance*
(a)	N 60° E	300.00 ft
(b)	S 41° E	295.63 ft
(c)	S 73° W	112.45 ft
(d)	N 34°11'20" W	200.00 ft
(e)	N 11°37'10" E	164.22 ft
(f)	S 82°58'43" E	2360.42 ft
(g)	S 52°21'17" W	3845.95 ft
(h)	N 22°13'40" W	95.11 ft

4. Determine bearing and distance from origin for points with coordinates listed here:

    (a) (200.00, 300.00)   (f) (35.80, −13.76)
    (b) (112.20, 90.00)   (g) (−220.85, −296.22)
    (c) (196.42, 484.91)   (h) (−195.13, −411.28)
    (d) (7364.28, 1008.50)   (i) (−3408.29, 698.37)
    (e) (45.33, 82.67)   (j) (29.91, −180.64)

5. In each case, compute bearing and distance of the second point from the first by trigonometry. All points are in the first quadrant.

    (a) (800.00, 1000.00)   (1000.00, 918.20)
    (b) (1100.00, 10000.00)   (1196.80, 1034.52)
    (c) (1090.99, 876.83)   (1175.22, 1053.01)
    (d) (1333.37, 1319.84)   (1408.48, 1035.11)
    (e) (362.24, 420.19)   (592.84, 111.45)
    (f) (219.91, 186.42)   (108.13, 24.26)
    (g) (864.22, 568.14)   (228.96, 638.28)
    (h) (246.34, 482.14)   (108.21, 409.17)

6. In each case, coordinates of a point are given, and bearing and distance to a second point are given. Determine the coordinates of the second point:

    (a) (1000.00, 1000.00); N 25° E; 1000.00 ft
    (b) (1000.00, 1000.00); N 12° E; 188.92 ft

(c) (974.89, 725.58); N 82°58'50" E; 275.47 ft
(d) (1175.43, 880.92); N 84°55'20" W; 171.79 ft
(e) (708.35, 420.21); S 25°18'37" E; 237.50 ft
(f) (140.29, 207.55); S 82°20'20" W; 98.36 ft
(g) (90.00, 250.50); S 45°22'13" E; 85.50 ft
(h) (334.91, 208.15); S 72°20'52" W 298.76 ft

7. What is the distance from station 7 + 31.28 to the following points?
   (a) sta. 8 + 79.91   (d) sta. 17 + 13.33
   (b) sta. 35 + 17.01   (e) sta. 46 + 11.19
   (c) sta. 0 + 18.43   (f) sta. 6 + 92.17

8. What is the distance from station 16 + 41.29 to the following points?
   (a) sta. 16 + 98.34, 42.34 ft right
   (b) sta. 14 + 87.72, 84.26 ft left
   (c) sta. 36 + 11.29, 17.00 ft left
   (d) sta. 10 + 80.00, 90.50 ft right

9. A line bears due east. What are the bearing and distance from station 6 + 54.31 to the following points?
   (a) sta. 7 + 91.12, 57.31 ft left
   (b) sta. 6 + 13.18, 67.45 ft left
   (c) sta. 5 + 28.59, 59.11 ft right
   (d) sta. 8 + 07.66, 61.47 ft right

10. A line runs from south to north. What are bearing and distance from station 4 + 10.00, 18.00 ft right to the following points?
    (a) sta. 5 + 63.17, 11.00 ft right
    (b) sta. 2 + 60.00, 37.66 ft left
    (c) sta. 6 + 18.91, 13.97 ft left
    (d) sta. 3 + 06.78, 56.00 ft right

11. Determine slope between two points defined by the following stations and elevations:

| | Beginning | | End | |
	Station	Elevation	Station	Elevation
(a)	0 + 00	2310.00	4 + 00	2318.00
(b)	1 + 50	242.00	6 + 00	260.40
(c)	2 + 37.62	91.42	18 + 06.28	117.91
(d)	3 + 22.86	3348.17	6 + 95.20	3449.82
(e)	7 + 17.45	150.28	2 + 48.62	160.58
(f)	4 + 83.36	1185.32	1 + 29.19	1183.98
(g)	5 + 50.29	260.45	7 + 88.11	253.26
(h)	8 + 30.25	1860.27	11 + 48.67	1836.48

12. Slope of line and elevation at one point are given. Determine elevation at second point.

	Slope	Station	Elevation	Second Station
(a)	0.0300	1 + 00	1740.00	3 + 50
(b)	0.0850	2 + 30	1126.48	8 + 20
(c)	-0.00021	3 + 85.16	140.21	9 + 34.67
(d)	-6.42%	11 + 19.48	785.41	13 + 07.42

| (e) | 28.28% | 40 + 82.18 | 626.83 | 36 + 22.89 |
| (f) | 3.48% | 1 + 82.55 | 518.74 | 0 + 11.78 |

13. What is the horizontal distance required to reach the second elevation from the first elevation at the given slope?

	First elevation	Second elevation	Slope
(a)	1100.00	1250.00	2.00%
(b)	1120.20	1110.50	−0.0200
(c)	450.36	458.22	0.0615
(d)	620.71	618.35	−0.42%
(e)	584.12	588.93	0.1280
(f)	791.26	783.47	−1.21%

2

ACCURACY AND ERROR

INSTRUCTIONAL OBJECTIVES

1. *Given an explanation of a source of error, the student should be able to decide whether it is systematic or accidental.*
2. *Given the magnitude of an accidental error and the number of operations, the student should be able to determine probable total error.*
3. *Given total horizontal and vertical errors and length of circuit for each, the student should be able to determine orders and classes of accuracy.*

Accurate surveying requires that errors be controlled, not eliminated. In fact, they cannot be eliminated. One mark of a skilled surveyor is understanding this. Errors must be controlled sufficiently to obtain the necessary accuracy, but the competent surveyor does not waste time in trying to eliminate errors nor in reducing errors unnecessarily.

2.1 DEFINITIONS

Errors.   Errors are inaccuracies in measurements caused by the type of equipment used or by the way in which the equipment is used.

Systematic Errors.   Systematic errors are errors that occur in the same direction, thereby tending to accumulate so that the total error increases proportionally as the number of measurements increases.

Accidental Errors.   Accidental errors are errors that occur randomly in either direction, thereby tending to cancel one another so that, although the total error does increase as the number of measurements increases, the total error becomes proportionally less when compared with the number of measurements, and the accuracy becomes greater as the number of measurements increases.

Note: It is not always possible to identify each error as systematic or accidental, although most fall under one type or the other.

Mistakes.   Mistakes are inaccuracies in measurements occurring because some part of the surveying operation is performed improperly.

Total Error.   Total error is the sum of the inaccuracies in a completed job.   Since inaccuracies are either positive or negative, it is an algebraic sum.

Surveying accuracy is determined by completing a circuit to the point of beginning (or another known point).   The **error of closure** is the difference between the actual position of the finishing point (either horizontally or vertically) and the location of the same point determined mathematically as a result of the circuit.

Accuracy.   Accuracy is the ratio of error of closure to the total distance of the survey or, in some cases, to the square root of the total distance.

Order of Accuracy.   The order of accuracy is the range of accuracy acceptable for particular surveys.   In some cases this range is divided into higher and lower categories called *Class I* and *Class II*.

2.2 ACCURACY AND SPEED

Accuracy is of primary importance in surveying—not maximum accuracy but accuracy of the required order.   Speed is also important.   However, achieving proper accuracy must always take precedence over working at the utmost speed.

Delay causes the surveying work to be more expensive; and design, construction, or transfer of ownership of land may be delayed at extra expense to those waiting for and depending on the survey for information.

However, by hurrying, the survey party may allow excessive total error, make a mistake, or forget to perform some part of the work.   A return visit to the field may then be required, which makes the surveying work more expensive.   If design, construction, or property transfer has proceeded based on inaccurate or incomplete surveying information, redesign or reconstruction may be required at great expense, or a lawsuit may be initiated because of an erroneous property transfer.   The surveyor will certainly be named a party to such a suit. Obviously, excessive haste can have more disastrous results than excessive effort to achieve high accuracy.

2.3 ERRORS AND MISTAKES

To control errors so that the total error is not excessive, sources of error must be understood and methods and equipment must be chosen that will reduce the total errors to allowable levels without wasting time. Sources of error are instrumental, personal (physical abilities and concentration of the surveyor), and natural (weather and ground conditions).

Size of total error depends on the precision of the equipment and the way in which the equipment is used. More precise equipment often requires more time to operate and normally costs more to buy or rent. More accurate field methods nearly always require more time. On the other hand, extremely precise equipment is available that takes less time for certain operations. In this case, the additional cost of expensive equipment must be weighed against the cost of extra time spent using less expensive equipment. With identical equipment and methods, some surveyors consistently achieve more accurate results than others, and all achieve poorer results with adverse weather conditions.

Systematic errors are generally caused by imperfections in the manufacturing of equipment—not mistakes in the manufacturing process but an inability to achieve absolute perfection. Equipment may also cause systematic errors because it is damaged or out of adjustment. Systematic errors may sometimes be due to field methods or weather conditions. Since systematic errors build up to larger values as the work progresses, some means must be taken to compensate for them whenever they can be identified and their magnitude determined.

Accidental errors are due to field methods and conditions of the work site. They are small, partially compensating errors that cannot be eliminated but can be reduced by choice of field methods.

Accidental errors tend to accumulate in proportion to the square root of the number of possibilities for their occurrence. Mathematically:

$$\frac{E_n}{E_1} = \frac{\sqrt{n}}{\sqrt{1}}$$

where

$$E_n = \text{error in } n \text{ measurements}$$

$$E_1 = \text{error in 1 measurement}$$

$$n = \text{number of measurements}$$

and

$$E_n = \pm E_1 \sqrt{n}$$

Example:
A tape measurement can be made to the nearest 0.01'. Therefore, the maximum probable error in one operation, E_1, is $\pm 0.005'$. If the taping operation is repeated 36 times in measuring a line,* the maximum probable total error is found as follows:

$$E_n = E_1 \sqrt{n}$$

where

$$n = 36$$

$$E_n = 0.005' \times 6$$

$$= \pm 0.03'$$

Note that the direction of the probable error is not known, and, therefore, no corrective measure can be taken.

Mistakes cannot be permitted. To avoid mistakes, proper field methods must be made habitual. These methods must include checks of all steps. Succeeding chapters will explain the usual methods and checks. When a mistake is not caught in the field, it usually requires a return trip to the field to correct it.

2.4 ORDER OF ACCURACY

Horizontal accuracy is computed by dividing the error of closure by the total measured distance of the survey; for example:

$$\text{Accuracy} = \frac{0.43' \text{ (error of closure)}}{7053.62' \text{ (total measured distance)}}$$

$$= \frac{1}{16,400} \text{ or } 1{:}16{,}400$$

Solve this way:

$$\frac{0.43'}{7053.62'} = \frac{1}{x}$$

$$x = \frac{7053.62'}{0.43'} \text{ or } 16{,}403.77, \text{ say } 16{,}400$$

*The beginning and end of the line are such a distance apart that the measuring tape must be stretched step by step 36 times to cover the distance.

Accuracy usually need not be computed exactly and is properly shown as a ratio with one as the first number or numerator. Allowable accuracies prepared by the Federal Geodetic Control Committee are shown in Table 2.1. The listed horizontal accuracies are minimum acceptable accuracies for each category.

Remember, accuracy is a ratio with one as the first number or numerator. A ratio (or fraction) with a small denominator is a larger number than a ratio (or fraction) with a larger denominator. A larger number indicates larger error and, therefore, less accuracy. An accuracy with a larger denominator than the one listed is, therefore, satisfactory for that category because it is more accurate than necessary.

The accuracy of 1:16,400 falls within the limits of third-order class I accuracy. It is more accurate than the minimum of 1:10,000 required for third-order class I but less accurate than the minimum of 1:20,000 required for second-order class II. It is also satisfactory for third-order class II but could qualify with a much lower accuracy.

If systematic errors are eliminated and no mistakes are made, accuracy will increase as the length of the survey increases. The reason for this is that the accidental errors (the only ones present) increase as the square root of the number of measurements (assumed to be proportional to total distance), which is a lower rate than the increase in total distance. Therefore, error of closure (numerator) increases at a lower rate than total distance (denominator), making the fraction smaller as the total distance increases.

Allowable vertical error of closure is also shown in Table 2.1. Note that the formulas for vertical control accuracy indicate maximum allowable error, not accuracy. The allowable error is equal to a constant multiplied by the square root of the distance between points in kilometers.

The formulas are of the same form as the formula for probable total error. That formula, $E_n = \pm E_1 \sqrt{n}$, states that the probable total error after more than one operation is the probable error in one operation multiplied by the square root of the number of operations. The formulas for allowable vertical error state that the allowable total error over a long distance is equal to the allowable error in one kilometer multiplied by the square root of the number of kilometers in the long distance. This method agrees mathematically with the method for probable total error if the number of operations is assumed to be proportional to the distance between points. In general, this is the case.

Assume that a survey is required to be completed with second-order class II accuracy. If the distance between points is 4 kilometers, the maximum error of closure that is acceptable is:

$$1.3 \text{ mm} \times \sqrt{4} = 2.6 \text{ mm}$$

If the error of closure is 2.6 mm or less, the survey is accurate enough to qualify as second-order class II work.

TABLE 2.1 Standards of Accuracy by the Federal Geodetic Control Committee

STANDARDS FOR THE CLASSIFICATION OF GEODETIC CONTROL AND PRINCIPAL RECOMMENDED USES

HORIZONTAL CONTROL

Classification	First-Order	Second-Order		Third-Order	
		Class I	Class II	Class I	Class II
Relative accuracy between directly connected adjacent points (at least)	1 part in 100,000	1 part in 50,000	1 part in 20,000	1 part in 10,000	1 part in 5,000
Recommended uses	Primary National Network. Metropolitan Area Surveys. Scientific studies.	Area control that strengthens the National Network. Subsidiary metropolitan control.	Area control that contributes to, but is supplemental to, the National Network.	General control surveys referenced to the National Network. Local control surveys.	

VERTICAL CONTROL

Classification	First-Order		Second-Order		Third-Order
	Class I	Class II	Class I	Class II	
Relative accuracy between directly connected points or benchmarks (standard error)	$0.5 \text{ mm } \sqrt{K}$	$0.7 \text{ mm } \sqrt{K}$	$1.0 \text{ mm } \sqrt{K}$	$1.3 \text{ mm } \sqrt{K}$	$2.0 \text{ mm } \sqrt{K}$

(K is the distance in kilometers between points.)

Classification	First-Order		Second-Order		Third-Order
Recommended uses	Basic framework of the National Network and metropolitan area control. Regional crustal movement studies. Extensive engineering projects. Support for subsidiary surveys.		Secondary framework of the National Network and metropolitan area control. Local crustal movement studies. Large engineering projects. Tidal boundary reference. Support for lower order surveys.	Densification within the National Network. Rapid subsidence studies. Local engineering projects. Topographic mapping.	Small-scale topographic mapping. Establishing gradients in mountainous areas. Small engineering projects. May or may not be adjusted to the National Network.

TABLE 2.1 (cont.)

STANDARDS OF ACCURACY AND GENERAL SPECIFICATIONS FOR THIRD-ORDER WORK

	TRAVERSE		VERTICAL CONTROL	
	Class I	Class II		
Recommended spacing of principal stations	Seldom less than 0.1 km in tertiary surveys in metropolitan area surveys. As required for other surveys.		*Principal uses* Minimum standards; higher accuracies may be used for special purposes.	Miscellaneous local control; may not be adjusted to the National Network. Small engineering projects. Small-scale topo. mapping. Drainage studies establishment in mountainous areas.
Horizontal directions or angles			*Recommended spacing of lines*	
Instrument	1".0	1".0	National Network	As needed
Number of observations	4	2	Metropolitan control	As needed
Rejection limit from mean	5"	5"	Other purposes	As needed
Length measurements			*Spacing of marks along lines*	
Standard error	1 part in 60,000	1 part in 30,000	Gravity requirement	Not more than 3 km

Reciprocal vertical angle observations

Number of and spread between observations.	2 D/R–10"	2 D/R–20"
Number of stations between known elevations.	10–15	15–20

Astro azimuths

Number of courses between azimuth checks.	20–25	30–40
No. of obs/night.	8	4
No. of nights.	1	1
Standard error.	3".0	8".0
Azimuth closure at azimuth check point not to exceed.	3".0 per station or 10" $\sqrt{N}$. Metropolitan area surveys seldom to exceed 6" per station or 15" $\sqrt{N}$	8" per station or 30" $\sqrt{N}$

Position closure after azimuth adjustment	0.4 m $\sqrt{K}$ or 1:10,000	0.8 m $\sqrt{K}$ or 1:5,000

Instrument standards — Geodetic levels and rods

Field procedures	
Section length.	Double- or single-run
Maximum length of sight.	1 to 3 km for double-run / 90 m

Field procedures	
Max. difference in lengths Forward & backward sights per setup	
per section (cumulative)	10 m
	10 m
Max. length of line between connections	25 km double-run / 10 km single-run

Maximum closures	
Section; fwd. and bkwd.	12 mm $\sqrt{K}$
Loop or line.	12 mm $\sqrt{K}$

Note: 12 mm $\sqrt{K}$ = 0.04'

The required accuracy must be known before a surveying project can be carried out properly. In many cases, the agreement to provide surveying services specifies an order of accuracy. In other cases, the surveyor might decide how accurately to place stakes for construction from his or her own knowledge of construction methods. In each case, the required accuracy will indicate which equipment to use and what procedure to follow. The greater the accuracy required, the higher the precision of the equipment and the more time-consuming and painstaking the procedures must be to reduce errors. Specific examples are given in succeeding chapters.

Being within the allowable error is not all that is required for a survey to qualify for a certain order of accuracy. Equipment and methods that are sufficiently precise must be used, and the field party must have sufficient experience to perform with that precision. It is possible at times to achieve an apparent accuracy that is beyond the capabilities of the equipment or methods and that is achieved only through lucky cancellation of one error by another. In these cases, the fact that the survey ends very close to the starting point does not prove that all points between start and finish are located that accurately.

The Federal Geodetic Control Committee also publishes specifications detailing the precision of equipment and methods for each order and class of accuracy. Their specifications for third-order traverses and third-order vertical control are included in Table 2.1.

2.5 ERROR IN LOCATING A POINT

In the field, objects are located in the horizontal position by angles or distances, or a combination of both. Any combination that can be used to plot a point on paper with compass and protractor can be used in the field. The location will not be mathematically exact, either on paper or in the field. The surveyor should appreciate the relative accuracy of the combinations of angles and distances that can be used.

Method 1. A point can be located in relation to one other point by a direction and a distance.

Method 2. A point can be located in relation to two other points by a direction from each of the two points or by a distance from each of the two points.

Method 3. A point can be located in relation to two other points by a direction from one point and a distance from the other point.

Any of the preceding methods will result in an intersection of two lines. While this is sufficient to locate a point, in practice a third line is often established for greater reliability. The least probable error will be obtained in any case if the angle between intersecting lines is 90°.   The more the angle varies from 90°, the greater the probable error becomes.

Examples are shown in Figs. 2.1 and 2.2.   Known points are shown as solid dots, and points being located are shown as circles.   Lines used to locate points are shown in heavy weight.

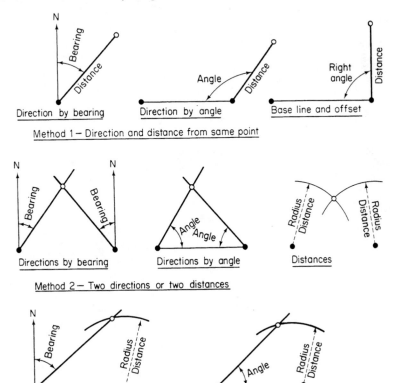

Figure 2.1   Methods of locating a point

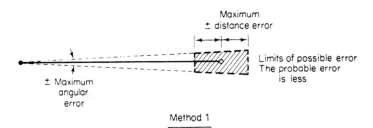

Figure 2.2   Relative accuracy of the methods

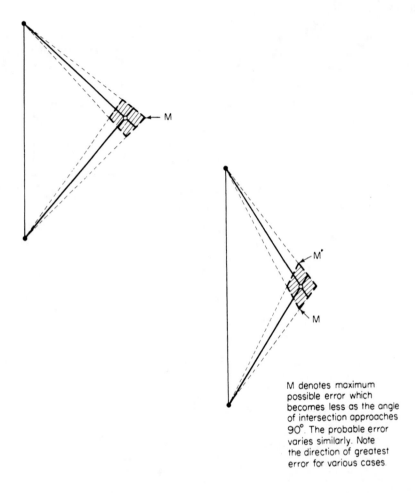

M denotes maximum
possible error which
becomes less as the angle
of intersection approaches
90°. The probable error
varies similarly. Note
the direction of greatest
error for various cases.

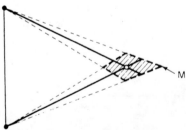

Method 2 — Directions from two points

Figure 2.2 (cont.)   Relative accuracy of the methods

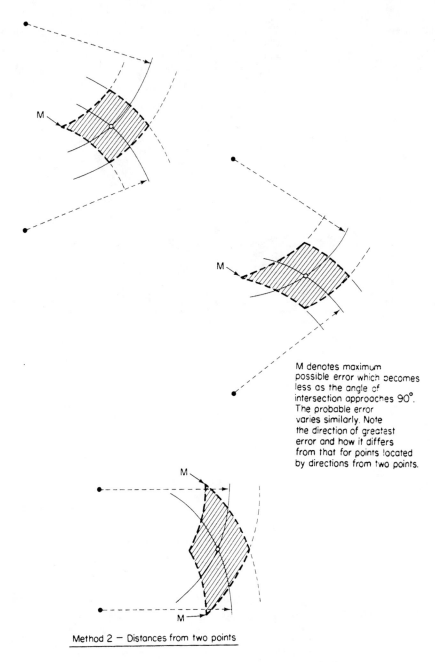

M denotes maximum
possible error which becomes
less as the angle of
intersection approaches 90°.
The probable error
varies similarly. Note
the direction of greatest
error and how it differs
from that for points located
by directions from two points.

Method 2 — Distances from two points

Figure 2.2 (cont.)   Relative accuracy of the methods

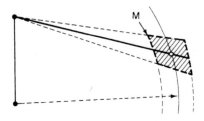

M denotes maximum possible error which becomes less as the angle of intersection approaches 90°. Note that the angle of intersection will be 90° (and error will be the least) if direction and distance are measured from the same point.

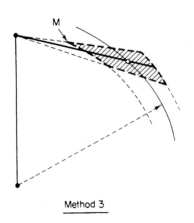

Method 3

Figure 2.2 (cont.) Relative accuracy of the methods

PROBLEMS

1. An accidental error of 0.01 ft is likely in each one of 80 separate measurements that are to be added to get the desired total. What is the probable total error? What is the probable total error if the individual accidental error is 0.02 ft? If it is 0.04 ft?

2. If the accidental error is 0.002 ft and there are 38 separate measurements, what is the probable total error?

3. A circuit is completed with a horizontal error of closure of 0.19 ft in a circuit of 6974.28 ft length. What are the accuracy and order and class of accuracy?

4. If the horizontal error is 0.21 ft and the length is 2784.94 ft, what are the accuracy and order and class of accuracy?

5. A circuit is completed with a vertical error of 11 mm in 36 kilometers. What are the order and class of accuracy?

6. If the vertical error is 0.1 mm and the length is 2.3 kilometers, what are the order and class of accuracy?

7. A level circuit is 7 kilometers long.   What is the maximum closure error allowed for a first-order class I survey?

8. A level circuit is 3.1 kilometers long.   What is the maximum closure allowed for a third-order survey?

3

HORIZONTAL DISTANCES

INSTRUCTIONAL OBJECTIVES

1. *Given the necessary equipment, the student, with a partner, should be able to tape on sloping ground, holding the tape and plumb bob in the various positions required for taping horizontally, employing voice signals, and recording entries in the field notebook. Distances should have an accuracy of 1:3000.*

2. *Given the true length of a tape, the student should be able to correct a given measured distance to the nearest one-hundredth of a foot.*

3. *Given an average temperature, the student should be able to correct a given measured distance or calculate the corrected length to set a point to the nearest one-hundredth of a foot.*

4. *Given a slope angle or difference in elevation between two points and the slope distance between the two points, the student should be able to compute the horizontal distance to the nearest one-hundredth of a foot.*

5. *Given any of the sources of error listed in the chapter, the student should be able to tell whether the resulting error is plus or minus or could be either plus or minus and should describe methods to control the error where appropriate.*

6. *The student should be able to enter notes in a field book for taping with any of the corrections.*

Horizontal distances are fundamental because plane surveying is based on the two mutually perpendicular directions—horizontal and vertical. There are two operations involving horizontal distances—*measuring a distance* and *setting a point.*

A *distance is measured* between two points that are already there; i.e., an unknown distance is determined.

A *point is set* from an existing point at a predetermined distance; i.e. the distance is known beforehand and the location of the new point is determined.

3.1 INTRODUCTION TO EQUIPMENT AND METHODS

Horizontal distances are ordinarily determined in the following ways:

1. *Pacing* is a quick, easy way for rough approximation.
2. *Taping* between two points with a tape calibrated in feet to the nearest one-hundredth. Steel or fiberglass tapes are commonly used, although cloth tapes with or without metal-wire reinforcing are used where high accuracy is not important. The tape may be marked in hundredths continuously from the zero mark to the opposite end, commonly a distance of 100, 200, or 300 ft. It may be marked only at each ft from zero to the opposite end with one ft before the zero mark calibrated in tenths or hundredths. See Fig. 3.1.
3. *Electronic distance measuring.* An accurately positioned transmitter sends an electromagnetic wave of known velocity to a receiver or reflector that returns the wave. The total time of travel at the known velocity provides a means of determining the distance between transmitter and reflector.

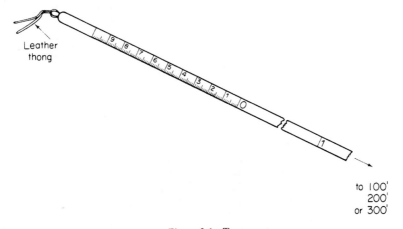

Figure 3.1 Tape

4. *Subtense bar.* The subtense bar of known length is set up horizontally at one end of a line to be measured and is aligned perpendicular to the line. The angle at one end of the line subtended by the known length at the other end of the line is used to determine the length of the line. See Fig. 3.2.

5. *Stadia.* The principle is the same as that of the subtense bar except that a constant angle is subtended by a length that varies in proportion to the length of the line to be measured. The stadia principle and procedure are covered in Chapter 7.

6. *Measuring wheel.* Length is determined by multiplying number of revolutions by the circumference of a wheel rolled along the surface. A vehicle odometer or a device consisting of a wheel with a revolution counter and a handle to push it along the surface can be used. The distance determined is along the surface so it is always longer than a level distance and can be adjusted with an estimated correction if necessary.

The methods listed according to accuracy are:

1. Electronic distance measuring
2. Taping
3. Subtense bar
4. Stadia
5. Measuring wheel
6. Pacing

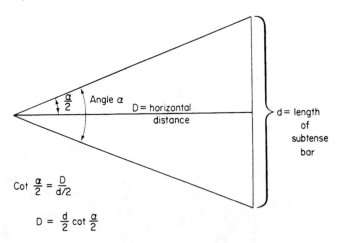

$$\text{Cot } \frac{\alpha}{2} = \frac{D}{d/2}$$

$$D = \frac{d}{2} \text{ cot } \frac{\alpha}{2}$$

Figure 3.2   Distance by subtense bar

3.2 PACING

Pacing is useful when a rough approximation is needed as in mapping and area determination of various kinds, e.g., for agriculture, forestry, or geology. It is also useful to check quickly for a large mistake in work done by another method. Paces are counted as they are stepped off and are later multiplied by the length of a pace to measure a distance. Number of paces is calculated ahead of time when setting a point.

The pacer can adjust the natural pace to a 3-ft length by practicing until the feeling is familiar; or measure the length of the normal pace to a tenth of a ft. Either is done by walking alongside a calibrated tape stretched out on level ground.

Practicing the pace up and down hill helps develop a feeling for adjusting the 3-ft pace or changing the value of the normal pace to produce a horizontal distance. An accuracy of 1 ft per 100 ft is good accuracy for pacing.

It is often useful to know how many paces per 100 ft to the nearest one-third of a pace because much surveying deals with stations. See Fig. 3.15 for pacing field notes.

3.3 ELECTRONIC DISTANCE MEASURING

An *electronic distance measuring device*, known as an *EDM*, is an instrument that emits a wave of electromagnetic energy to a receiver from which the wave returns to the source. The EDM, which is a transmitter-receiver-computer, determines the time of travel of the wave and converts time to distance between the EDM and receiver in both feet and meters.

Because the EDM and receiver are not at the same elevation, the distance is a slope distance and the EDM also computes horizontal distance and difference in elevation. The information is displayed in digital form or print-out or both. Some models do not compute horizontal distances and elevation differences. These must then be computed according to methods in this chapter for converting slope distances.

The EDM and receiver are set up over points using plumb bobs or optical plumb lines so that the distance computed is the distance between those points. Setups are the same as described for transits or theodolites in Chapter 5. If elevations are to be determined, the elevation of the EDM must be determined as described in Chapter 4.

Length can be determined for any line if one end of it can be seen from the other, and even distances beyond eyesight can be measured with some types of EDM. Advantages of the EDM are that measurements can be made over longer distances, faster, and more accurately than by any other means, and over obstructions such as water, steep-walled ravines, and posted property where no other method may be possible.

EDM's are capable of measuring distances of hundreds of miles with one setup using radiowaves. Microwave EDM's are used for distances of ten miles or so. However, the EDM's most often used are electro-optical instruments using lightwaves, either infrared or laser, with ranges up to two miles or so and sometimes less.

The longer-range setups include a transmitter-receiver at each end of the line because the signal is transmitted, then received and retransmitted to be received at the original transmitter. The electro-optical EDM's require only a reflector at the opposite end to return the lightwave the way a mirror does. The reflector consists of glass prisms mounted on a tripod and constructed to reflect waves back in the direction from which they came. A reflector requires more prisms for greater distances.

Laying off the distance for setting a point can be done by trying points until the correct point is found. The reflector is set up on line close to the unknown correct point (estimated by pacing, for example), and the distance is measured. The reflector position is moved the distance needed (determined by taping), and the distance is measured again. Several trials are needed. Taping might be more efficient at distances under 100 ft, but not nearly as efficient or accurate over longer distances.

Setting points by trial and adjustment is more efficient with the reflector mounted on a pointed staff that is easily handled and with the use of a *tracking EDM* repeatedly measuring the distance as the staff is moved to new trial points.

The distance at which to set the point is punched into the tracking EDM, which indicates the difference between staff position and desired position until, by successive trials, the correct point is established.

EDM's are powered with portable 12-volt batteries rechargeable overnight. In general, the longer the range of the EDM, the higher the cost and the greater the weight to carry in the field.

The velocity of electromagnetic waves varies with changes in atmospheric pressure, temperature, and humidity. The latest EDM's adjust automatically when these variables are dialed into them. For other models, a correction must be determined from a chart and entered into the EDM before measuring or applied to the results after measuring. Humidity has negligible effect on lightwaves, so electro-optical instruments require only pressure and temperature corrections.

EDM measurements are subject to instrumental errors that include a constant error at any distance plus a small error that increases in proportion to the distance. Thus EDM's are extremely accurate at distances near their maximum range but may be no more accurate than taping over short distances. A typical accuracy for an electro-optical EDM is ±0.03 ft plus one part per million. An EDM instrument and reflector are shown in Figs. 3.18 and 3.19.

3.4 TAPING OPERATION

Taping is simple in theory but requires more skill and practice than any of the other methods because accuracy is dependent on the surveyors' skills rather than on properties built into the equipment.

Terminology

Certain terminology is customary.   The point at which measuring begins is toward the *back*, and measurements proceed *forward* to the other point. The *tape person* at the back is the *rear tape person*, and the one at the front is the *head tape person*.   Any point on the straight line between the two points is *on line*, and if not on line, it is *right*, or *left*, looking forward from the back.

A *range pole* (see Fig. 3.3) may be stuck into the ground just beyond the point ahead to enable the rear tape person to keep the head tape person on line by line of sight.   Points for measurement are often marked by driving into the ground 1/2 in. to 3/4 in. steel reinforcing rods, 1 in. to 1 1/2 in. pipes, or wooden stakes with nails in the tops.   Temporary points are marked with nails or *surveyor's pins* driven into the ground.   Surveyor's pins, shown in Fig. 3.3, are straight wires with a point at one end and a circular eye at the other.

Use of Plumb Bob

Tape measurements are usually not made with the tape held on the points.   Normally, each end is held above a point and is located vertically over the point by means of a plumb bob and string.   See Fig. 3.4 for the

Figure 3.3   Range pole and surveyor's pins
(*Courtesy of Keuffel and Esser Company*)

Figure 3.4 Tape and plumb bob

proper method of holding the tape and plumb bob. The thumb and forefinger
pinch the string against the top of the tape. The string must hang vertically
from the tape edge opposite the surveyor without touching the finger under
the tape.

Proper Tension

A steel tape stretches when pulled. Its length changes if the tension
changes. For this reason, it should be pulled with the tension for which it
is designed. Only at this tension can its actual length be expected to be the
same as its calibrated length. The proper tension is normally 20 lb for a 100-
ft length of tape suspended at the two ends. For lengths other than 100 ft,
it is usually satisfactory to vary the tension in proportion to the length used.
For example, the proper tension for a 50-ft length is

$$\frac{50}{100} \times 20 = 10 \text{ lb}$$

If the tape is supported throughout its length, as when it is lying on a
level sidewalk, the tension should be one-half as much. In the case of full
support, it is necessary to pull just hard enough to straighten the tape. With
the tape suspended, its actual length is on a curve that is longer than a straight
line. Therefore, the tape must be elongated enough by the tension so that
the length along the curve is longer than the tape reading and the level distance
under the tape is the same as the tape reading. Thus, with proper tension,
the tape reads the correct level distance.

There is a tendency for the inexperienced surveyor not to pull hard
enough. Thus, the error due to improper tension is likely to be a plus error

because the end of the tape being read is not stretched far enough and indicates a reading greater than the level distance.

Proper tension may be maintained by attaching to the zero end of the tape a spring balance that indicates the tension in pounds. In ordinary work with experienced personnel, the tension is usually estimated by the head tape person; the rear tape person resists the tension by holding over the point.

Tapes of material other than steel require different tensions as described by manufacturers.

Proper Alignment

In order to measure accurately the distance from one point to another, the distance must be measured in a straight, level line. When the tape is shorter than the distance to be measured, intermediate points must be used. Either the points are set a certain distance apart (100 ft usually), or they are placed at convenient locations and the distances between them are measured. The points must be in a straight line. Even though the partial measurements are not made along a continuous level line, their total is the same as the level line distance as long as each measurement is level.

Some means must be devised to stay on line. Usually lining up the head end of the tape with the forward point by eye from the rear tape person's position will be sufficiently accurate. See Fig. 3.5. Generally it is not difficult to stay close enough to the line so that there is no significant error due to misalignment. A range pole may be stuck into the ground behind the

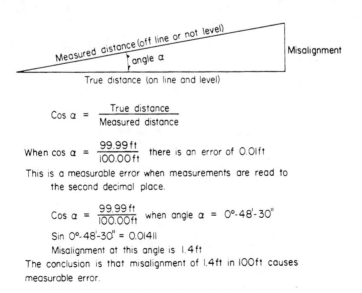

$$\text{Cos } \alpha = \frac{\text{True distance}}{\text{Measured distance}}$$

When $\cos \alpha = \dfrac{99.99\,\text{ft}}{100.00\,\text{ft}}$ there is an error of 0.01 ft

This is a measurable error when measurements are read to the second decimal place.

$\text{Cos } \alpha = \dfrac{99.99\,\text{ft}}{100.00\,\text{ft}}$ when angle $\alpha = 0°\text{-}48'\text{-}30''$

Sin $0°\text{-}48'\text{-}30'' = 0.01411$

Misalignment at this angle is 1.4 ft

The conclusion is that misalignment of 1.4 ft in 100 ft causes measurable error.

Figure 3.5 Significant error caused by tape misalignment

forward point to be used as a guide in staying on line. A good method is to hold a plumb bob by the string over the back point and to line the string up by eye with the range pole. The rear tape person can easily see whether the forward end of the tape is on line with the string and range pole.

Taping on a Level Line

It is necessary to hold both ends of the tape on the same horizontal line in order to measure a level distance. This often requires the tape person standing on lower ground to hold the tape farther above the ground than the other tape person. Except for short distances of 30 or 40 ft, the tape can be held steady only by bracing the hand on some part of the body. Figure 3.6 shows several common holding positions. These or other comfortable positions should be used whenever possible. The tape person must be solidly in position and well-balanced to resist tension on the tape with a minimum of movement.

The head tape person or downhill tape person should call for the other tape person to hold the tape in a position that makes the tape level.* As an example, the head tape person might call, "Hold at your knee." The proper position may be determined with a hand level (shown in Fig. 1.1) or by eye.

The principle by which accuracy can be estimated is shown in Fig. 3.5. The error caused by being 1.4 ft too high or too low is the same as that caused by being 1.4 ft right or left. However, it is more difficult to line up the tape accurately in elevation, and not keeping the tape level is more likely to be a source of significant error. This means that if one end is off 1.4 ft right, left, high, or low in a distance measured as 100.00 ft, the distance is really 99.99 ft and there is a plus error of 0.01 ft. The accuracy will be the same (1/ 10,000) if one end of the tape is 0.7 ft off in a taped length of 50.00 ft.

Taping Operation Described

Surveyor's pins or nails may be used to mark intermediate points. Surveyor's pins should be stuck into the ground at an angle of 45° with the ground and perpendicular to the tape. Thus, they are accurate in the direction of the distance being measured but may be off line (in a direction perpendicular to the direction of the measurement, where slight inaccuracies are negligible). The spot at which the surveyor's pin enters the ground is the point for measurement. See Fig. 3.3 for an illustration of surveyor's pins.

A set of surveyor's pins contains eleven pins. They are used only for long distances or where stations are being marked. A pin is placed at the

---

*The more experienced tape person or the party chief acts as head tape person on most work and directs the operation. However, on a steep slope, it is easier for the tape person downhill to estimate a horizontal line, and it is much easier to use a hand level for alignment from the downhill position.

Figure 3.6 Positions for holding tape at various heights

starting point, and the head tape person goes forward with the other ten pins. Full stations are marked with pins, and the rear tape person picks up and keeps each pin after the measurement is made and checked. Thus, the number of pins that the rear tape person has when coming to a new point is the number of that station or the number of hundreds of ft from the starting point. This is a check on the notekeeping.

Nails stuck into the ground at each point are left there. They can be referred to again if necessary, but they do not provide a running check on the number of the station.

It is convenient and sometimes necessary to pull the grass, to clear a small area, and to smooth the ground before establishing a point. Grass catching the plumb bob prevents the string from hanging in a straight line. Also rough ground and litter cause difficulty in setting a nail or pin firmly in place. In setting a point, the plumb bob must stick into the ground to mark the point. This can be done accurately only if the ground is smooth. If surveyor's pins are used, the point at which the pin intersects the ground surface is the point for measurements, and it can be identified accurately only on smooth ground.

When taping on pavement, the head tape person writes the station number next to each point. After a new point is marked by the head tape person, the rear tape person calls the number written at the rear point, and the head tape person adds one station mentally and calls the new station number while writing it. The rear tape person repeats the new station number as a check.

When stations are being marked, a full 100-ft distance is taped whenever possible. This means that the tape person must *set a point* 100 ft from an existing point. If stations are not needed, a nail is set on line at a convenient point, and the tape person *measures a distance* from the previous point to it. Measuring a distance is generally simpler than setting a point, so surveyors usually do not count stations without a good reason.

It is sometimes impossible to tape a full 100 ft because of the slope of the ground. A process called *breaking tape* may be used when stations are being counted. A point is set by the head tape person at a convenient number of whole ft from the back point. The rear tape person comes forward and holds that same ft mark over the newly set point, and the head tape person goes forward and sets another point at a convenient number of whole ft. The rear tape person again comes forward and holds the new ft mark over the new point. The process is repeated until 100 ft are accumulated, and then a station is set. If surveyor's pins are being used, one is placed only at the station.

The term *breaking tape* is often loosely used to mean measuring short horizontal distances up or down a slope whether stations are counted or not.

Teamwork is required to tape efficiently and accurately. Voice and hand signals are needed. Each measurement must be checked and immediately recorded.   Good systems for measuring a distance and for setting a point are described here step by step.   Refer to Fig. 3.7 while following the method for measuring a distance.

Mistakes can be made for several reasons when reading the tape.   If the tape is viewed so that the numbers are upside down, a two-digit number may be read backwards.   With certain digits, such as 1, 3, 6, 8, and 9, this can easily happen.   An 18 may look like 81 or a 39 like 63.   Certain numbers look alike when the tape is worn, especially 3, 8, and 0; they can be mistaken for one another.   The person reading the zero end can mistake the direction in which the hundredths increase and misread the tape.   In Fig. 3.7, the head tape person's final reading is 0.32.   It could be misread as 0.48.   All these mistakes can be prevented by looking at the number on either side of the number being read.

Note that every measurement is checked by three means:

1. Reading it a second time.

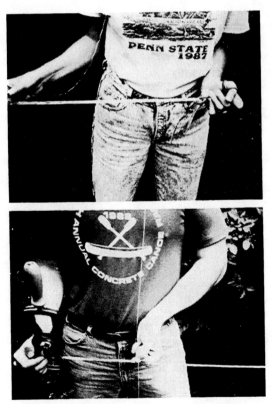

Figure 3.7   Holding numbers on both ends of tape

2. Saying it aloud.

3. Hearing it repeated.

STEP-BY-STEP PROCEDURE FOR MEASURING BETWEEN TWO EXISTING POINTS

Rear Tape Person (holding reel)

Head Tape Person (holding zero end of tape)

1. Holds zero approximately over point and calls, "Holding zero."

2. Holds plumb bob on point and observes where tape lines up with point. Either a number is over the point or the tape must be moved toward the rear so that the lower number is over the point. In Fig. 3.7 the point is approximately halfway between 96 and 97. The tape must be held with the 96 over the point so that tenths and hundredths can be read over the other point. Calls, "Give me half a foot."

3. Slacks off on tape until 0.5 is held approximately over the point. If the space between 0 and 1 is over the point, calls, "Take a foot." The rear tape person pulls the tape to the next lower foot, and the head tape person has the decimals over the point. Sometimes, it might be necessary for the rear tape person to "give a foot" to accomplish this.

4. Holds plumb bob string on 96 over point, braces self, and calls, "Mark" while plumb bob is over point or is silent if it swings away from point. Must watch plumb bob point constantly.

5.   Applies proper tension (20 lb), and, with the tape pulled tighter, the distance read is a little less. Slides plumb bob string until plumb bob is over point at same time rear tape person calls, "Mark." Watches plumb bob point, not tape.

6.   Resists tension. Repeats, "Mark, mark" while on point.

7.   When satisfied that the number is correct, slacks off on tape, holding string on tape with thumb and forefinger while checking number on each side of string and reading number under string.

8.   Checks number on each side of 96. Calls, "Nine six."

9.   Looks at 0.32 to verify it. Calls, "Nine six point three two" and records it in notebook while saying it.

10.   Looks at 96 to verify it. Repeats, "Nine six point three two."

11.   Listens to the number called while reading it in notebook. Signals to move on.

12.   Picks up surveyor's pin if used.
13.   The measurement may be taken again as a further check.

STEP-BY-STEP PROCEDURE FOR SETTING A POINT 86.30 FEET FROM EXISTING POINT

Rear Tape Person (holding reel)

Head Tape Person (holding zero end of tape)

1.   Holds 86 roughly over point.

2.   Roughly locates 0.30 on line. Clear surface of grass and other interfering objects within area large enough to include the point. Calls, "Hold eight six."

3. Holds 86 over point after checking adjacent numbers on tape. Calls, "Holding eight six."

4. Calls, "Holding point three oh" after checking adjacent numbers. Holds plumb bob string on 0.30 with thumb and forefinger and applies proper tension.

5. Resists tension, and calls, "Mark" while plumb bob is over point or is silent if it swings away from point.

6. While rear tape person is over the point, the head tape person drops the plumb bob so that it sticks into the soil and he/she places a nail in the hole made by the plumb bob.

The procedure must be repeated to verify the position of the nail.

Tapes divided into hundredths of a foot over the entire length simplify the procedure. The rear tape person holds zero and calls, "Holding zero" when ready. When measuring a distance, the head tape person reads the

Figure 3.8 Setting a point on pavement

distance and calls it to the note keeper or calls it while writing it.   To set a point, the party chief calls the distance to the head tape person who repeats it while taping it.

If the point is to be set on a hard surface such as pavement, the plumb bob is dipped until its point touches the surface.   It is held in this position by the string until it can be reached with the other hand and a scratch can be made at the point (see Fig. 3.8).

Hand signals are sometimes needed when conditions are poor for voice communication, such as on noisy city streets or construction sites.   Signals to "take a foot" or to "give a foot" are the hand motions that come naturally— waving the hand in the direction of desired movement.   A signal to move right or left to get on line is a waving motion of the hand in the appropriate direction.   A large, slow motion means a long distance; a short, quick motion means a short distance.

3.5 CORRECTIONS

Significant errors should be corrected whenever their magnitude and direction can be determined.   A *significant error* is one that could reduce the total accuracy below the required level.   Accidental errors cannot be corrected because their direction is not known.   Some systematic errors can be corrected and may have to be corrected to obtain the required accuracy.

Temperature Correction

Steel, like other solid material, expands or contracts with changes in temperature.   The *coefficient of expansion* is an index of the amount of change in size that a material will undergo because of a change in temperature.   Each material has its own coefficient of expansion.   The coefficient of expansion indicates the percentage that any length will expand or contract with a change in temperature of one degree.   A coefficient of 0.01 indicates a one percent change in length for a one degree change in temperature.   Thus, one ft would expand to 1.01 ft with a one degree rise in temperature and to 1.05 ft with a five degree rise.   A length of 100 ft would increase to 101 ft with a one degree rise in temperature, and decrease to 99 ft with a one degree drop in temperature.

Steel tapes have a coefficient of expansion of 0.00000645.   In other words, a steel tape lengthens 0.00000645 ft for each ft of its original length with each degree increase in temperature and shortens similarly with each degree drop in temperature.   The starting point is 68°F, the temperature at which the tape should be of correct length according to manufacturing practice.   Two examples follow:

1. A tape that is truly 100.00 ft long at 68°F is used at 95°F. A distance is measured as 1308.37 ft. The true distance is greater than the amount read on the tape since the tape increased in length and the inscribed numbers became farther apart. The error is negative, the correction is positive, and the corrected distance is as follows:

Measured distance plus correction = 1308.37' + 0.00000645

$$\times \ 1308.37' \times (95 - 68)°F = 1308.37' + 0.23' = 1308.60'$$

The correction is subtracted for temperatures below 68°F.

2. A point is to be set 1308.37 ft from a known point with the same tape at the same temperature. The true distance is greater than the amount read on the tape. Therefore, the length read on the tape must be less than 1308.37 ft. The distance to be laid out is:

True distance minus correction = 1308.37' − 0.00000645 × 1308.37'

$$\times \ (95 - 68)°F = 1308.37' - 0.23' = 1308.14'$$

The correction is added for temperatures below 68°F. Table III in the Appendix can be used to determine temperature corrections directly.

The average temperature during the time a distance is measured is used, or for highly accurate work, a temperature is recorded for each tape measurement. The temperature of the tape might not be the same as the air temperature. The tape can be warmer because it is in the direct rays of the sun or cooler because it is cooled by evaporation in wet grass. The appropriate temperature is obtained by using a tape thermometer that is clamped to the tape with the bulb in contact with the tape.

Tape Correction

A tape may be shorter or longer than the total length inscribed on it. A new tape, although manufactured with high precision, may have a discernible error. During use, small kinks occur that shorten the tape slightly. Dragging the tape wears it thinner so that it stretches a little longer with standard tension than it did when new. These two sources of error might balance each other, or either one might outweigh the other.

If significant error is suspected, the size of error can be determined by comparing the *field* or *working tape* with a *standard tape* that is precisely 100 ft long at 68°F when it is fully supported along its length and is under a tension of 10 lb. The standard tape is made of *invar* or *lovar* metal. These are steel alloys with very low coefficients of expansion, but are not strong enough for field use.

If the field tape reads 100 ft for a length determined to be 99.995 ft with the standard tape, the field tape is short and a distance measured as 100 ft has a true length of 99.995 ft.

The error can be eliminated by applying greater tension when using the tape so that it stretches to the full 100 ft.   The correct tension is determined by applying tension until the 100-ft calibrations on the field tape match those of the standard tape.   Correct tension is greater than 20 lb for a short tape and less than 20 lb for a long tape.   The revised tension may be adjusted by proportion for lengths other than 100 ft.   The tape should be labeled with the correct tension, or the correct tension should be recorded in a record book.

Another method is to apply a correction to the distances measured with standard tension and recorded in the field as measured.   The error is determined with standard tension, and the error is recorded in the record book.

Error is assumed to be uniformly distributed throughout the length of the tape.   This is not necessarily true.   The error may be in one part of the tape.   Because the zero end is used more, the error is likely to be near that end, especially if the tape is carried on a reel and unreeled for each taping. The assumption is valid for either correction method when the entire tape length is used because correct tension is determined for the entire tape and total error is included within the entire tape.

Allowing for error when less than a full tape length is used for measuring may not improve the accuracy.   It could lessen the accuracy if the error is in the part of the tape not being used.   Even so, it is customary to adjust the tension or to reduce the correction in proportion to the length of tape being used.   Any reduction in accuracy that might occur is not significant with ordinary tape error.   See Fig. 3.9 for the method of determining error. Two examples follow:

1. A distance is measured between two points and recorded as 1273.42 ft. The true distance is

$$1273.42' - (0.005 \times 12.73)$$

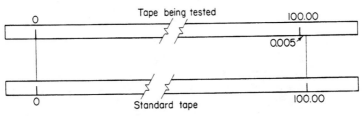

Tape being tested is 0.005 ft short and therefore has a length of 99.995 ft causing a plus error of 0.005 ft in every 100.00 ft read.

Figure 3.9 Determining tape error

Tape correction

	Short tape	Long tape
Measuring a distance	−	+
Setting a point	+	−
	Below 68°F	Above 68°F

Temperature correction

Figure 3.10   Correct signs for tape and temperature corrections

or

$$1273.42' - 0.06' = 1273.36'$$

2. A point is to be set 1273.42 ft from a known point. The tape readings will be greater than the true distance. The distance to be taped in order to establish a true distance of 1273.42 ft is

$$1273.42' + (0.005 \times 12.73)$$

or

$$1273.42' + 0.06' = 1273.48'$$

In ordinary surveying and for short distances (under approximately 100 ft) of high-order accuracy, a tape correction is not necessary. As indicated in the example, the error is small. It is preferable to replace an old tape with a new one when the error becomes too large. See Fig. 3.10 for aid in deciding whether to add or subtract temperature and tape corrections.

Slope Correction

In some cases, it is faster and more accurate to measure a distance at an angle with the horizontal and to calculate the horizontal distance than to measure it with several horizontal steps. The angle up or down from the horizontal is called *slope angle*, and the distance is called *slope distance*. The slope distance is always longer than the corresponding horizontal distance. Practical aspects of measuring slope distances are covered in Chapter 6.

Two methods of making a slope measurement and calculating the horizontal distance are described here.

METHOD 1

A slope distance may be measured from one point to another, the slope angle determined, and a horizontal distance computed. The slope is along

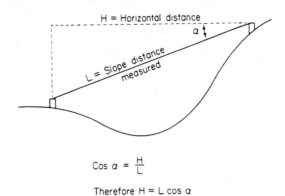

$$\cos \alpha = \frac{H}{L}$$

Therefore $H = L \cos \alpha$

Figure 3.11   Determining horizontal distance from slope distance and slope angle

a line that passes through both ends of the tape and does not necessarily follow the ground surface. The horizontal distance (adjacent side) can be calculated by multiplying the slope distance (hypotenuse) by the cos of the slope angle. See Fig. 3.11.

Sometimes a correction, C_S, is subtracted from the slope distance to find the horizontal distance. See Fig. 3.12.

$$C_S = L - L \cos \alpha$$

where

$$L = \text{slope distance}$$

Radius of
arc = H

$H = L \cos \alpha$

C_s

$L = $ Slope distance measured

$H = L - C_s$ (from figure)
$C_s = L - L \cos \alpha$ (from figure)

The advantages of using C_s are that it can be taken from a table and it can be combined with other required corrections to make one composite correction.

Figure 3.12   Determining horizontal distance with slope correction, C_S, derived from slope angle

$$\alpha = \text{slope angle}$$

$$L \cos \alpha = \text{horizontal distance}$$

This correction is found in Table IV in the Appendix for various slope angles. A correction taken from this table can be combined with tape and temperature correction and applied to the taped distance in one step.

METHOD 2

A slope distance can be measured from a point of known elevation to another point of different known elevation, and the horizontal distance computed. The Pythagorean Theorem can be used directly. See Fig. 3.13.

$$H = \sqrt{L^2 - d^2}$$

where

$$L = \text{slope distance}$$

$$d = \text{difference in elevation}$$

$$H = \text{horizontal distance}$$

A correction C_S can be computed by using the Pythagorean Theorem. The correction is convenient to use, and there is little loss of accuracy except at steep slopes where d equals one-tenth or more of L. See Fig. 3.14.

$$C_S = L - H$$

$$d^2 = L^2 - H^2 = (L - H)(L + H) = C_S(L + H)$$

$$C_S = \frac{d^2}{2L} \text{ (approximately)}$$

$$L = \text{slope distance}$$

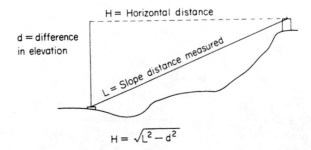

Figure 3.13 Determining horizontal distance from slope distance and elevation difference

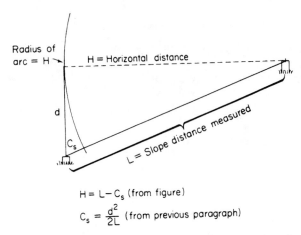

$$H = L - C_s \text{ (from figure)}$$
$$C_s = \frac{d^2}{2L} \text{ (from previous paragraph)}$$

Figure 3.14 Determining horizontal distance with slope correction, C_S, derived from Pythagorean Theorem

H = horizontal distance

d = difference in elevation

Total Correction

When more than one correction is needed, there is a logical sequence that can be followed. Because the tape correction adjusts the recorded distance to conform to the actual tape length, it should be made first. The temperature correction adjusts for expansion or contraction of the actual length of material in the tape. It should be based on the actual length determined by applying the tape correction. The applying of these two corrections determines the actual slope distance. Therefore, the slope correction should be applied after the other two have been made.

Only with a long distance, large tape correction, extreme temperature, and a very steep slope is it necessary to follow this sequence. Usually each of the three corrections is determined from the recorded distance, and all are added algebraically to it. An example follows.

A distance is measured as 754.81 ft with a 100-ft tape on a slope with an angle of 8° − 42′. The true length of the tape is 99.992 ft and the temperature is 35°F. Calculations with all corrections based on the recorded length are shown first:

$$C_L = 7.5481 \, (-0.008) = -0.06$$

$$C_T = 7.5481 \, (-0.021285) = -0.16 \text{ from Table III}$$

$$C_S = 7.5481 \times 1.15 = -8.68 \text{ from Table IV}$$

Corrected horizontal distance = 745.91 ft

Calculations in logical progression are also shown. Even though recorded length is long and all corrections are rather large, there is no difference in the answer. However, there can be a difference for larger distances or larger corrections.

$$C_L = 7.5481 \, (-0.008) = -0.06$$

Distance corrected for C_L = 754.75 ft

$$C_T = 7.5475 \, (-0.021285) = -0.16$$

Distance corrected for C_L and C_T = 754.59 ft

$$C_S = 7.5459 \times 1.15 = -8.68$$

Corrected horizontal distance = 745.91 ft

3.6 NOTEKEEPING

Notekeeping is shown for various conditions in Figs. 3.15, 3.16, and 3.17.

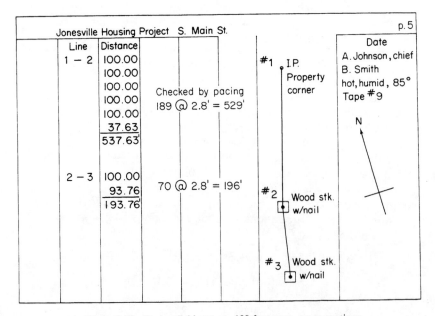

Figure 3.15 Taping field notes—100-foot tape, no corrections

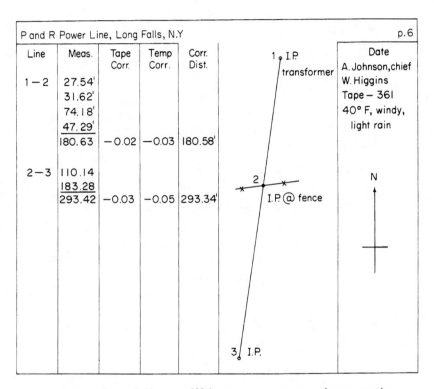

Line	Meas.	Tape Corr.	Temp Corr.	Corr. Dist.
1 − 2	27.54'			
	31.62'			
	74.18'			
	47.29'			
	180.63	−0.02	−0.03	180.58'
2 − 3	110.14			
	183.28			
	293.42	−0.03	−0.05	293.34'

P and R Power Line, Long Falls, N.Y   p. 6

1 • I.P.
transformer

2
I.P. @ fence

3 I.P.

N

Date
A. Johnson, chief
W. Higgins
Tape − 361
40° F, windy,
light rain

Figure 3.16   Taping field notes—200-foot tape, temperature, and tape corrections

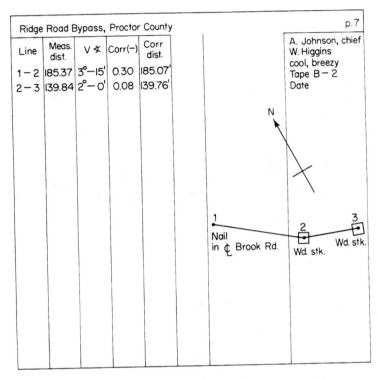

Figure 3.17 Taping field notes—200-foot tape, slope distances

3.7 ERRORS AND MISTAKES

Systematic Errors

The two truly systematic taping errors and their corrections have been discussed. They are:

1. Difference between working tape length and standard tape length.
2. Change in tape length due to temperature variation.

Accidental Errors

The most common sources of accidental errors are:

1. Imperfectly estimating the second decimal place on the tape.
2. Inexact plumbing over a point.
3. Using incorrect tension.

These are truly accidental errors. Neither direction nor magnitude can be determined, although incorrect tension is usually too little, which results in a reading greater than the actual distance.

Other sources of error are not so readily categorized as systematic or accidental. They cause error of an unknown magnitude but always cause the reading to be greater than the actual distance. Two of the most common are:

1. Misalignment—vertical or horizontal. This source can be controlled as described earlier in the chapter.
2. Wind causing the tape to curve out to the side. This source can be controlled by applying greater tension and by taping shorter distances.

Common Mistakes

1. Misreading a number. This can be avoided by reading the number on each side of the number to be recorded. Look at the distance and estimate it before measuring. A large mistake like reading 69 ft for 96 ft can be avoided this way.
2. Recording a number incorrectly. This can be avoided by saying the number out loud while recording it. The other tape person should listen and verify the number.
3. Using an incorrect location for zero. Zero may be at the end of the ring or on the tape. Be sure before starting the work. Verify it with another tape or a ruler if necessary.
4. Omitting a tape length. This is more likely to happen when taping full tape lengths such as 100-ft increments. Each distance should be re-

Figure 3.18 Electronic distance measuring instrument (*Courtesy The Lietz Company*)

Figure 3.19   Reflector
(*Courtesy The Lietz Company*)

corded immediately after being measured.   The methods described in this chapter act as a check.

5. Using the tape with ends reversed.   Check for this before work begins. It will be noticed as soon as a measurement is made if proper taping procedures are used.   However, time is saved if it is noticed and corrected at the start.

6. Allowing the tape to touch the ground, brush, a fence, or any other object so that it is not straight and hanging freely between plumb bobs. Look at the tape just prior to making the measurement.

PROBLEMS

1. One pace is 2.8 ft.   A distance is measured as 117 paces.   What is the distance in feet?

2. A point is set at 132 ft with a 3-ft pace.   How many paces?

3. A line is measured with 46 paces of 3-ft length over level ground and 31 paces of 2.6 ft over rugged ground.   What is its length?

4. A point is to be set at 250 ft.   Thirty-five paces of 2.3 ft are stepped off over rugged ground.   How many 2.8-ft paces over level ground are required?

5. One hundred eighty sidewalk squares (6-ft squares) are counted in a block.   How long is the block?

6. Three hundred twenty furrows are counted across a plowed field.   Furrow widths average 3.5 ft.   What is the width of the field?

7. Eighty paces of 2.4 ft are counted between telephone poles along a road.   After driving past six poles from the first pole, what distance has been traveled?

8. A measuring wheel with a 3.5-ft circumference indicates 83 revolutions on a slope judged to be 15%. Calculate horizontal distance by slope correction methods 1 and 2.

9. A point is to be set at 390 ft. A measuring wheel with 3-ft circumference indicates 26 revolutions on a 10% slope. How many more revolutions over level ground?

10. A point is to be set at 500 ft. A measuring wheel with 2.75-ft circumference indicates 120 revolutions over level ground, and the rest is to be placed over rugged terrain at 2.2 ft per pace. How many paces?

11. What is the tension to use for a distance of 79 ft with a 100-ft tape if recommended tension is 20 lb?

12. What is the tension to use for a distance of 120 ft with a 200-ft tape if recommended tension is 30 lb?

13. What is the tension to use for a distance of 30 ft with a 100-ft tape if recommended tension is 7 lb?

14. A distance is measured in two increments of 75 ft and 86.32 ft, and the intermediate point is 2.5 ft off line. What are the error and corrected distance.

15. A distance is measured in two increments of 25.36 ft and 48.97 ft with the intermediate point 1.2 ft higher than the end points that are at the same elevation. What are the error and corrected distance?

16. A distance is measured as 100 ft with the 50-ft mark over a fence so that it is 1.5 ft higher than the end points. What are error and corrected distance? What if the 31-ft mark is at the fence?

17. A distance is measured as 1000 ft in 100-ft lengths with the difference in elevation between ends of the tape being 1.5 ft each time. What are total error and corrected distance? What are total error and corrected distance if a 50-ft tape is used with 1.5-ft difference in elevation of the ends? What about using a 200-ft tape?

18. A point is set with taped distances of 75 ft and 75 ft with the intermediate point 1.4 ft out of line. What is the actual distance to the point?

19. After stations are set from 0 + 00 to 6 + 00 it is learned that tape misalignment averaged 2.7 ft per 100-ft measured length. What is total error using the methods of Fig. 3.11 and 3.12?

20. A 100-ft tape is determined to be 100.05 ft long when checked against a standard tape. A distance is measured as 149.96 ft. What is the distance after applying the tape correction?

21. A distance is measured as 1000.00 ft with a steel tape when average temperature is +08°F. What is the distance when corrected for temperature?

22. A point is to be set at a distance of 100 ft. The true length of the tape is 100.01 ft, and the temperature is +91°F. What length should be laid off with the tape?

23. A distance is measured as 180.73 ft with a slope angle of 6°-05′. What is the horizontal distance?

24. A distance is measured as 776.86 ft on a slope of 3°-05′ when the temperature is +97°F with a 200-ft tape having a true length of 199.99 ft. What is the corrected horizontal distance?

25. A slope distance is measured as 576.59 ft between two points, one of which is 24.63 ft higher than the other. What is the horizontal distance?

26. A slope distance is measured as 1200.00 ft between two points with an elevation difference of 42.21 ft at a temperature of − 18°F with a 300-ft tape having a true length of 300.02 ft. What is the corrected horizontal distance?

27. A distance is measured as 396.17 ft with a slope of 1°-11′ with a 100-ft tape having a true length of 99.98 ft. What is the corrected horizontal distance?

28. A distance is measured as 797.46 ft with a tape having a true length of 99.996 ft. The temperature is 19°F. What is the correct distance?

29. A distance is measured as 87.62 ft at a temperature of 12°F with a slope angle of 13°-14′. What is the corrected horizontal distance?

30. A point is to be set at a distance of 790.35 ft at a temperature of 7°F. What length should be laid off with the tape?

31. A point is to be set at 90.45 ft from a higher point. An intermediate point is set at 90.00 ft on a slope of 8°-52′. What additional distance should be taped horizontally to set the point?

32. A point is to be set at 165.00 ft from a lower point with a temperature of 10°F. An intermediate point is set at 165.00 ft at a slope of 4°-18′. What is the remaining horizontal distance?

33. A point is to be at a distance of 860.50 ft with a tape having a true length of 200.009 ft. A slope distance measured from the starting point to a temporary point is 192.13 ft. What is the remaining distance to be taped to set the point if the slope angle is 5°-36′?

34. A point is to be set at a distance of 320.00 ft from a point at elevation 5481.16. An intermediate point is set at 5474.03 and a slope distance of 176.32 ft measured to it. What is the remaining horizontal distance to set the point?

4

VERTICAL DISTANCES

INSTRUCTIONAL OBJECTIVES

1. *Given the necessary equipment, the student, with a partner, should be able to complete a level circuit of four turning points with an error not greater than .01 ft.*
2. *Given an engineer's level, the student should be able to demonstrate the proper procedure for setting it up and for reading the rod.*
3. *Given a level rod, the student should be able to select a satisfactory turning point, to hold the rod properly, and to wave the rod properly.*
4. *Given a series of rod readings as seen through the engineer's level (either slides or pictures), the student should be able to read them correctly.*
5. *Given field data, the student should be able to keep complete notes including an arithmetic check.*
6. *Given an object to be used as a bench mark, the student should be able to write an adequate description.*

Vertical direction is the second of the two directions on which all plane surveying is based. Understanding it requires an ability to visualize relationships in space. The study of surveying will assist greatly in developing this ability, which is of primary importance in technical work. The necessity of visualizing space relationships becomes apparent in this chapter.

4.1 METHOD

The vertical distance between two points can be determined by first finding the vertical distance of each point below a level line as shown in Fig. 4.1. The difference in elevation between the two points can then be calculated. If the elevation of one of the points is known with reference to a datum, then the elevation of the other can be determined with reference to the same datum. The level line could be established with the hand level described in Chapter 1 or with a more precise instrument. The procedure illustrated in Fig. 4.1 is called *leveling*.

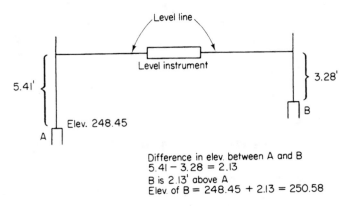

Difference in elev. between A and B
5.41 − 3.28 = 2.13
B is 2.13' above A
Elev. of B = 248.45 + 2.13 = 250.58

Figure 4.1   Leveling procedure

4.2 DEFINITIONS

Bench Mark. (B.M.) is a permanent or semipermanent point of known elevation that can be used to establish other elevations. See discussion in Chapter 1 under Sea Level and Elevation. In Fig. 4.1, point *A* is a bench mark. Bench marks are set by surveyors and are described in field books so that other surveyors can find them and use them.

    A description includes two parts: (1) complete directions so that some-one who has never been there can find the B.M.; and (2) a complete description of its appearance so that when it is found, there is no doubt about it. Sample field notes in this chapter include B.M. descriptions.

    The description should first state the largest area or political subdivision necessary and then narrow the area step by step until there can be only one possible point intended. For example, the description of a B.M. in a state-wide benchmark system could begin with the county, then town, then nearest highway intersection, then further details narrowing the location to one point, and describing the appearance of the B.M.

Height of Instrument.   (H.I.) is an elevation, established at a known vertical distance above another point of known elevation, from which other elevations can be determined.   It is established with a level instrument so that the elevation can be extended in any direction along a horizontal line. In Fig. 4.1, the level line is at the height of instrument.

Turning Point.   (T.P.) is a point of fixed elevation used temporarily in the process of leveling.   The point need not be permanent.   In Fig. 4.1, point B is a turning point.

Backsight.   (B.S.) is a reading taken with a level instrument on a point of known elevation in order to establish the height of instrument.   It is taken in a back direction.   In Fig. 4.1, the reading 5.41 ft is a backsight. It is read on a calibrated rod placed on point A.

Foresight.   (F.S.) is a reading taken with a level instrument on a new point in order to establish the elevation of the new point from the height of the instrument.   It is taken in a forward direction.   In Fig. 4.1, the reading 3.28 ft is a foresight.   It is read on a calibrated rod placed on point B.

4.3 INTRODUCTION TO EQUIPMENT

The *engineer's level* shown in Fig. 4.2 is used for surveying work of ordinary accuracy.   It includes a telescope that defines the line of sight between the eye and the object viewed and that magnifies the object.   The telescope

Figure 4.2   Engineer's level (*Courtesy of Teledyne Gurley, Troy, N.Y.*)

consists of a metal tube containing four main parts. They are shown schematically in Fig. 4.3.

The *objective lens* is fixed at the end toward the object being sighted (object end). Its purpose is to admit light rays into the telescope to form an image. This image is upside down.

The *focusing lens* is attached within a slide that can be moved longitudinally on rack and pinion gears by turning the *focusing screw*. Its purpose is to focus the image so that it is seen in the plane of the cross hairs.

The *reticle* is stationary and includes a ring and cross hairs. The cross hairs are made of spider web, fine wire, or lines etched on glass. The ring that holds the cross hairs is held in position by capstan screws so that it can be adjusted vertically or horizontally within the tube but only in a plane perpendicular to the axis of the tube. It can also be rotated slightly so that the horizontal hair can be maintained truly horizontal.

The *eyepiece* is a microscope containing four lenses close to the observer's eye. Its purpose is to enlarge the image of the object and to invert it so that it appears right side up. The object image is at the cross hairs. The eyepiece is movable in a longitudinal direction so that it can be focused on the image to suit each individual eye.

The *line of sight* through the telescope is a line from the eye through the center of the cross hairs and through the optical center of the objective lens. This line must be horizontal when the level vial is horizontal. The cross hairs and level vial can be forced out of alignment if the instrument is jarred, and they are difficult to manufacture with perfect accuracy. There-

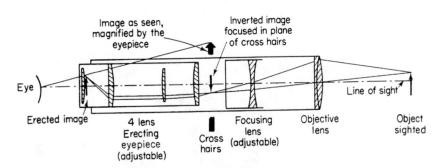

The diagram shows paths of two representative rays from a point at the top of the object sighted. Rays from this point and from every other point on the object are distributed across the entire face of the objective lens. Where rays from a point on the object are brought to a point within the telescope that point is in focus and a visible image of it is formed. The lenses are designed to bring the object into focus by bending (refracting) rays from all points on the object to a focus in the same plane. For accurate sighting this must be the plane of the cross hairs. The instrument man sees the image enlarged because of the wide angle at which the refracted rays come to his eye.

Figure 4.3 Internal focusing telescope with erecting eyepiece

fore, the line of sight is made adjustable by providing movable cross hairs, and the level vial can be adjusted by moving one end of it up or down until the line of sight and the axis of the level vial are parallel.

Some telescopes focus the image in the plane of the cross hairs by sliding the objective lens in and out and therefore have no focusing lens. This is called *external focusing* because the objective lens projects beyond the tube when it is focused on nearby objects. External focusing instruments are not generally available now, but some may still be in use. The external focusing instruments are open to the atmosphere so that dust and moisture can enter the telescope tube and can cause abrasion of moving parts and decreased visibility. The modern *internal focusing* telescope is sealed against dust and moisture.

The eyepieces of some telescopes do not reverse the image but show it upside down. These are called *inverting eyepieces* and provide a somewhat clearer image than the *erecting eyepieces*. This is because each lens absorbs some light, which therefore does not get through to the eye, and because the inverting eyepiece has only two lenses instead of four.

The telescope is joined to a base plate by a *half-ball joint* and is rotated into level position about the half-ball by four *leveling screws* arranged at 90° intervals around a circle and bearing on the *base plate*. Refer to Figs. 4.4 and 5.7 and note that the elevation of the telescope is not changed by adjusting the leveling screws because of the half-ball connection. The telescope rotates about the center of the spherically shaped half-ball and is centered at the highest point when level. It cannot go lower without being out of level.

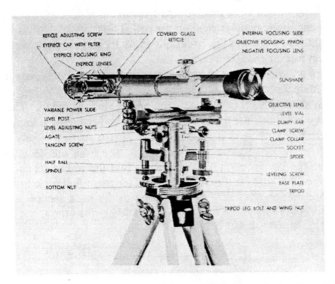

Figure 4.4   Inside of engineer's level (*Courtesy of Teledyne Gurley, Troy, N.Y.*)

The base plate is mounted on three long legs called a *tripod*. The legs include pointed steel shoes and are pivoted at the top. Their purpose is to provide a stable platform at eye height for the instrument.

The level position is indicated by the centering of an air bubble in a level vial containing alcohol or ether, attached to the telescope and parallel to the line of sight through the telescope. The curve of the vial is flatter and therefore more sensitive to a small change in direction than that of a hand level, and thus it is also more accurate. To facilitate aiming, the instrument includes a clamp to stop unwanted rotation and a tangent screw to rotate the line of sight to the position desired. A similar level of less accuracy called a *builder's level* is used in simple construction work.

The *self-leveling level* permits faster operation because it requires only approximate leveling to a stage where it levels itself and remains level even if moved slightly. The instrument is leveled with three leveling screws until a bubble in a hemispherical vial is centered roughly within a circular "bull's eye." The instrument's mechanism then maintains a level position despite unequal settlement of tripod legs or construction vibrations. Leveling with three screws is discussed in Chapter 5.

The *tilting level* is the most accurate. It is leveled only approximately to start and then leveled precisely with one screw by viewing the bubble through prisms while reading the rod.

The *level rod* is read through the level instrument to get backsights and foresights. The rod is calibrated to 0.01 ft in a bold, easy-to-read style with zero at the bottom of the rod. A level rod is shown in Fig. 4.5. The rod is held vertically with the bottom on the bench mark or turning point so that the horizontal line of sight through the instrument intersects it at the height of instrument. The number read on the rod at this elevation is the backsight or foresight. In Fig. 4.1, the backsight (5.41 ft) and the foresight (3.28 ft) are read on a level rod.

There are many styles of level rod. One of the most widely used, the 13-ft Philadelphia level rod, is described here and is shown in Fig. 4.5. The Philadelphia rod consists of two sections, one behind the other. The rod can be extended by sliding the back section upward and clamping it in place. For ordinary accuracy, the rod is used at either of two settings—fully extended (high rod) or not extended at all (short rod). The front section is calibrated to 7 ft, and the back section is calibrated so that the rod reads continuously from zero to 13 ft when it is extended its full length. A short part of the top of the front section reading 7 ft is attached to the back section so that the 7-ft mark is at the top where a 13-ft mark should be when the rod is extended.

Figure 4.5 Level rod with target (*Courtesy of Keuffel and Esser Company*)

Mistakes can be prevented by reading the number below the 7 before deciding whether it means 7 ft or 13 ft.

Vernier and Its Use

Although the rod is calibrated to read to 0.01 ft, it can be read to 0.001 ft by the use of a vernier. The *vernier* is a device that allows more exact measurement with an instrument than is possible with the scale of that instrument. It is a scale constructed with equal spaces of a size such that N spaces on the vernier are equal in length to $N - 1$ spaces on the instrument scale. A common type of vernier contains 10 spaces with each vernier space being equal to $\frac{9}{10}$ of the instrument space. Thus, 10 vernier spaces equal $10 - 1$ or 9 instrument spaces. This type of vernier will allow accurate readings of $\frac{1}{10}$ the size of the smallest instrument space. See Fig. 4.6 for an illustration of this vernier.

Visualize the index arrow on the vernier moving to the right until the 0.1 of the vernier lines up with the 1 of the instrument. Since the vernier space is $\frac{9}{10}$ the length of an instrument space, the index has moved $\frac{1}{10}$ the length of an instrument space when these line up. This could be estimated but not read accurately by noting the movement of the arrow. It can be read accurately by noting the position of the vernier line marked 0.1.

If the index moves farther until the 0.2 lines up with the 2 of the instrument, it has moved $\frac{2}{10}$ of a space on the instrument scale. As the index moves to the right, the vernier marks line up with marks on the instrument one by one in succession, indicating the length of movement in tenths of an instrument space. The same vernier is shown in Fig. 4.7 with a reading of 1.9. The instrument is read by noting the position of the arrow for whole numbers and the vernier number that lines up with any scale number for the fraction or decimal part to be added to the whole number.

The rod is equipped with a stationary vernier reading to 0.001 ft attached to a sleeve through which the back section slides. The reverse side of the back section is calibrated from 7 ft to 13 ft from top to bottom so that the farther the rod is extended, the higher the number at the vernier. The vernier

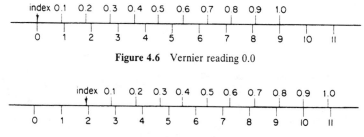

Figure 4.6   Vernier reading 0.0

Figure 4.7   Vernier reading 1.9

reads 7.000 when the rod is closed, and when the rod is extended, it reads
7.000 plus the length of the extension.

Thus, if the rod is adjusted while at a point so that the line of sight
intersects 7.000 on the front when the rod is extended, the rod person can
read the B.S. or F.S. to the nearest 0.001 ft with the vernier on the reverse
side of the rod. The instrument person signals up or down to the rod person,
who adjusts the length of rod until the instrument person reads 7.00 exactly.
The rod person then clamps the extended section in place and reads it at the
vernier. The rod person keeps notes or calls readings to the note keeper.

A *target* with alternating red and white sectors arranged to define a
horizontal line sharply can be fixed on 7.000 to improve the instrument person's accuracy. The target is removable and can be used with its own vernier
below 7 ft when the back vernier cannot be used. It is adjusted to the line
of sight by the rod person, who can then read the rod to 0.001 ft by using
the vernier on the target.

4.4 DIFFERENTIAL LEVELING

Method

It is often necessary to set a new B.M. (at a construction site, for
example). This is done by converting the elevation of an already established
B.M., step by step, as shown in Fig. 4.1, to the elevation of the new B.M.,
which is built before its elevation is determined. The new elevation is then
checked by converting, step by step, back to an elevation on the first B.M.
This process is called running a *level circuit*. The difference between the
starting and final elevations at the first B.M. is the error of closure. Accuracy
is computed as described in Chapter 2.

Differential leveling is the process of determining the elevation of a new
point from the known elevation of an existing point. It is started from a
bench mark of known elevation or from one that is installed specifically for
the project and is assigned an arbitrary elevation such as 100.00 ft. The level
is set up, and a backsight is read on the rod on the bench mark. A foresight
is then read on the rod on a convenient turning point. The turning point
may be a natural object or a stake driven solidly enough into the ground to
be used for the foresight and a subsequent backsight without any movement.
It should have an easily identifiable small high point that will not break or
move in any way while it is in use.

The recording of the foresight establishes the elevation of the turning
point and the level may then be moved. The level is moved to a new location,
and a backsight is read on the same turning point to establish a new height
of instrument. The process is repeated until the elevation is established for
the desired point. Often, the desired point is a new bench mark. See Fig.

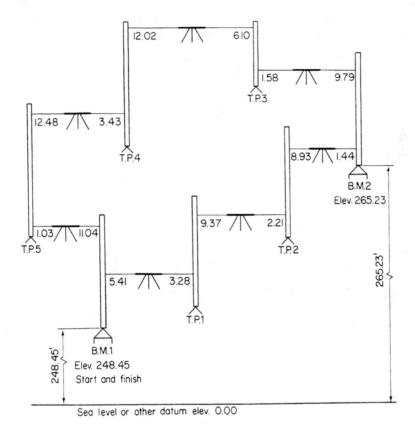

See Fig. 4-9 for field notes

Figure 4.8   Differential leveling showing elevations but not true horizontal relationships

4.8 for an illustration of differential leveling. It is necessary to complete a circuit by returning to the original B.M. in order to check the accuracy of the work. If the work is perfectly accurate, the elevation determined for the B.M. at the end of the level circuit is the same as the starting elevation.

Notekeeping

A level circuit begins with a known elevation at a bench mark, and succeeding elevations are computed as follows:

$$\text{Elevation of B.M. 1} \quad 248.45$$

$$\text{plus B.S.} \quad +5.41$$

$$\text{Elevation of H.I. (line of sight)} \quad 253.86$$

$$\text{minus F.S.} \quad -3.28$$

$$\text{Elevation of T.P. 1} \quad 250.58$$

$$\text{plus B.S.} \quad +9.37$$

$$\text{H.I.} \quad 259.95$$

Differential leveling notes for Fig. 4.8 are shown in standard form in Fig. 4.9. Note that each backsight and foresight is on the same line as the bench mark or turning point on which that sight was taken. If they are not, notes are being improperly kept. The closing elevation on B.M. 1 is not the same as the starting elevation. The difference is the error of closure and is equal to $+0.01$ ft. This is caused by accidental errors and, therefore, cannot be avoided.

In this case, the elevation of B.M. 2 is accepted as 265.23 since it is not known where the error is. If the error of closure had been $+0.02$, it could be assumed that the error is $+0.01$ going out from B.M. 1 to B.M. 2 and $+0.01$ returning from B.M. 2 to B.M. 1. B.M. 2 could then be adjusted by adding a correction equal and opposite in sign to the error from B.M. 1 to B.M. 2 ($265.23 - 0.01 = 265.22$).

Fairview Ave. Intersection, Albany   P.10

Sta.	B.S.(+)	H.I.	F.S.(−)	Elev.
B.M.1	5.41	253.86		248.45
T.P.1	9.37	259.95	3.28	250.58
T.P.2	8.93	266.67	2.21	257.74
B.M.2	9.79	275.02	1.44	265.23
T.P.3	6.10	279.54	1.58	273.44
T.P.4	3.43	270.95	12.02	267.52
T.P.5	1.03	259.50	12.48	258.47
B.M.1			11.04	248.46
	+44.06		−44.05	

Arithmetic check

Starting elev.	248.45
+ total B.S.	+ 44.06
	292.51
− total F.S.	− 44.05
Answer	248.46

equals closing elev.

Date
Level # 2
Rod # 3
Light snow 15° F
Chris P.
Maura T.

B.M.1 Fairview Ave. West, north side 600' fm center of intersection w/ Main, "X"cut into NE corner of top of stone wall.

B.M.2 Center of Fairview Ave. in inter- section w/Main, bead welded on SE section of circular frame of manhole opening.

Figure 4.9 Differential leveling field notes

Note that the final elevation will be the same as the starting elevation if the total of all the backsights (positive sign) is equal to the total of all the foresights (negative sign). Any difference in the closing elevation is due to a difference between the total backsights and the total foresights unless a mistake is made in adding or subtracting. The closing elevation should be higher (in a positive direction) than the starting elevation if the sum of backsights is greater than the sum of foresights and vice versa.

In computing the elevation as the work progresses, there is a chance for an arithmetic mistake. The difference between the sum of backsights and the sum of foresights will equal the difference between starting and closing elevations (error of closure) unless a mistake is made in arithmetic.

A convenient method of checking is shown in Fig. 4.9. If the final result does not equal the closing elevation, a mistake has been made in addition or subtraction. The check only shows whether or not a mistake has been made in arithmetic. It does not indicate whether or not the field work is satisfactory. The rod can be misread or a rod reading recorded incorrectly without affecting the arithmetic check. The use of correct field procedures and careful attention while performing the work are necessary to prevent mistakes. The fact that the closing elevation is the same or nearly the same as the starting elevation indicates that the field work is accurate. The arithmetic check should be performed before leaving the field.

4.5 PROFILE LEVELING

For design of highways, pipelines, and other long, narrow projects, it is necessary to plot a continuous representation of the ground surface called a *profile*. The profile is a section view of the surface along the center line of work. The information needed to plot the profile is obtained in the field by the process of profile leveling. *Profile leveling* consists of differential leveling with additional elevations being obtained at locations needed to plot the profile. The locations are often at 50-ft or 100-ft intervals along the project center line and are designated by stationing. Rod readings are taken at the desired points from a known H.I. The rod is read only to the nearest tenth of a ft when the rod is placed on the ground. The readings are called *rod shots* to differentiate them from foresights, which are part of the level circuit and must be used in calculating turning point elevations around the circuit. Rod shots are not part of the circuit and are not used in the arithmetic check.

Figures 4.10, 4.11, and 4.12 show a plan view of a profile leveling circuit, field notes, and a plot of the profile from the field notes. Notice that the B.M. and T.P.'s are not part of the profile. There is no reason for them to be located on the line of the profile. Instead, each T.P. should be located so that the maximum number of rod shots can be taken with each instrument setup.

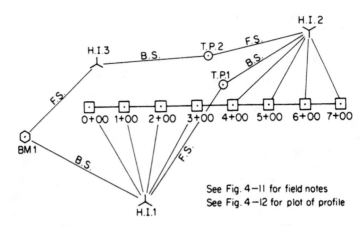

See Fig. 4–11 for field notes
See Fig. 4–12 for plot of profile

Figure 4.10   Plan view of profile leveling along a straight route

The sequence is important. All rod shots from any one instrument position should be read and recorded before a foresight is read in order to prevent possible confusion of numbers. When working on soft ground or other soft surfaces, the instrument might sink slightly and, therefore, change its elevation between the time of reading the B.S. and the time of reading

Fairview Ave. Sewer, Albany						
Sta.	B.S.(+)	H.I.	F.S. (−)	Rod(−)	Elev.	p.11
B.M.1	11.82	111.82			100.00	Date
0+00				5.3	106.5	Level # 2
1+00				5.2	106.6	Rod # 4
2+00				4.1	107.7	Warm, clear
3+00				3.0	108.8	Joe B. ⊼ ⊏⊐
T.P.1	5.32	115.18	1.96		109.86	Kathy H. ∮
4+00				7.9	107.3	
5+00				6.7	108.5	
6+00				5.6	109.6	
7+00				4.5	110.7	
T.P.2	2.11	109.80	7.49		107.69	
B.M.1			9.81		99.99	B.M.1
	+19.25		−19.26			See page 1 for description.

```
   100.00          Arithmetic
 + 19.25              check
  119.25
 − 19.26
   99.99 ◄
```

Figure 4.11   Profile leveling field notes

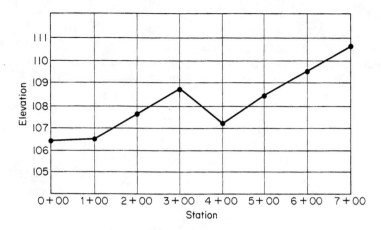

Figure 4.12 Plot of profile

the F.S.   In this case, a different procedure may be required.   This is discussed in the section on systematic errors.

4.6 CROSS-SECTION LEVELING

It is often desirable for the designer to have a representation of the surface
on both sides of the center line of work.   This is usually shown by plotting
short profiles at right angles to the line of work.   These are called *cross
sections* and are plotted at regular intervals and are designated by stationing.

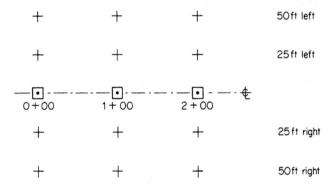

Instrument positions, bench mark, turning points
and rod shots are the same as in Fig. 4 −10
with additional rod shots at specified offsets
from each station.

See Fig. 4 − 14 for field notes
See Fig. 4 − 15 for plot of cross sections

Figure 4.13 Plan view of cross-section leveling showing only rod shot locations

The information needed is obtained in the field by the process of *cross-section leveling*. Everything written in the preceding section about profile leveling applies to cross-section leveling. In addition, other rod shots are taken adjacent to each rod shot taken in profile leveling. The shots are taken at

Round Hill Rd. Storm Drain Cross Sections.									p.14
Sta.	B.S.(+)	H.I.	F.S.(−)	Elev.	Left		¢	Right	
B.M.1	11.82	111.82		100.00					
0+00					105.7 6.1 50'	106.0 5.8 25'	106.5 5.3	106.8 5.0 25'	107.3 4.5 50'
1+00					105.3 6.5 50'	106.2 5.6 25'	106.6 5.2	106.8 5.0 10'	107.3 4.5 50'
2+00					105.8 6.0 50'	106.6 5.2 16'	107.7 4.1	107.4 4.4 8'	108.2 3.6 50'
3+00					106.0 5.8 50'	106.8 5.0 22'	108.8 3.0	107.8 4.0 20'	107.6 4.2 50'
T.P.1	5.32	115.18	1.96	109.86					
4+00					106.4 8.8 50'	106.7 8.5 32'	107.3 7.9	108.0 7.2 19'	107.4 7.8 50'
5+00					107.2 8.0 50'	107.4 7.8 18'	108.5 6.7	108.2 7.0 31'	107.4 7.8 50'
6+00					108.8 6.4 50'	109.2 6.0 25'	109.6 5.6	109.8 5.4 38'	109.6 5.6 50'
7+00					109.2 6.0 50'	108.7 6.5 25'	109.7 5.5	108.2 7.0 25'	107.7 7.5 50'
T.P.2 B.M.1	2.11 <u>+19.25</u>	109.80	7.49 9.81 <u>−19.26</u>	107.69 99.99	B.M.1 − E. side of Round Hill Rd. 500' N. of Mill Creek. Spike in N.side of 24" oak in S. fence line.			Date Level # 3128 Rod #3 Warm, hazy C.B. 𝛑 R.M ⊡ W.H. ф	

100.00
+ 19.25
119.25
− 19.26
99.99

Arithmetic check

Note: Some rod shots are at a change in ground slope instead of a 25 ft offset. No shots are needed beyond 50 ft offset.

Figure 4.14   Cross-section leveling field notes

prescribed lateral distances from the center line and at breaks in the ground slope on a line perpendicular to the survey line at the location of the profile shot.   See Figs. 4.13, 4.14, and 4.15 for a plan of the field locations, field notes, and a plot of cross sections.

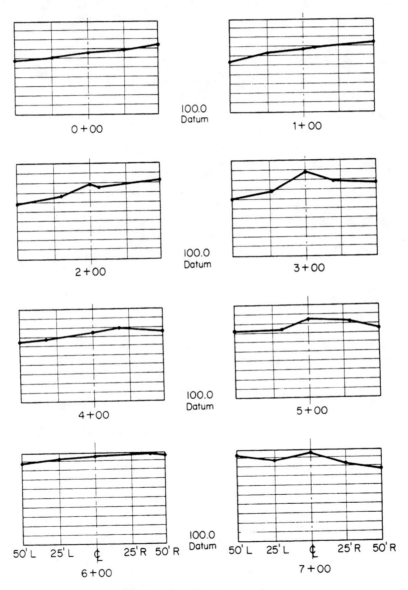

Figure 4.15   Plot of cross sections

4.7 INVERTING THE ROD

Conventional leveling requires that the level instrument be higher than any point on which the rod is placed. It is sometimes necessary to obtain the elevation of an object higher than the instrument. Any reading, B.S., F.S. or rod, can be obtained as illustrated in Fig. 4.16. Notekeeping is standard except that a B.S. is minus and an F.S. or rod reading is plus. A note should be put on the right-hand side of the page to explain the reversal of signs.

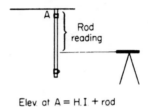

Elev. at A = H.I. + rod

Figure 4.16 Sighting rod above instrument

4.8 SIGNALS

When the members of a survey party cannot hear each other because of distance or noisy working conditions, they can use hand signals. The following signals are in general use.

The instrument person signals the rod person to establish a T.P. by holding an index finger in the air and rotating it in a horizontal circle. This signal is used to prevent the rod person from going so far up or down a hill that the level line of sight falls below or above the level rod; it is also used by the rod person to notify the instrument person and note keeper that the rod is on a turning point and not in a position for a rod shot. The instrument person must know this because the rod is read more accurately for a T.P. than for a rod shot, and the note keeper must know in order to keep notes properly.

The party chief signals to move the instrument to the next location by extending both hands downward and outward and then raising them in a motion similar to lifting an instrument by the legs. This signal is used to indicate that all readings needed from this instrument position have been obtained and that the instrument should be moved to the next position. The instrument should not be moved until so decided by the party chief who is responsible for obtaining complete field information.

The signal that an operation is completed is given by raising both hands above the head, and then waving them outward and back to the original position. This signal, given by the instrument person or party chief, indicates that a rod reading is completed and that the rod should be moved to the next position. This signal does not mean that the instrument may be moved.

If the instrument person sees that the rod is not plumb, he or she should call, "Plumb the rod" or signal by extending the arm vertically and moving it in the direction in which the top of the rod should move.

The instrument person cannot tell if the rod is leaning out of plumb toward or away from the instrument; but if it is suspected, the rod person can be signalled to *rock* the rod slowly toward and away from the instrument. As the rod leans farther toward the instrument, the reading becomes greater. As the rod starts back, the reading becomes lower until the rod is plumb and then becomes greater as the rod leans farther away from plumb.   Therefore, the lowest reading is most accurate.   The signal for this is to hold the arm over the head and wave it slowly forward and back or to call, "Rock the rod."

If an obstruction prevents reading the rod, it might be read with sufficient accuracy if the top of the rod is moved clear of the obstruction by *waving* it slowly back and forth in a direction perpendicular to the line of sight with the bottom of the rod remaining on the point.   The signal for this is to wave the arm slowly from side to side above the head or to call, "Wave the rod." Note that rocking and waving are in different directions.

Sometimes, when the rod is close to the instrument, the short length of rod that is visible through the telescope does not include a foot number.   In this case the rod should be raised slowly in a vertical line until a whole foot can be read.   The signal for this is to hold the hand out palm up and raise it a short distance or to call, "Raise for red."   The signal that the rod has been raised enough and should be returned is the signal that an operation is completed.   The rod is then lowered to the original point so that the reading of tenths and hundreths can be verified.

4.9 STEP-BY-STEP OPERATION—INSTRUMENT PERSON

Steadiness of the instrument depends on proper adjustment of the hinge thumbscrews at the top of the legs.   If they are too loose, the entire instrument will be unsteady.   If they are too tight, they might bind and cause slight distortion when the legs are moved into position.   The distortion might relieve itself suddenly and put the instrument out of level or change its elevation. The legs of a properly adjusted tripod fall slowly of their own weight from a horizontal position toward the vertical.

Tripod legs should be set rigidly in place so that the footplate appears level by eye.   Rigidity is obtained by driving the shoes into the earth, or if the legs rest on a hard surface, by tightening the hinge thumbscrews after the legs are in place.   The footplate is leveled by moving the legs in or out relative to the center under the instrument.   On a hillside, the uphill leg or legs must be farther away from the center than the downhill leg or legs.   Setting up is easier if the level is placed so that two legs are an equal distance downhill from the instrument and one leg is uphill. The telescope should be at such a height that the instrument person can use it comfortably,

The telescope is leveled by adjusting the leveling screws until the level bubble remains centered no matter which way the telescope is pointed. This is done by aligning the scope over one pair of leveling screws and centering the bubble by turning the two screws in opposite directions, then aligning the scope over the other pair of leveling screws and centering the bubble by turning those screws. The operation is repeated until the instrument is leveled satisfactorily. The level bubble will move in the direction in which the left thumb moves while turning the screw.

The cross hairs are then brought into focus by adjusting the focusing ring on the eyepiece while looking at the cross hairs. The cross hairs will vary from extremely thin to thick and fuzzy within the adjustment range. They are in focus when they appear thick with a sharp outline. It will help the eye to concentrate on the cross hairs if the background is of a solid light color such as the sky or a concrete wall. It might be necessary to occasionally make this adjustment. The condition of the cross hairs can easily be observed each time the telescope is used, and an adjustment can be made when needed.

The rod is sighted and its image is brought into focus by adjusting the focusing screw until the image is in the same plane as the cross hairs. This adjustment must be made for each change in distance to the rod. The test for proper focusing is to move the eye up and down slightly. When the image and cross hairs are in the same plane, there will be no movement between the cross hairs and the rod image. If they are not in the same plane, movement called *parallax* will be noticed. *Parallax* is the apparent movement between two objects at different distances caused by movement of the eye of the observer. Parallax is illustrated in Fig. 4.17.

After focusing, the instrument person checks the telescope level vial just before reading the rod, and an adjustment with one or two screws is made if necessary. The rod is then read without touching the instrument. The rod should be read at the point of intersection of the horizontal and vertical cross hairs. If the horizontal hair is not exactly horizontal, this intersection is the only point on it that lies in a level line of sight. The rod may be read to 0.01 ft or estimated to 0.001 ft. Always check numbers above and below the reading to assure that the rod is read correctly. If the instrument is used with both eyes open, the eye being used will not tire so soon. The natural tendency is to close one eye, and practice is required to learn to read the rod with both eyes open.

If the rod is not plumb by comparison with the vertical cross hair, if the rod cannot be read because of obstructions such as leaves or branches, or if no red whole number can be seen, the appropriate signal or instruction is given to the rod person until a satisfactory reading is obtained. The rod person is then sent to the next location with a signal.

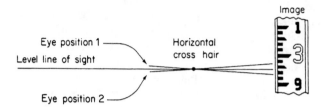

With the eye at position 1, the horizontal cross hair
    intersects the image at 2.93.
With the eye at position 2, the horizontal cross hair
    intersects the image at 2.97.
Although only the eye has moved, it appears the
    cross hair has moved across the image.
The closer the image is to the cross hairs, the
    smaller the possible error. When the image
    coincides with the cross hairs there can be no
    parallax.

Figure 4.17   Parallax in surveyor's telescope

The instrument person calls the reading to the note keeper while continuing to look at the rod through the telescope and checks the reading while saying it. The note keeper as a check repeats the reading aloud while writing it. The instrument person listens for the repetition and acknowledges it. If the instrument person is keeping notes, the reading is recorded immediately while saying it as a check.

4.10 CARE OF THE INSTRUMENT

The instrument should be kept in its carrying case until the work site is reached and, even then, should be carried in the case if it must be transported a long distance or over rough terrain before it will be used. Note how the manufacturer has placed the instrument in the case or read the manufacturer's instructions on how to store the instrument so that you can return it properly to the case. Precautions should be taken to prevent jarring the instrument even while in the case.

Most level instruments should be lifted from the case by gripping just below the telescope. The tripod should be set up solidly before the instrument is taken from the case. The instrument should be held firmly until it is attached to the tripod. The sunshade should be placed on the telescope. This improves visibility whether the sun is out or not. Once the instrument is in place on the tripod, it should not be left unattended.

The instrument is normally carried with the tripod on the shoulder and the instrument in back when moving from setup to setup, but it should be carried with the tripod held under one arm and the instrument in front supported by the other hand when there is danger of the instrument bumping something, such as when inside a building or in high brush. The clamp screw should be clamped lightly before the instrument is picked up on the tripod so that the telescope does not rotate when carried but will give without breaking if it hits something.

A level instrument can be used in rain or snow. After use, it should be allowed to dry off in the most dustfree place available.

Storing in the carrying case with the cover ajar will provide protection while drying. Modern instruments are built to prevent dust from entering and generally are not harmed by use in a dusty atmosphere. When it is used in rain or dust, the instrument should still be kept covered when it is not actually in use.

If either the objective lens or the eyepiece lens becomes so dirty that vision is impaired, it can be cleaned with a camel's-hair brush or lens paper but nothing rougher than these.

4.11 DUTIES OF ROD PERSON

The duties of the rod person appear simple compared with those of the instrument person. However, the rod person must understand the leveling process and must employ proper procedures if the work is to be completed without mistakes. It should be realized that work of unacceptably low accuracy is often caused by the poor performance of the rod person.

The rod person is responsible for placing the rod at the proper point for all shots, selecting turning points, and holding the rod vertical. Points are located with a tape and the help of another person, by measuring with the level rod laid flat on the ground or by pacing. The rod person should watch the instrument person or party chief for signals and comply promptly.

The rod person should stand on the side of the rod opposite the instrument and should balance the rod lightly with the fingertips of both hands. In this way, the rod is seen and can be held plumb while watching the instrument person for signals, and the fingers will not block the instrument person's view of the rod. The rod is held plumb by balancing it so that it does not lean against the fingertips of either hand. If a wind is blowing, the rod will be in balance while leaning into the wind. The rod person should learn to compensate for this and to keep the rod vertical. Several kinds of devices called *rod levels* are available for indicating when the rod is vertical by the location of a level bubble.

4.12 DUTIES OF NOTE KEEPER

Level surveys are often made by a party of three. If there are three people in the party, the third one is the note keeper. Notes must show the correct elevation for the starting B.M. and describe it completely. The note keeper records each rod reading immediately and repeats it while writing it to verify it with the originator. Each station must be recorded correctly. Elevations are computed as the work progresses, and an arithmetic check is made at the end of the project and at the end of each day.

4.13 MISTAKES

1. The rod may be read incorrectly. When the next higher foot mark can be seen through the telescope, it is sometimes read accidentally, causing a one-foot mistake. To prevent this, the instrument person should read the foot numbers above and below the cross hairs and should also count the hundredth place from the tenths numbers above and below the cross hairs to check the tenths and hundredths.

2. Notes may be entered incorrectly. To prevent this, the note keeper must understand the leveling process and visualize the operation before making each entry. Remember that the backsight and foresight are entered on the same line as the station being sighted.

3. The rod must be extended for shots with a large difference in elevation. Unless the numbers on the upper section of the rod are an accurate continuation of the numbers on the lower section, the reading will be incorrect. The rod person should extend the rod fully, hearing or feeling the click as the proper position is reached, and should look at the joint just before each shot to see that the numbers are in correct alignment.

4. By mistake, the rod may be placed on different points for the foresight and backsight of a turning point. To prevent this, the rod person should mark the T.P. with crayon or paint before using it the first time and be careful to use the same spot both times. If all rod shots are taken before the F.S. on the T.P., there will be little delay between F.S. and B.S. and little chance of losing the T.P. location before the B.S. is read.

5. The rod may be set down on chewing gum, mud, or another object that sticks to it. Each reading taken with the object stuck to the rod is lower than it should be. The error is minus for each B.S. and plus for each F.S. and rod shot. Therefore, a rod may be used for a complete level circuit, including rod shots, with a constant error in each reading and still provide accurate results because each backsight error is cancelled by the following foresight or rod shot error. However, if the object

falls off between the B.S. and F.S. or rod shot, an error results. When surveying in an area where something is likely to stick to the bottom of the rod, it is a mistake not to check before each reading to be sure nothing is there.

These mistakes cannot ordinarily be corrected without repeating the level circuit, or at least part of it. The exception is that notekeeping mistakes can sometimes be discovered and corrected in the office.

4.14 ERRORS AND CORRECTIONS

Systematic

1. If the telescope level vial and the line of sight are not perfectly parallel, the line of sight points up or down when the level bubble is centered. The result is an error consistently plus or consistently minus with magnitude in proportion to the distance between instrument and rod. Therefore, all B.S. and F.S will be larger or all will be smaller than the correct value. Since a positive B.S. and a negative F.S. are entered in the notes for each instrument location (H.I.), the errors will partially cancel each other and will exactly cancel each other if the distances from rod to instrument and instrument to rod are equal for each instrument setup. Then, the elevation of each T.P. or B.M. will have no error from this source. See Fig. 4.18.

    It is good practice to equalize the B.S. and F.S. distances from each instrument location by measuring, pacing, or estimating, depending on the accuracy needed. In ordinary work, the distances are paced where convenient and are estimated where pacing is inconvenient.

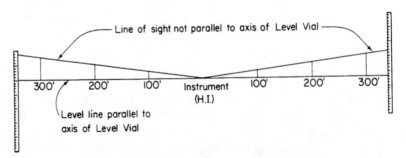

Error increases as distance from instrument increases.
B.S. error equals F.S. error if distances from instrument
are equal and therefore one cancels the other.

Figure 4.18   Error due to line of sight being out of level

When an elevation is to be carried from one B.M. to another, with no intermediate elevations to be determined, is is not necessary that the B.S. and F.S. distances be equal for each instrument setup as long as the total of B.S. distances equals the total of F.S. distances.

If the total of all B.S. distances in the survey equals the total of all F.S. distances, then total plus error will equal total minus error because error is directly proportional to distance, and the result will be no error from this source.

2. If the rod has an accurately calibrated scale but the zero mark is not exactly at the bottom of the rod, there will be an error, with the same direction and magnitude, for every reading regardless of distance. This situation occurs if the bottom of the rod is worn excessively or if the scale, which may be printed on a plastic tape and attached to the wood rod, is not attached correctly. This error cancels itself in the same way that the previous error did but is unaffected by distances to B.S. and F.S. Elevations determined by rod shots are also unaffected because the B.S. and the rod shot contain equal errors that cancel each other because of their opposite signs.

3. The instrument sinks downward over a period of time when it rests on a surface such as swampy ground, frozen ground, ice, or bituminous paving, which allows settlement under the weight of the instrument. The F.S. is then always read from a lower point than the B.S. The F.S. is less than it should be, giving a plus error to the new T.P. The total error increases with each setup on a yielding surface.

The effect can be minimized by providing a foundation of flat stones or blocks of wood for the tripod and by taking the F.S. as soon as possible after the B.S. The error can be made compensating by taking the F.S. before the B.S. on alternate instrument setups.

Accidental

1. The accuracy of a rod reading depends on many factors. Among these are the skill of the instrument person and rod person, distance to rod, clearness of the atmosphere, heat waves rising from the ground, and wind that may shake the instrument. The required accuracy can generally be obtained by shortening the distance between instrument and rod to suit the weather conditions and the capabilities of the party members. Weather conditions may sometimes be so bad that leveling work should not be done. A distance of 200 ft is about the longest ever permissible for level readings, and it should usually be shorter. Accuracy may be increased by estimating readings to the third decimal place even though no vernier is used. The end result will not be accurate to the third decimal place, but accuracy will be improved.

2. If the rod is not held plumb, the reading will be too high.   The error from this source is always in the same direction and of unknown size. Since some errors will apply to B.S. (+) and some to F.S. (−), they tend to cancel one another.   The correct reading can be determined by rocking the rod toward and away from the instrument while it is read. The reading will be lowest when the rod is plumb.

4.15 LONG SIGHTS

Very long sights are sometimes required because no intermediate points are accessible.   Three factors cause difficulty on extremely long sights.

1. It is difficult to read a level rod accurately at distances greater than about 200 ft.
2. A misalignment between the line of sight and the level vial results in a large error since the error is proportional to the distance.   Equalizing B.S. distance with F.S. distance eliminates this error but it may not be possible.   When it is possible, there are then two very long sights with the accompanying loss of accuracy due to difficulty in reading the rod.
3. The line of sight is a level line only at the point where it is perpendicular to a plumb line.   It deviates from the level because it is theoretically straight, while a level line curves to remain perpendicular to plumb lines at all points.   The line of sight is actually bent because of refraction and is not truly straight.   The relationships of the theoretically straight line of sight, the slightly curved actual line of sight, and the level line following the curve of the earth are shown in Fig. 4.19.

The deviation of the actual line of sight from a truly level line is insignificant in ordinary surveying for any one shot at distances up to 400 ft.   If readings are taken to 0.001 ft, the deviation is significant at about 200 ft. However, if B.S. and F.S. can be equalized, the errors caused by this deviation will cancel each other.

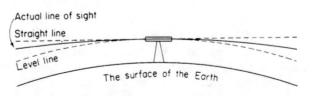

Figure 4.19   Diagram of actual line of sight

The method for accurately determining an elevation using two widely separated points is shown in Fig. 4.20 for two consecutive turning points, T.P. 1 and T.P. 2. The new elevation is found by reading B.S. and F.S. from an instrument setup close to T.P. 1 then by reading B.S. and F.S. from an instrument setup close to T.P. 2. The long sights must be of equal length. If the instrument is set the same paced distance from each T.P. toward the other T.P. the long lengths are equal. The error in the long sight causes the F.S. to be too high by an unknown amount from H.I. 1 (a minus error) and the B.S. to be too high by the same amount from H.I. 2 (a plus error). The errors cancel each other if an average of the two elevations of T.P. 2 is used. Field notes are shown in Fig. 4.21. This method eliminates systematic error caused by misalignment in the instrument and curvature of the earth.

In order to eliminate accidental errors as much as possible on long sights, a target should be used, and the average of several readings taken.

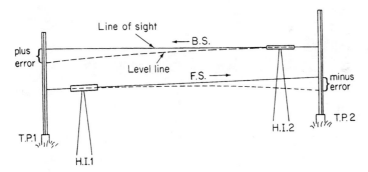

Figure 4.20 Method for accurate leveling over a great distance

Sta.	B.S.(+)	H.I.	F.S.(−)	Elev.	
B.M.1	5.22	342.64		337.42	
T.P. 1	5.72*	344.05	4.31	338.33	
T.P.2			2.10*	341.95	minus error in F.S.
T.P. 1	6.30**	344.63			plus error in B.S.
T.P.2			2.62**	342.01	
T.P.2	5.17	347.15		341.98	Average elevation
T.P. 3			4.98	342.17	

    * sighted from H.I.1
   ** sighted from H.I.2

Figure 4.21 Field notes for leveling method of Figure 4.20

PROBLEMS

1. Prepare acceptable field notes, including an arithmetic check, from the following field data. Can you visualize that both circuits run up hill and back down?

	Sta.	B.S.	F.S.	Known Elevation
(a)	B.M. 7	6.42		347.36
	T.P. 1	8.43	1.77	
	T.P. 2	12.49	2.08	
	T.B.M. 7–1	0.27	3.48	
	T.P. 3	2.76	11.86	
	T.P. 4	3.92	7.98	
	B.M. 7		7.10	347.36
(b)	B.M. 16	10.75		144.62
	T.P. 1	11.96	2.21	
	T.P. 2	10.43	3.61	
	T.P. 3	6.22	10.84	
	T.B.M. 1	2.04	11.79	
	T.P. 4	1.18	9.91	
	B.M. 17		0.08	148.77

2. Prepare complete field notes from the following field data.

	Sta.	B.S.	F.S.	Rod	Known Elevation
(a)	B.M. 1	3.42			3421.16
	T.P. 1	2.67	2.90		
	T.P. 2	3.16	3.51		
	T.P. 3	2.79	2.84		
	Rod 1			8.22	
	Rod 2			8.19	
	B.M. 2		3.38		3421.57
(b)	B.M. 3	9.46			3841.11
	T.P. 1	1.23	11.13		
	Rod 1			4.5	
	T.P. 2	2.19	8.31		
	Rod 2			6.8	
	Rod 3			9.7	
	T.P. 3	3.49	10.95		
	Rod 4			2.2	
	B.M. 4		11.46		3815.62

3. Prepare field notes and plot profiles from the following field data.

	Sta.	B.S.	F.S.	Rod	Known Elevation
(a)	B.M. 1	7.91			2100.68
	T.P. 1	8.42	6.24		
	0 + 00			6.42	

Sta.	B.S.	F.S.	Rod	*Known* *Elevation*
T.P. 2	8.10	5.13		
0 + 50			5.41	
1 + 00			5.98	
T.P. 3	7.52	4.55		
1 + 50			5.02	
B.M. 3		4.08		2112.63

Sta.	B.S.	F.S.	Rod	*Assumed* *Elevation* 100.00
(b) B.M. 1	6.33			
6 + 00			4.2	
T.P. 1	6.59	8.28		
6 + 50			5.8	
T.P. 2	7.88	4.45		
6 + 25			1.2	
6 + 75			8.0	
T.P. 4	3.92	8.08		
B.M. 1		3.91		

4. Prepare field notes and plot profiles for the level circuits and rod shots shown here schematically.

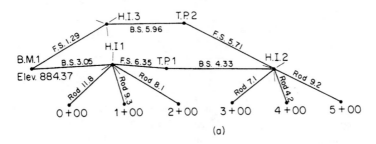

(a)

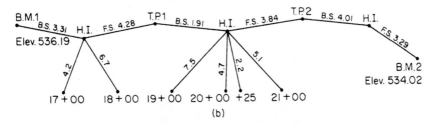

(b)

5. Finish the following field notes and plot cross sections from them. Often the first one or two digits of elevations can be omitted to save time and space if no confusion will result.

Sta.	B.S. +	H.I.	F.S. −	Elev.	Left 50'	Left 25'	₵	Right 25'	Right 50'
B.M.8	10.18			843.22					
9+00					9.8	8.1	7.3	6.3	5.9
9+50					10.7	9.2	8.4	6.2	5.1
10+00					10.5	9.0	8.1	5.8	4.8
10+50					9.8	8.6	7.6	6.5	5.4
11+00					10.4	8.0	6.9	5.6	4.2
TP 1	8.89		5.70						
11+50					12.0	10.6	9.3	8.1	6.7
TP2	5.44		9.13						
BM8			9.68						

(b)

Sta.	B.S. +	H.I.	F.S. −	Elev.	Left		₵	Right	
BM 31	3.13	37.34		2134.21					
0+00					$\frac{1.0}{5.0}$	$\frac{3.6}{3.5}$	4.8	$\frac{4.9}{2.5}$	$\frac{7.3}{5.0}$
1+00					$\frac{9.3}{5.0}$	$\frac{3.3}{2.5}$	3.1	$\frac{1.9}{1.5}$	$\frac{6.7}{5.0}\,\frac{6.3}{5.0}$
2+00					$\frac{1.2}{5.0}$	$\frac{4.4}{2.0}$	5.3	$\frac{2.4}{2.0}$	$\frac{3.4}{3.3}\,\frac{5.0}{5.0}$
TP 1	1.03		2.89						
3+00					$\frac{9.3}{5.0}$	$\frac{1.1}{3.5}$.	2.4	$\frac{3.4}{2.5}$	$\frac{4.6}{5.0}$
4+00					$\frac{0.8}{5.0}$	$\frac{1.7}{2.5}$	2.1	$\frac{2.4}{2.5}$	$\frac{4.3}{5.0}$
5+00					$\frac{1.7}{5.0}$	$\frac{3.4}{2.5}$	4.7	$\frac{4.4}{2.5}$	$\frac{7.8}{5.0}$.
TP 2	2.17		8.94						
TBM 31–1			7.66						

Elev. TBM 31–1 = 2121.05

(a)

6. The elevation of the bottom of a beam is needed. The H.I. is determined by reading 3.97 on the rod in a normal way with the rod on a B.M. of 739.08 elevation. The rod is then held upside down against the bottom of the beam and 7.31 is read. What is the elevation of the bottom of the beam?

7. In a mine, a B.M. on the ceiling has an elevation of 213.19. A rod is held upside down against the B.M., and a H.I. is determined by reading 4.81. A turning point on the floor is used with the rod in normal position, and a F.S. of 5.01 and a B.S. of 4.76 are read to establish a new H.I. A new B.M. is set on the ceiling, and a F.S. of 6.92 is read on it. What is the elevation of the new B.M.?

8. From one instrument setup, a rod reading of 11.4 is read on the underside of a bridge, and a rod reading of 10.8 is read on the water surface under the bridge. What is the clearance? Draw a sketch if needed to visualize this.

9. B.S. on an overhead B.M. (elev. 789.10) is 6.22. F.S. on T.P. 1 (normal) is 3.86, and B.S. is 11.46. Rod shot in normal position on a point is 4.19. What is the elevation of the point?

10. A rod with a 0.02-ft gap between bottom of rod and bottom of scale is used up to and including the B.S. on T.P. 4. Starting with F.S. on T.P. 5, a rod with no

gap is used to complete the circuit of 12 turning points.   What is the total error caused by changing rods?

11. A level circuit is run using a level rod with the numbers printed on a plastic strip. Part way through the circuit, it is noticed that zero on the plastic strip is 0.10 ft above the bottom of the rod.   What is the total error from this source if the circuit of 14 turning points is completed with no alteration to the rod?   What is the total error if zero on the strip is adjusted to coincide with the bottom of the rod between reading a B.S. on T.P. 8 and reading a F.S. on T.P. 9?   What if the adjustment is made between B.S. and F.S. at any setup?   What is the total error if the adjustment is made between F.S. and B.S. on the same T.P.?

12. A wad of bubble gum 0.01-ft thick is stuck to the bottom of the rod from the B.S. on T.P. 3 through the F.S. on T.P. 6.   What error is caused?

13. The instrument settles 0.01 ft between the B.S. on T.P. 5 and the F.S. on T.P. 6.   What error is caused?

14. After two level circuits are run, it is discovered that all readings on the extended rod were 0.02 ft low.   Using the notes shown, what corrections should be made to the closing elevation and rod elevations?

B.S.	F.S.	Rod	B.S.	F.S.	Rod
1.15			8.33		
8.24	4.22		6.14	6.25	
		5.13			11.19
9.61	5.16		9.46	5.21	
		8.89			10.80
11.21	8.63		10.98	8.01	
		9.17			6.27
	0.49			11.42	

15. After running two level circuits it is discovered that the new rod is calibrated with the 5-ft mark adjacent to the 3-ft mark (the length from 4.00 to 4.99 is missing). What are the corrections needed with these readings?

B.S.	F.S.	Rod	B.S.	F.S.	Rod
6.61			2.24		
		7.81	1.47	11.19	
8.29	5.42				6.73
5.26	3.21		2.43	12.28	
7.48	2.88				1.10
		3.37	1.93	14.26	
	2.26			10.82	

16. Prepare acceptable field notes, including an arithmetic check, from the following field data:

Sta.	B.S.	F.S.	Known Elevation
(a) B.M. 1	3.762		1576.230
T.P. 1	4.914	4.192	
T.P. 2	8.373	5.723	
T.P. 3	7.525	8.298	
B.M. 2	9.768	10.117	
T.P. 4	8.207	7.243	
T.P. 5	5.391	8.032	

Sta.	B.S.	F.S.	Known Elevation
T.P. 6	4.131	4.894	
B.M. 1		3.568	1576.230
(b) B.M. 5	7.211		174.372
T.P. 1	8.496	4.119	
T.P. 2	10.137	3.862	
T.P. 3	8.412	4.381	
T.P. 4	9.139	2.938	
T.B.M. 5–1	10.941	3.467	
T.P. 5	11.822	4.842	
T.P. 6	9.436	3.178	
T.P. 7	8.197	2.673	
B.M. 6		2.412	226.293

17. A city B.M. with an assumed elevation of 100.00 has been used to set other B.M.s with elevations as follows: 117.65, 97.42, 46.21, −1.29 and −13.72. The city B.M. is later determined to have an elevation of 97.42 based on a datum of zero at mean sea level. Convert the other B.M. elevations to the mean sea level datum.

18. A city has a B.M. with assumed elevation of zero and an industrial plant has a B.M. with assumed elevation of 100.00. The city B.M. elevation is 2624.23 and the plant B.M. elevation is 2601.56 based on mean sea level. What is the difference in elevations of the 2 B.M.s? What is the sea level elevation of a point with city datum elevation of 26.48? What are the city datum elevations of points with plant datum elevations of 147.50, 46.21, 0.00, and −12.47?

19. A level rod is run over by a train and loses 1.37 ft from the bottom. What error is introduced when the level circuit is continued if the first reading after the accident is a B.S.? If it is a F.S.? Decide how to adjust field notes to correct the error in each case.

20. From the following sequences of readings, describe the ground as sloping downward, sloping upward or generally level.

B.S.	F.S.	B.S.	F.S.	B.S.	F.S.
2.02		2.02		10.24	
3.48	7.55	4.61	2.97	12.75	8.22
1.10	8.91	6.85	4.18	11.38	9.98
	6.04		7.18		9.44

5

MEASURING ANGLES

INSTRUCTIONAL OBJECTIVES

1. *Given a transit of a type decided on by the instructor and a point the size of a nail head, the student should be able to set up the transit over the point.*

2. *Given a transit already set up over a point and two additional points, the student should be able to:*
   a. *Turn an angle between the two points to the left or right or in deflection as directed.*
   b. *Double the angle between the two points and read it on the vernier.*

3. *Given a transit already set up over a point and one additional point, the student should be able to:*
   a. *Determine the vertical angle to the point from a horizontal line.*
   b. *Extend a line by double centering.*

4. *Given a field notebook and horizontal and vertical angle data, the student should be able to enter satisfactory notes, including a sketch.*

5. *Given a transit, with a compass, already set up over a point and one additional point, the student should be able to determine the magnetic bearing to the other point.*

Distance alone is not sufficient to establish relationships between points. Direction is also needed. A review of Chapter 1 shows that this is true whether the relationship is shown by direction and distance, by coordinates, or by stationing and offset.   Once a reference direction, such as north, is established, other directions are determined by angles from the reference direction—by bearings or azimuths, for example.   Angular measuring is covered in this chapter.

5.1 KINDS OF ANGLES

An *angle* is formed by two lines drawn from one common point called the *vertex*.   The size or measurement of the angle is the amount of divergence between the two lines.   It is helpful to think of the angle as being formed by a stationary line and a revolving line that starts at the stationary line and swings about the vertex a certain distance in either direction to define the angle.

Angles used in surveying are either vertical or horizontal; i.e., the revolving line either rotates in a vertical plane or it rotates in a horizontal plane. For horizontal angles, the stationary line is the *backsight*, and the revolving line is the *foresight*.

Horizontal angles are turned to the right or left starting at the backsight or to the right or left looking forward 180° from the backsight.   The second type is called a *deflection angle*.   Figure 5.1 shows the four ways in which a horizontal angle may be turned.

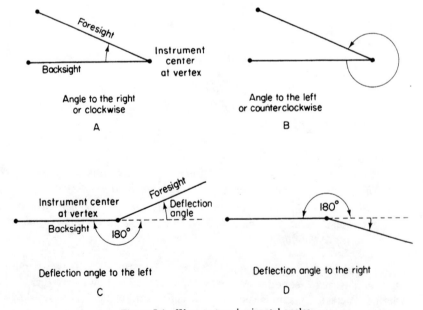

Figure 5.1   Ways to turn horizontal angles

The same angle is shown at *A* and *B*. The only difference is that it is turned in opposite directions. Any particular angle can be turned by any of the four methods. Often, one way is most convenient. For example, it is convenient to turn a small deflection angle rather than a larger angle right or left. From Fig. 5.1, it can be seen that a deflection angle is equal to 180° minus what the angle would be if turned the closest way.

Instead of "right" and "left," the terms *clockwise* and *counterclockwise* are sometimes used. However, in the field, it is easier to visualize right and left while turning angles than it is to visualize clockwise and counterclockwise motion.

Vertical angles are measured up or down from a horizontal line. If the vertical angle is turned upward, it is a *plus angle*, and it is a *minus angle* if turned downward. An angle measured downward from a vertical line is called a *zenith angle*. These angles are measured from the major surveying reference directions (horizontal or vertical) and not between two points as horizontal angles are measured. See Fig. 5.2 for illustrations.

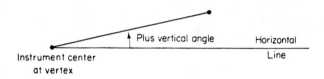

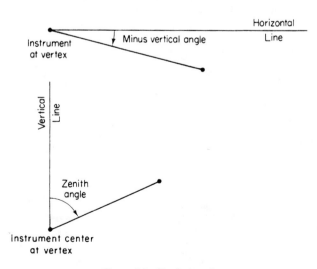

Figure 5.2   Vertical angles

5.2 THE ENGINEER'S TRANSIT

Horizontal and vertical angles are measured with a transit. The transit is designed so that horizontal and vertical angles have their vertex at a common center. This *instrument center* is the intersection of three lines: one vertical, one horizontal, and one variable. The vertical line is the center line of two vertical concentric tapered cylinders called *spindles*, on which all the measuring devices of the transit are mounted. The horizontal line is the center line of the *horizontal axle*, and the variable line is the line of sight through the telescope. The instrument center is the vertex for any angle turned with the transit.

Geometric Relationships

The vertical line can be moved, while remaining vertical, so that it coincides with a vertical line through a point that is to be used as the vertex of a horizontal angle. The horizontal line can be rotated in a complete circle about the vertical line while remaining horizontal. Thus, an angle turned in the plane of rotation of the horizontal is a horizontal angle. The variable

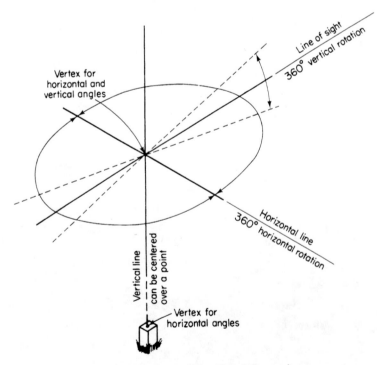

Figure 5.3 Basic relationships of the transit

line of sight can be rotated in a vertical plane, but it always passes through the instrument center and always is perpendicular to the horizontal line. The line of sight can thus turn a vertical angle or a horizontal angle or both at once. See Fig. 5.3 for illustration.

The line of sight can be rotated to point in any direction, but its rotation always consists of horizontal and vertical components. Therefore, any change in direction consists of a horizontal angle only, a vertical angle only, or a horizontal angle plus a vertical angle.

The transit shown in Fig. 5.4 is of the kind known as *American type transits*. There are other transits differing greatly in details and appearance, but the basic principles of operation and methods of use are similar. The American type is discussed in this chapter.

The transit telescope is the same as the telescope of the level instrument described in Chapter 4. A level vial is attached parallel with the telescope, as on the level instrument, to indicate whether or not the line of sight is horizontal. This is the *telescope level*.

The transit telescope is mounted on trunnions, much like an old-fashioned cannon, and is rotated on the trunnions, in a vertical plane. The trunnions, called the *horizontal axle* in this book, are supported by two frames called *standards*, one at each end of the axle.

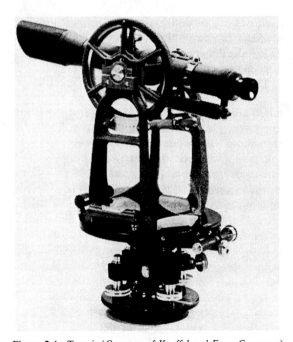

Figure 5.4 Transit (*Courtesy of Keuffel and Esser Company*)

The purpose of the standards is to hold the horizontal axle level so that a vertical angle can be turned in a vertical plane and so that a horizontal angle can be turned accurately, regardless of a difference in elevation between backsight and foresight.

Measurement

A vertical circle calibrated in degrees and minutes is attached to the telescope and rotates with it. Note in Fig. 5-4 how the telescope and vertical circle rotate about the horizontal axle. The vertical angle up or down is indicated by the rotation of the vertical circle past a stationary index mark. The index is supplemented by a vernier on each side of it, and the index and verniers together are called the *vertical vernier*. Any vertical angle turned on the instrument has its vertex at the instrument center.

Vertical motion is stopped approximately at the proper position with the *vertical motion clamp*, and the cross hairs are trained exactly on the object with the *vertical tangent screw*.

The transit may be used for leveling since it has a level vial parallel with the line of sight. It is more cumbersome to use than an engineer's level and is generally not as accurate. See Fig. 5.5 for the relationship of the devices used in turning vertical angles and leveling.

The telescope along with the base on which it is mounted is called the *upper plate* or *alidade*. This entire assembly rotates horizontally as a unit on the *inner spindle*. The assembly includes two additional level vials called *plate levels*, which indicate when the plate is level. One is parallel with the telescope, and one is perpendicular to it. Both are perpendicular to the axis of the spindle. Therefore, the axis of the spindle is made vertical by leveling the upper plate.

Also included are two index marks 180° apart that indicate how far the upper plate is turned. Each mark has a vernier on either side of it for a more precise indication. Each mark including its verniers is called simply a *vernier*. One vernier is located adjacent to the eyepiece where it is easily used by the instrument person and is called the *A vernier*. The opposite vernier is called the *B vernier*. The entire upper plate rotates within a calibrated horizontal circle so that the angle turned can be read with a vernier on the circle. See Fig. 5.5 for details of the upper plate.

The rotary motion of the upper plate is stopped at approximately the proper position with a clamp, and the cross hairs are trained exactly on the object with a tangent screw. These are called the *upper motion clamp* and the *upper tangent screw*. The upper plate is often called the *upper motion*.

Below the upper plate is a horizontal circular plate divided around its circumference into 360 degrees and subdivided into smaller parts, generally half degrees, one-third degrees, or quarter degrees. This plate, called the *lower plate*, can be held stationary while the upper plate is rotated or can be

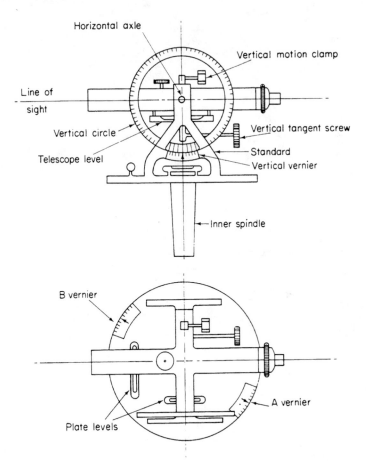

Figure 5.5   Transit upper plate

rotated independently of the upper plate. It can also be rotated as one unit with the upper plate. Its level position is controlled by the upper plate because it is attached to a vertical *outer spindle* that is hollow and encloses the inner spindle of the upper plate. Both spindles are tapered and have a common axis. As they wear with use, they settle slightly lower, but because of the tapered bearing surfaces, neither one can become loose. They, therefore, continue to rotate truly about their common center. The rotary motion of the lower plate is stopped with a clamp and moved to exact position with a tangent screw. These are called the *lower motion clamp* and the *lower tangent screw*. The lower plate is often called the *lower motion*. See Fig. 5.6 for details of the lower plate.

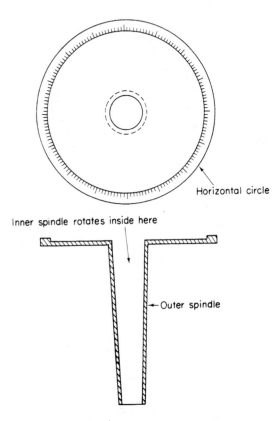

Figure 5.6   Transit lower plate

With the lower plate clamped, the upper plate can be rotated, and the A vernier can be made to mark any desired angle. Generally, the A vernier is set approximately on zero, clamped, and then set precisely on zero with the upper tangent screw. The lower plate is then loosened and turned so that the line of sight is on the stationary line of the angle to be measured. It is clamped with the lower clamp and aimed precisely on line with the lower tangent screw. While the lower plate is turned, the upper plate remains firmly clamped with the vernier marking zero. Thus, the vernier reads zero at the stationary side of the angle.

Next, the upper plate is loosened, and the telescope (with the entire upper plate) is rotated until the line of sight is on the point at the other side of the angle. Here, the upper plate is clamped and then adjusted with the upper tangent screw. The upper plate has now turned from one side of the angle to the other, and the A vernier has moved from zero to the angle turned, which is read and recorded.

Transit Orientation

Some device is needed to align the upper and lower plates in a horizontal plane, or put in another way, to position the concentric spindles in a vertical line. The device that serves this purpose is called the *leveling head*. It contains a vertical *socket* in which the outer spindle fits. The socket is attached through a *half-ball joint* to the *shifting plate*, which is free to move horizontally within the *footplate* that is fixed in position. The socket and thus the entire upper and lower plate assembly can be rotated in any direction about the half-ball joint. Thus, these plates can be made precisely level even though the footplate is not quite level. The leveling head is mounted on a three-legged stand called a *tripod*.

Levling is accomplished by means of four vertical screws called *leveling screws* arranged 90° apart on a circle around the spindle socket. Sometimes, there are three leveling screws 120° apart. The screws, encased in *shoes*, press against the footplate. Be lengthening one of a pair of opposite screws and shortening the other, the instrument can be rotated about the ball joint until it is level, at which position the axis of the spindles will be vertical. Once the spindle axis is vertical, the upper plate and lower plate will remain level when they are rotated on their spindles.

At the bottom of the leveling head, on the spindle axis, is a hook from which a plumb bob is hung. When the transit is level, its center line is a continuation of the vertical line of the plumb bob string, which means that the instrument center is in the vertical line through the plumb bob point.

It is necessary for the instrument to be level and centered vertically over a point. This is accomplished by properly manipulating the shifting plate and the leveling screws. When the instrument is thus located, the point below the instrument is the vertex of any horizontal angle turned by the instrument. See Fig. 5.7 for details of the leveling head and plumb bob attachment.

Some instruments are equipped with an optical centering device in which the line of sight passes downward along the vertical center line of the two spindles. When the instrument is level, the line of sight is vertical, and, by means of it, the instrument center can be located over the vertex point.

The Vernier

The principle of the vernier described in Chapter 4 applies to the three transit verniers even though they measure min and sec of arc. Transit verniers usually have 15, 20, or 30 spaces, and, in some cases, these spaces are divided into two of three subdivisions. Therefore, it is not so readily apparent that N spaces on the vernier equal $N - 1$ spaces on the instrument scale.

To apply the principle, first determine the value of the smallest space on the circle. The vernier is capable of dividing this value into the number

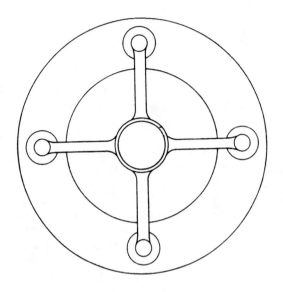

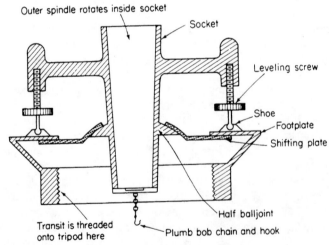

Outer spindle rotates inside socket

Socket

Leveling screw

Shoe

Footplate

Shifting plate

Transit is threaded
onto tripod here

Plumb bob chain and hook

Half balljoint

Figure 5.7   Transit leveling head

of spaces on the vernier. The value of one space on the vernier is called the *least count* of the vernier. The angle to read is the mark on the circle that the vernier index has passed plus the vernier spaces in the same direction beyond the index up to the point where a vernier line coincides with a line on the scale.

Some of the verniers commonly provided on transits are shown in Fig. 5.8. Note that these are double verniers, designed so that angles can be read

GRADUATED 30 MINUTES READING TO ONE MINUTE
DOUBLE DIRECT VERNIER

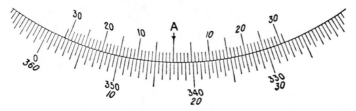

GRADUATED 20 MINUTES READING TO 30 SECONDS
DOUBLE DIRECT VERNIER

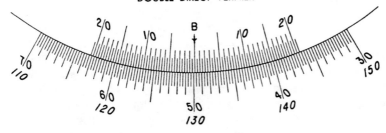

GRADUATED TO 15 MINUTES READING TO 20 SECONDS
DOUBLE DIRECT VERNIER

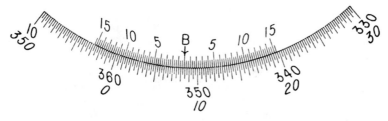

Figure 5.8   Three verniers (*Courtesy of Keuffel and Esser Company*)

to the right or left.   The vernier shown in Figs. 4.6 and 4.7 is marked to be read to the right.   If the arrow is moved to the left the 0.9 lines up with a division on the instrument scale when the movement is one-tenth of an instrument division.   Thus, the vernier divisions are the same size to right or left, but they must be properly numbered for a right or left movement.   The numbers on the correct side of the transit vernier are usually slanted in the same direction as the numbers on the angle being read in that direction. Look at the transit in Fig. 5.3 to help to visualize that the vernier moves to the right when the angle is turned to the left and to the left when the angle is turned to the right.

A small magnifying glass is used to read the vernier. Sometimes the angle is estimated to one-half of the least count of the vernier.

Clamps and Tangent Screws

The position and appearance of clamps and tangent screws indicate their functions. This is deliberate since the instrument person cannot look at them while using them. The clamp and tangent screw for the lower plate are below those for the upper plate, and those for the vertical motion are near the horizontal axle. The clamp screws turn inward toward the center of the part they stop, and the tangent screws turn in a direction tangent to the motion they control. Clamps are sometimes equipped with hexagonal heads and tangent screws with round ones, denoting smoother or finer adjustment.

The upper motion clamp and tangent screw are attached to the upper plate and rotate with it. This clamp is a screw that turns inward to tighten a collar around the outer spindle of the lower plate, thus stopping motion between the upper plate (inner spindle) and the lower plate (outer spindle). The two plates can still rotate together. The tangent screw bears against the clamp housing in a direction tangential to the rotary motion of the plates, causes rotary motion between upper and lower plates by pushing when turned clockwise, and allows motion forced by a spring acting in the opposite direction when withdrawn by a counterclockwise turn. It operates over a very small distance.

The lower motion clamp and tangent screw are attached to the leveling head and do not rotate. This clamp also tightens a collar around the outer spindle and thus stops the motion between the lower plate (outer spindle) and leveling head. The upper plate (inner spindle) can still rotate within the outer spindle unless the upper motion is tightened. The lower tangent screw operates the same way as the upper one, but it is housed separately from the clamp and bears against an extension of the clamp housing.

The vertical motion clamp and vertical tangent screw operate the same way but connect the axle to a standard to stop and adjust the axle motion.

The clamps should not be forced. They are designed to hold fast with very little pressure. The tangent screws should not be forced when they reach their limits. Since the tangent screws push when turned clockwise and merely release and allow a spring to push when turned counterclockwise, it is possible for some looseness to occur when the screw is released slightly against a weakened spring. A good habit to develop is that of finishing each fine adjustment with a clockwise turn. If you turn past the mark, return and come up to it again with a clockwise turn.

The Leveling Head and Plumb Bob

The leveling head is designed to permit the instrument to be leveled and centered on a vertical line over a point.

The transit is leveled with the upper plate aligned so that each of the two plate levels is parallel with a pair of leveling screws. The two screws 180° apart are considered as a pair since they operate together to rotate the entire instrument in an arc about the center of the half-ball joint. The screws are always operated in pairs and are always turned in opposite directions. They rotate the transit in a plane that passes through both screws and through the axis of spindles so that a plate level parallel with the two screws indicates only the rotation caused by those two screws.

The plate levels indicate the rotation perfectly only if the plane of rotation is vertical. Since this plane is vertical only when the other plate level is leveled, a small component of the rotational movement will usually exist perpendicular to the major movement through the two screws being used and will cause the other plate level bubble to move also.

The bubble in the parallel level is approximately centered with the two screws, and they are left slightly loose. Before these can be operated, the other pair of screws usually must be loosened. After one bubble is nearly centered, the other bubble is nearly centered with the opposite pair of screws. This process is continued, each time leveling more accurately and each time leaving the screws a little tighter until the instrument is leveled.

An experienced instrument person adjusts each bubble two or three times in making a setup. A handy rule to remember when leveling the transit is that the bubble moves in the direction that the left thumb moves when turning the screws.

The rotational movements may cause the plumb bob to move off the point, and the leveling operation must be interrupted to reposition the transit over the point by moving the shifting plate without moving the footplate or tripod. The shoes on the leveling screws readily slide across the footplate when they are slightly loose, thus allowing the transit to move in any direction.

An experienced instrument person sets up the instrument with one or two such movements. The student can expect to make half a dozen such movements on the first few attempts. The leveling and shifting must be coordinated so that the transit is both level and centered at the end of the operation.

Figure 5.9 shows the relationship between the half-ball joint on which the upper and lower plates rotate and the plumb bob chain attachment. In the figure, the center line of the plumb bob chain and string always passes through the center of the half-ball because this is also the center of the *half-ring* the chain hangs on; also, it is always vertical because it is directed by gravity. The transit vertical center line always passes through the center of the half-ball and is vertical only when the plates are leveled. Therefore, a continuous vertical line is formed from the instrument center to the tip of the plumb bob when the transit is level.

This construction is ideal, and not all transits are constructed this way. The center of plumb bob rotation may be vertically above or below the half-

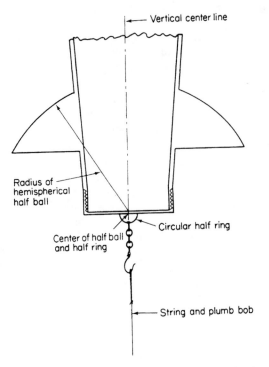

Vertical center line

Radius of hemispherical half ball

Center of half ball and half ring

Circular half ring

String and plumb bob

Figure 5.9 Detail of half-ball and plumb bob attachment

ball center a slight amount, but it cannot be to one side. If the centers are displaced vertically, any rotation of the half-ball (by turning leveling screws) causes horizontal movement of the plumb bob because the half-ring center rotates about the same center with the half-ball. Setting up the instrument is more difficult in this case because the shifting head must be moved more to compensate for horizontal movement caused by leveling. If the centers are displaced horizontally (through being damaged since they are not manufactured this way), the instrument center cannot be aligned vertically over the plumb bob.

When an optical plumb line is used, the sight line is fixed as an extension of the vertical center line, and, therefore, it moves more during leveling than a plumb bob hanging on a vertical string does. It is important that the instrument be nearly level the first time it is centered over a point. A *shifting-head tripod* is available with a shifting plate in the head of the tripod to allow greater movement in centering over a point.

Optical centering is usually faster than centering with the plumb bob because fastening the plumb bob and stopping its swinging take time. The optical method is more accurate, especially in wind. However, with the optical plumb bob line, the beginner has difficulty getting the point within the field of vision, and often a plumb bob is used for approximate centering and the optical line for final centering.

Tripod

The tripod serves as a base to prevent movement of the instrument after it is set up and to facilitate making a setup. The tripod is equipped with pointed *shoes* that are forced into the ground by pressing with the foot. They should be pressed in deeply enough so that the tripod will not settle while standing. Usually a *spur* is provided on each shoe to facilitate pushing the point in. On hard surfaces, the shoes must rest on the surface. In either case, the legs should be spread wide enough to provide a stable platform for the instrument. If a shoe becomes loose, it must be tightened before the tripod can be used with accuracy.

The tripod legs are hinged at the top. If the hinges are loose, the instrument will move while being used. However, the hinges must be loose enough to adjust readily while the shoes are being set into the ground. If they are bolted too tightly, they may bind instead of adjusting when the tripod is set up and may later spring free while in use, thereby moving the instrument. Each hinge should be snug enough so that the leg will almost stand out horizontally with no support. Many tripods have legs that are adjustable in length. These are easier to set up than tripods with fixed-length legs. An experienced instrument person can very nearly center and level an instrument with tripod leg adjustments. This leaves little adjusting with the leveling screws and the shifting plate.

Compass

A transit is usually equipped with a compass that is used to establish *magnetic north* as a reference direction. See Chapters 1 and 6 for discussion of directions referred to north.

A compass consists of a magnetized steel needle mounted in such a way that it is free to align itself with the earth's magnetic field. When so aligned, it is said to point toward magnetic north. The magnetic North Pole is located in the Hudson Bay area of Canada roughly 1000 miles from the true North Pole.

However, the compass needle does not necessarily point directly to the magnetic North Pole, but usually approximately toward it. The needle's direction is different at different places on the earth and is constantly changing slowly at any one location.

The earth's magnetic field pulls the compass needle downward as well as horizontally. The downward direction of the needle is called *dip*. It is balanced by a weight (coil of wire) on the south end of the needle. The weight may sometimes have to be adjusted to balance the needle and to allow free movement.

The needle must move freely to give accurate readings. It is fitted with a cup-shaped jewel bearing that rests on a finely pointed steel pivot. It is equipped with a lever to lift the bearing off the pivot and a screw to hold it in place against the glass cover of the compass. The bearing should rest on the pivot only when it is being used in order to avoid wear or damage to the jewel bearing.

The difference between compass, or magnetic, north and true north is called *declination*. Declination is said to be east or west according to whether the compass points east or west of true north.

Charts showing declinations throughout the United States and the predicted variations in the declinations are prepared by the National Geodetic Survey. True north can be determined by the use of one of these charts called *isogonic charts* in conjunction with the observed magnetic north as demonstrated in Fig. 5.10.

True north can be determined more accurately by observation of the sun or North Star using the transit. True north and magnetic north may be established with the transit from the same point, and the observed declination may be used to determine true direction of other lines in the area from their magnetic direction. See Fig. 5.10 for illustration.

The bearing system of designating directions is easy to use with a compass. The north and south lines are provide by the compass, and the direction

Prob. 1   Given : Magnetic bearing of line 1 − 2 38° E
                   Declination   7° East

           Find : True bearing of line 1 − 2

Prob. 2   Given : Magnetic North 38° left of line 1 − 2
                   True North   45° left of line 1 − 2

           Find : Declination
                   See diagram for solutions

Figure 5.10 Relationships, true and magnetic bearings

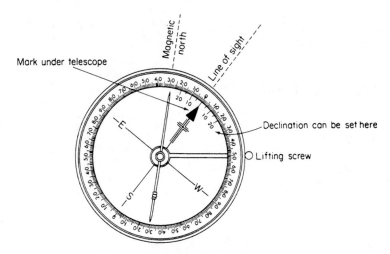

Mark under telescope

Magnetic north

Line of sight

Declination can be set here

Lifting screw

Figure 5.11   Compass face

of any point can be read as a bearing.   Bearings are discussed in Chapters 1 and 6.   Compasses are usually calibrated from 0° to 90° to east and west of the north arrow and to east and west of the south arrow.   See Fig. 5.11 for a typical compass face.

The compass is used in the following way.   With the instrument set up over a point, the compass needle is released, and the telescope is aimed at a point.   A mark on the edge of the compass circle, at the north point, is under the line of sight and, therefore, points at whatever object the cross hairs are fixed on.

Note that east and west are reversed on the compass.   This is so that the bearing direction can be read at the north or south needle.   In Fig. 5.11, the needle points to magnetic north (remember that the needle does not move; the compass circle moves with the telescope), and the zero is toward the point sighted.   The compass needle indicates the magnetic bearing of the point sighted.

The magnetic declination can be set into the compass with as set screw so that the compass needle reads the true bearing.   This is done by setting zero on the compass circle to the left of the mark for west declination and to the right of the mark for east declination.   The setting is made before the needle is released.   This operation can be visualized with the help of Fig. 5.11.

The compass needle must settle down before a bearing can be read. Even then, the accuracy is probably no better than one degree, although the compass is commonly read to the nearest quarter of a degree.   Iron, steel, or electric current nearby causes a variation in the expected declination.   Cars passing, power lines overhead, a steel tape, or a pocket knife near the instrument can be the source of what is called *local attraction*, which deflects the needle from magnetic north.

5.3 PURPOSE OF TURNING AN ANGLE

The operation of turning an angle is performed either to *measure an angle* or to *lay off an angle*.

To determine the location of an existing point an angle must be *measured*. A backsight is taken on a known line, an angle is turned to sight the existing point, (this is called a foresight) and the angle is read on the vernier.

To set a new point, an angle must be *laid off*. The angle is known ahead of time and the point is established at that angle from a given line. A backsight is taken on the given line, the telescope is moved to set the known angle with the vernier, and the new point (called a foresight) is placed at that angle from the backsight.

Backsight and foresight are taken by the processes of *giving line* and *taking line*. The instrument person must *take line* from a point on the known line to measure an angle or to lay one off. If the point cannot be seen another person *gives line* by holding an object vertically over the point for the instrument person to sight. A plumb bob and string are often used.

If an angle is being measured, the instrument person *takes line* again for the foresight to complete the angle. If a point is being set, the instrument person *gives line* in a predetermined direction to another person who *takes line* in order to set the second point.

The instrument person *gives line* by directing the other person to line up a plumb bob string (or other vertical object) with the vertical cross hair of the instrument. The other person *takes line* simply by taking directions and marking a point under the plumb bob.

5.4 STEP-BY-STEP OPERATION

The processes of measuring and laying off angles are covered here. These are the most common operations performed with the transit. They consist of setting up the transit over a point, backsighting a point, and turning an angle to a foresight on another point. A point may be marked by a pipe or steel-reinforcing rod stuck in the ground, a tack in a wooden stake, an *X* chiselled in a concrete walk or pavement, or in many other ways.

Before starting a setup, the leveling screws should be adjusted to the same length so that the upper and lower plates are parallel with the footplate, and the shifting plate should be centered in the footplate. The tripod legs should be adjusted to equal length. The plumb bob should be attached. In this way, each setup is begun with standard conditions.

1. Set the legs firmly in place with the footplate level by eye and the plumb bob over the point as nearly as your skill permits. If the instrument is being set up on sloping ground, plant two legs the same distance downhill from the point and the same distance outward from the point. Raise the third leg and pass it uphill directly over the point so that the plumb bob follows it and swings up to the point. Plant the third leg in the position where it stops the plumb bob over the point. Adjust the legs as desired to keep the footplate level and to bring the plumb bob more accurately over the point. The eyepiece should be at such height that it can be used comfortably. Always use the sunshade. Attach and remove it with a clockwise motion to avoid loosening the objective.

2. Bring the instrument level and over the point with leveling screws and shifting plate.

3. Clamp lower plate. Set vernier to zero with upper motion clamp and tangent screw. Release lower motion clamp. Turn to B.S. and focus telescope on it. Set cross hairs on B.S. with lower motion clamp and tangent screw.

The transit now reads zero at the stationary line of the angle (B.S.). It is ready to measure or to lay off an angle. Measuring an angle to right or left involves these additional steps:

4. Release upper motion clamp. Turn to F.S. and focus telescope on it. Set cross hairs on F.S. point with upper motion clamp and tangent screw. Vernier now marks the angle turned.

5. Read the vernier and record the angle.

6. Center the shifting plate and adjust the leveling screws so that the same length of each screw shows. Turn the telescope up and clamp it lightly. This makes the telescope less likely to be hooked on something while being carried. Pick up the transit and carry it to the next point.

Laying off an angle to right or left involves these additional steps after step 3:

4. Release upper motion clamp. Turn in appropriate direction until the vernier marks the correct angle. Set this angle with upper motion clamp and tangent screw. Telescope cross hairs now point to the opposite side of the angle that has been laid off.

5. Set a point (such as a nail) on this line.

When the point is set, the transit should be adjusted as in the previous step 6 before moving it.

A deflection angle is measured or laid off by the process of *plunging the telescope* and then turning the angle. Plunging consists of turning the telescope about the horizontal axle from the normal or direct position to the inverted or reversed position so that it is still aligned on the same line, but with the ends of the telescope reversed. It is thus pointed forward 180° horizontally from the B.S. The upper and lower plates remain clamped during the plunging operation. The upper plate is then released, and the deflection angle is turned.

Once the transit is set up, it should not be touched any more than is absolutely necessary to operate it. When reading the vernier with a magnifying glass, brace the hand by placing the little finger against the transit.

If the instrument or a tripod leg is brushed even by clothing such as a hat brim or shirt tail, the instrument must be releveled and resighted. Do not walk near the instrument any more than necessary, especially on soft ground. Accomplish the work as rapidly as it can be done while maintaining the required accuracy because the tripod feet often settle unevenly while the instrument is standing.

5.5 SIGHTING POINTS

The instrument person should sight the actual point whenever possible, but he or she is often unable to see the point and must be given a vertical line directly above it to sight. A pencil may be held vertically on the point. The instrument person should sight as close to the bottom of the pencil as possible to eliminate error caused by the pencil being out of plumb. A plumb bob point may be held on the point, or a plumb bob may be suspended by a string over the point. The string should be kept as short as possible for greater accuracy.

If swinging of the plumb bob cannot be prevented, every effort should be made to equalize the swinging to both sides of the point, and the instrument person should read the average. The person holding the plumb bob should be comfortable; should be able to see the point of the plumb bob; should steady hands on a firm support (using both hands) whenever possible; and should call, "Good" or "Mark" when the plumb bob crosses the point if the swinging cannot be stopped.

A range pole may be held on the point and balanced in a vertical position in the same way a level rod is balanced. On long sights, a range pole may be needed if a string cannot be seen. No accuracy is lost on long sights by the thickness of the pole. For greater accuracy, some transits have two parallel vertical cross hairs that are positioned such that one is on each edge of the range pole.

When a point that cannot be seen is going to be needed again, a semi-permanent mark may be established above the point or on line with it.

Examples are a range pole left stuck in the ground on line directly behind a point; a nail projecting next to a flat tack and bent so that the head is directly over the tack; and a plumb bob or metal rod suspended over the point from a tripod.

5.6 CARE OF TRANSITS

Transits should be cared for much as engineer's levels, whose care is discussed in Chapter 4.   Transits should be lifted by the standards from the carrying case to the tripod.   Generally, carrying cases are designed to hold the instrument firmly in one position so that it need not be clamped.   Clamping any part of the instrument puts a strain on the instrument if it then has to be forced to fit the case.   The dustcap should be put on the objective before the transit is stored in the case.

All motions should be clamped lightly before the instrument is picked up on the tripod.   Thus, there will be no loose motion, yet the clamp will give if the instrument hits an object.   Do not carry the instrument while crossing a fence or similar obstruction.   When the instrument is set down, the legs should be well spread so that it is stable even if it is to be left only momentarily.   Do not leave the instrument set up with no one watching it. Graduated circles and verniers should not be touched with fingers.

5.7 COMMON MISTAKES

The mistakes usually made are:

1. Confusing clamps or tangent screws and turning the wrong one.
2. Reading the horizontal circle in the wrong direction.
3. Read the wrong side of the vernier.
4. Forgetting part of the angle from the circle while reading the vernier. For example, the 20″ vernier in Fig. 5-8 could mistakenly be read 351°60′00″ instead of 351°36′00″ if the instrument person is not careful.

After practice is acquired in reading horizontal angles, it may be doubly difficult to read a vertical angle correctly.   The vertical vernier is outside the vertical circle while the A and B verniers are inside the horizontal circle. This reverses the appearance and causes confusion if the instrument person is not careful.   In addition, all the mistakes that can be made in setting and reading horizontal angles must also be guarded against in setting and reading vertical angles.

The instrument person must visualize fully what is being done and constantly check the work. The ability to visualize in space what is being done with the instrument comes only with practice.

5.8 SOURCES OF ERROR AND COMPENSATION

All the possible sources of error—instrumental, human, and natural—should be understood. Those errors that are carried from one point to another as small offsets with no increase in size from one point to another are not as dangerous as angular misalignments that cause small errors at short distances and large errors at greater distances. The difference should be understood so that precautions that are justified by the size of the potential error can be taken. See Fig. 5.12 for illustration.

Angles turned with longer sights will be more accurate than those turned with shorter sights. This applies until extreme range reduces visibility because of limitations of the telescope or the instrument person's eyes. At longer distances, the object appears smaller compared with the thickness of the vertical cross hair, and, therefore, the hair is more accurately centered. In addition, the same linear inaccuracy (caused, for example, by swinging of the plumb bob being sighted) results in greater angular error at short distances, as illustrated in Fig. 5.13.

For the same reasons, when an angle is being laid off, it is important to take a long backsight. If there is a choice, a long B.S. and short F.S. are preferable to a short B.S. and long F.S. Figure 5.14 illustrates the reason for this.

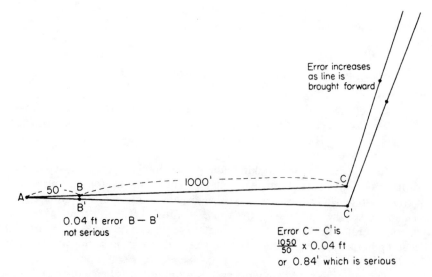

Figure 5.12   Demonstration of seriousness of small angular error

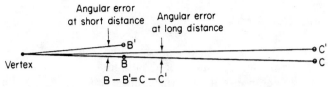

Sighting errors of equal size result in a smaller angular error at the longer distance.

The error in measuring an angle is equal to the algebraic sum of the errors in the B.S. and F.S.

Figure 5.13   Long sights improve accuracy in measuring an angle

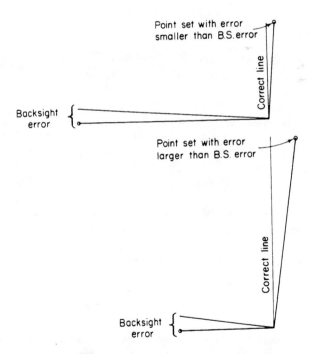

Size of error in laying off an angle is illustrated. It is assumed there is an error in the B.S. and no error in turning the angle. With equal B.S. errors, the angular error is smaller with a long B.S. The angular error of the B.S. is carried forward. The longer the F.S. is the farther the new point is from the correct line.

Figure 5.14   A long backsight improves accuracy in laying off an angle

Instrumental Errors

The operation of a transit depends on precise relationships among all its parts. It is, therefore, manufactured with great precision.

The design and use of the transit require the following relationships:

1. The telescope center line must be perpendicular to the horizontal axle.
2. The horizontal axle must be perpendicular to the vertical center line of the spindles.
3. The center lines of all three must pass through a common point within the telescope (the instrument center).
4. The upper and lower plates must be perpendicular to the spindle axis.

These relationships assure that the parts of the transit constitute a vertical-horizontal framework among themselves. If the transit is to be of practical use, two other relationships are needed:

1. The line of sight must coincide with the telescope center line.
2. The plumb bob string or optical plumb line must coincide with the spindle axis.

These last two must also be precisely aligned because they bring the transit, the instrument person, and the area being surveyed into one vertical and horizontal reference system.

Adjustable connections are built into transits because manufacturing cannot be perfect and because misalignment may be caused by handling or transporting a transit. If the parts were attached together rigidly with no allowances for adjustment, there would be no way to eliminate built-in errors, and a factory repair would be required to realign a transit that was jarred into misalignment.

Transits as now built can be adjusted to greater precision than could be built into them without adjustable parts; and some misalignments that occur can be corrected by a skillful instrument person instead of requiring factory repairs that are more costly and more time-consuming.

Adjustments are made with screws fitted with capstan heads that require special small steel pins to turn them. These screws are located at strategic points for positioning one part with respect to another to achieve the relationships described in this section. Not all movable parts are provided with adjustments.

1. The reticle holding the cross hairs is equipped with adjustment screws so that the cross hairs can be centered at the center line of the telescope, thus assuring that the line of sight passes through the instrument center.

The vertical hair can be made perpendicular to the horizontal axle with these screws.

2. The telescope can be rotated about the horizontal axle, and thus it is perpendicular to the vertical center line of the spindles at only one position. That position must be where the vernier marks zero. The vertical vernier is equipped with an adjustment screw to position it.

3. There is no adjustment to align the telescope with the horizontal axle. Construction is such that misalignment can be caused only be a severe blow, and when this happens, factory repair is required.

4. The horizontal axle is adjusted perpendicular to the vertical center line of the spindles by an adjustment screw in one of the standards to raise or lower one end of the axle until it is properly aligned.

5. There is no screw to adjust the plates relative to the spindles. Misalignment can be caused only be a severe blow, and factory repairs are then required.

6. All level vials are equipped with adjustment screws to align them parallel to the appropriate part of the transit—the plate levels to the upper and lower plates and the telescope level to the telescope center line.

The entire transit is oriented for use by leveling the plate levels. If all parts of the transit are in adjustment, then the plates are horizontal, the spindle axis is vertical, the horizontal axle is horizontal, and the telescope is horizontal with the telescope level bubble being centered and the vertical vernier marking zero. The instrument is then in agreement with the basic surveying references—vertical and horizontal directions.

Transit adjustments should be made in certain ways and in a particular sequence so that an adjustment does not disturb any previous adjustment. Procedures are explained in detail in more advanced surveying books.

Just as instruments cannot be manufactured perfectly, neither can they be adjusted perfectly. The adjustments provide sufficient accuracy for almost all surveying. For higher order work, special methods are used that can completely eliminate errors caused by manufacturing imperfections or imperfect adjustments. Some of these methods will even compensate for the instrument being out of adjustment and will produce results free from instrumental error. Ways in which a transit may be out of adjustment are discussed here with surveying methods of eliminating the resulting errors.

Note that very little can be done to obtain accurate vertical angles if the instrument is out of adjustment; but in nearly all situations, accurate horizontal angles can be obtained by turning the angle twice, once with the scope direct and once with the scope reversed. The error is in the opposite direction when the scope is reversed, and, therefore, the error is eliminated by averaging the two angles. This operation is called *doubling an angle*, and it is described in more detail in this chapter under the section entitled "Important Operations."

If the vertical vernier does not mark zero when the telescope line of sight is horizontal, the vernier can be adjusted to read zero. Vertical angle accuracy does not depend on vernier alignment, however, and angles can be turned accurately with the vernier misaligned. They can be read accurately if the vernier is read when the line of sight is level and after the angle is turned. The vertical angle is the difference between the readings, taking into account the direction (plus or minus) of each reading.

The line of sight may not be perpendicular to the horizontal axle because either the telescope has been knocked out of alignment by a blow or the cross hairs are not correctly aligned. The first case requires factory repair, and the second requires that the cross hairs be adjusted to the center line of the telescope.

The transit can be used while the line of sight is out of alignment. If the line of sight still passes through the instrument center, the misalignment causes error only when a straight line is extended by plunging the scope. If the line of sight passes to left or right of the instrument center, which is likely, an error is introduced into horizontal angles also. Error can be eliminated in either case by doubling the operation. Doubling an angle and extending a straight line by double centering are both discussed in this chapter.

There will be no error from this source in turning vertical angles unless the line of sight passes above or below the instrument center. However, this is also likely.

Doubling the vertical angle, or when feasible, taking the average of a plus vertical angle between two points from one of the points and a minus vertical angle from the other point without reversing the scope improves accuracy, but error is not eliminated.

The horizontal axle may not be level when the plate levels are. This can be caused by one of several misalignments. If the horizontal axle is not perpendicular to the standards, the axle can be adjusted. If the plate levels are not parallel to the plates, the level vials can be adjusted. If the standards are not perpendicular to the plates, the upper plate is not perpendicular to the spindles, the inner spindle does not fit accurately within the outer spindle, or the outer spindle does not fit accurately within its socket, then factory repair is necessary.

When the horizontal axle is out of level, error is introduced into all operations performed with the transit. See Figs. 5.15 and 5.16 for illustration. Error in turning horizontal angles or extending a straight line by plunging the scope can be eliminated in all cases by doubling the operation unless the source of error is a part that is worn so much that looseness results.

The error cannot be eliminated from vertical angles by doubling because the angle turned is always too large.

If the plumb bob does not hang from a point on the vertical center line

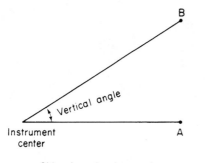

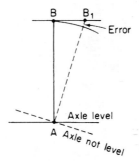

Side view showing angle
between points A and B

End view showing longer arc (and
greater angle) traveled by telescope
when axle not level. The line of
sight is turned horizontally to left
to sight B; but, A – B₁ represents
arc that is measured always with
a plus error.

Figure 5.15   Error in vertical angle when horizontal axle is not level

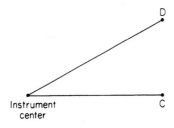

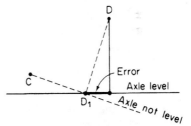

Side view showing points C and
D which are separated
horizontally and vertically.

End view showing horizontal and
vertical relationship of C and D.
When scope turns from C to D
vernier turns from C – D₁.
Error is shown approximately

Figure 5.16   Error in horizontal angle when horizontal axle is not level

or the optical plumb line does not coincide with the vertical center line, error
results when horizontal angles are turned or a line is extended by plunging
the scope.   The error cannot be eliminated by field methods, and factory
repair is required if the error is significant.

The graduated circle is manufactured with division marks cut at equal
spacing radially from its center.   This center is not precisely at its center of
rotation, which is on the center line of the spindles.   Thus, an eccentricity
exists that causes slightly different readings at different locations on the circle
when an angle is turned.   If the angle is read at opposite sides of the circle,

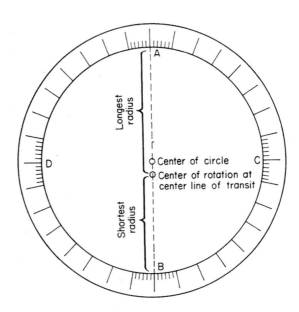

Scale divisions are inscribed in factory from center of circle.
Horizontal circle rotates in use about center line of transit.

Figure 5.17 Eccentricity in horizontal circle

the average angle is the true angle turned. See Fig. 5.17 for further explanation.

An angle generates a longer arc when the radius is longer. The longer arc includes more scale divisions. Of all points around the circle in Fig. 5.17, the longest radius about the center of rotation is at point A, and the shortest is at point B. During any movement between the circle and the upper plate, more division marks pass point A than any other point, and fewer pass point B than any other point. At points C and D, nearly perpendicular to a line from A and B, the correct number of scale divisions pass because, at these two points, the radius of the circle as manufactured equals the radius of rotation of the circle about the vertical center line of the transit.

Vernier readings for an angle depend on where the verniers are in relation to the two centers. The readings vary around the circle from readings with maximum plus error at A to maximum minus error at B with zero error at C and D. As long as the verniers are 180° apart, the true angle turned is the average of their readings regardless of what part of the circle the are on. The error is accidental and is so small that it is ignored in ordinary work, and only the A vernier is read.

When the B vernier is used, it must be read at B.S. and F.S. When the A vernier is zeroed for the B.S., the B vernier will not read at some

Sta.	Degrees	A	B	Avg.	
1,2,3	0	00–00	00–20	00–10	⋞ R
1D	65	27–20	27–20		
2R	130	55–00	54–40	54–50	
Avg.	65°–27'–20"				
2,3,4	0	00–00	59–40	59–50	⋞ L
1D	113	42–20	41–40		
2R	227	24–20	23–40	24–00	
Avg.	113°–42'–05"				
3,4,5	0	00–00	00–40	00–20	⋞ R
1D	146	03–20	03–20		
3D,3R	156	19–20	19–40	19–30	
Avg.	146°–03'–11.7"				

Figure 5.18 Field notes when *B* vernier used, angles doubled and turned six times

settings.   Notes must be carefully kept.   Sample notes are shown in Fig. 5.18.

Degrees are the same at *A* and *B* verniers with few exceptions.   Seconds and, sometimes, minutes differ.   In the notes in Fig. 5.18, the *A* and *B* vernier readings are recorded and averaged in separate columns.   The first two angles are doubled.   The averages of *A* and *B* vernier readings are computed first and are used to determine the total angle turned.   Then the average angle is computed.

The notes also include an angle turned six times.   The vernier may go past 360° several times in this process.   Each time, 60° (360° divided by 6) is allocated to the average angle.   The final angles indicated by the verniers are recorded, and the average is divided by six to compute the total average angle.   In turning this angle, the vernier turned two complete circles plus the angle noted.   It is not necessary to record all repetitions nor to record the number of times the vernier turns a full 360°.   The number of times to add 60° can be determined by the size of the angle turned once since the average angle will approximately equal it.   The notation indicates how many times the angle is repeated and whether direct or reversed.

Human Errors

The main source of human error is in the eyesight of the instrument person.   Steadiness of the instrument person's hands and the eyesight and

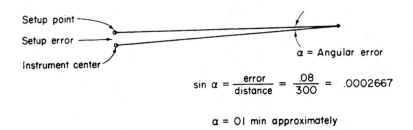

$$\sin \alpha = \frac{\text{error}}{\text{distance}} = \frac{.08}{300} = .0002667$$

$$\alpha = 01 \text{ min approximately}$$

The setup error is perpendicular to the direction of the sight.
The angular error would be less with an equal setup error
in any other direction.

Figure 5.19 Maximum error in sighting a point caused by inaccurate transit

steadiness of the person marking backsights and foresights are also important.
All the human errors are accidental.

1. If the instrument is not centered over the point that should be the vertex
   of an angle, the angle will be turned from another vertex—the instrument center. The size and direction of error are completely random,
   so the error is accidental. This condition is similar to that resulting
   from the plumb line not coinciding with the vertical axis, although that
   error is not accidental. Refer to Fig. 5.19 for illustration of the maximum probable error in one sight. The setup error shown is in a direction to cause maximum angular error. A setup off one in. (0.08 ft)
   and a distance of 300 ft result in a maximum angular error of approximately one min. The same setup error in any other direction results
   in less angular error. Decreasing the error in the setup decreases the
   angular error. The fact that 2 in. at 300 ft results in 2 min angular error
   is worth remembering. Other relationships are roughly proportional
   up to 5 min. Thus, ¼ in. at 300 ft results in ¼ min angular error while
   ¼ in. at 150 ft results in ½ min angular error, conforming to the principle
   that longer sights result in greater accuracy. All these figures are approximate.
   a. The error in turning an angle is not the same as the error in one
      sight. The error in turning an angle caused by inaccurate location
      of the instrument may vary from zero to twice the maximum angular
      error in one sight, depending on the direction of setup error compared
      with the two sides of the angle. See Fig. 5.20 for examples.
   b. The linear error in setting a point by laying off an angle may vary
      from zero to many times the setup error. The amount depends on
      the relationship between the direction of the setup error and the
      directions of the sides of the angle. The probable error in laying

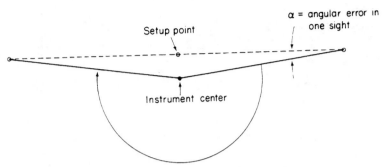

The error in the angle measured is twice as large as α.
The error increases as the angle increases.
An angle of approximately 90° would have an error equal to α.

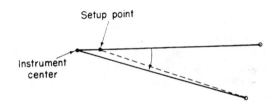

The error in the angle measured is almost zero.
An angle of 180° would have no error.
An angle of approximately 90° would have the largest error.

Figure 5.20   Probable error in measuring an angle caused by inaccurate transit setup

    off an angle will be less if B.S. is longer than F.S. and more if B.S. is shorter than F.S.   In measuring an angle between two points, the error is the same from either direction.   See Fig. 5.21 for illustration.

2. Some error is introduced each time the vernier is set and each time the vernier is read.   Generally, the maximum probable error is one-half of the least count of the vernier.   When the vernier count is small, the difficulty of reading may result in a maximum probable error greater than one-half of the least count.   The probable size of offset error resulting from an inaccurate angle can be estimated by the rule of one in. per min at 300 ft.   Often, the vernier can best be read by observing the vernier marks on both sides of the one that seems to line up.   The two marks adjacent to the one that lines up will be offset by the same amount in opposite directions.

3. A sight might not coincide with the point, or a point might not be set in coincidence with the line of sight.   Accurate results depend on teamwork.   The person indicating a point for measuring an angle should

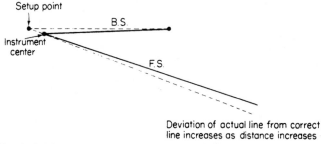

Error in B.S. is inversely proportional to distance to B.S.
Therefore longer B.S. means less error.
Error in F.S. is proportional to F.S. distance
Therefore longer F.S. means more error.

Figure 5.21   Error in laying off an angle caused by inaccurate centering of the instrument

call, "Good" or "Mark" while on the point, and the instrument person should be satisfied that the angle is accurate before signalling, "Finished." The person setting a point should call for as many repetitions as needed to be satisfied that the point is set as accurately as required before signalling "Finished."

4. Parallax is a source of error and should be eliminated as described in Chapter 4 for the level telescope.

5. Inaccurate leveling of the instrument causes error in turning vertical and horizontal angles and in extending lines by plunging. This condition is the same as that caused by the horizontal axle being out of adjustment. This error is an accidental one, and that caused by the horizontal axis being out of adjustment is not. The quantity of error depends on the direction of the operation relative to direction of the leveling error.

All the human errors are accidental and must be controlled by care and proper methods. Some people have a tendency to favor one side when sighting a point or reading a vernier. Such practice must be avoided because it causes systematic error.

Natural Errors

Natural sources of error are:

1. Wind, which blows the plumb bob string out of plumb and even vibrates the transit.

2. Dust, fog, or poor light, which obscure vision.

3. Temperature changes, which cause unequal expansion and contraction of the parts of the transit.

4. Heat waves, which bend the line of sight.

5. Soft ground, which allows the transit to move by settlement.

Poor weather conditions, such as wet brush, very low temperature, and heat with high humidity, cause surveyors such discomfort that a high level of accuracy is not possible.

5.9 IMPORTANT OPERATIONS

In surveying work, some operations are required frequently. Procedures have been devised for these operations that are accepted practice in the surveying field, and they should be understood and used when appropriate.

Repeating an Angle

An angle turned with a transit can be read with confidence to the least count of the vernier. It may be estimated to one-half of that value. In addition, there is a way in which any desired accuracy can be achieved. When an angle is turned and read, there is usually some small difference between the actual angle and the vernier reading that cannot be separated with the human eye. Nevertheless, it is there, on the ground, and indicated on the horizontal circle of the instrument.

If the lower motion clamp is released and the telescope is returned to the backsight while the original angle is still marked by the vernier, the lower motion can be clamped and the angle turned again, and the vernier will indicate twice the angle. The small difference that could not be picked up by the human eye will now be twice as large and may be large enough to be read on the vernier. If it is not yet large enough to be significant on the vernier, repetitions of the operation will increase it until its effect is noticeable on the vernier.

For example, if 20°00'07" is read with a 20-second vernier, it will be read as 20°00'00". This reading is correct to the nearest 20" or the least count of the vernier. If the angle is accumulated two times on the vernier as described here, it will be 40°00'14" and will be read as 40°00'20". Dividing by two gives 20°00'10", which is correct to the nearest 10" or one-half of the least count of the vernier. The accuracy is doubled.

If the angle is accumulated four times, it will be 80°00'28" and will be read as 80°00'20". Dividing by four gives 20°00'05", which is correct to the nearest 5" or one-fourth of the least count of the vernier. The accuracy is quadrupled.

It is theoretically possible to accumulate the angle enough times to achieve one-second accuracy or even more with the 20" instrument referred to in the example. However, inaccuracies in the manufacturing of the transit and in the operation preclude such accuracy.   In practice, angles are seldom turned more than six times.

After several repetitions, further increases in accuracy can be prevented by very small errors in the transit or in setting up.   It is customary to turn half the angles with the telescope normal and half with the telescope inverted in order to eliminate error as discussed in the "Instrumental Errors" section of this chapter.

Doubling an Angle

Doubling an angle eliminates many instrumental errors as explained in this chapter under "Instrumental Errors" and also eliminates any error caused by the horizontal axle being set up out of level.   The procedure also serves to prevent mistakes in reading the angle and is probably used more often for this purpose.

Using this procedure, the instrument person reads two different angles, and if the first angle is misread, it is not likely that a comparable mistake will be made reading the second.   A mistake in reading either angle causes a discrepancy in the notes and so is immediately apparent.   The same angle could be read twice as a check.   However, people have a tendency to make the same mistake again when faced with the same situation.

Doubling an angle is an important procedure and should be understood. The steps are as follows:

1. Turn the angle from B.S. to F.S. in the normal way.
2. Plunge the telescope.
3. Loosen the lower plate.
4. Sight the B.S. with the first angle held in the instrument.
5. Turn the angle from B.S. to F.S. with the telescope reversed.
6. Read the doubled angle on the *A* vernier where it was originally read (since the telescope was reversed for the second turning, the *A* vernier will be on the opposite side).

Notes are kept as shown in Fig. 5.22, and the final angle is compared with the original angle before the transit is moved.   Reversing the telescope is a refinement that may not be necessary when the instrument is in proper adjustment, and the purpose of doubling is solely to catch a possible mistake in reading the angle the first time.

Extending a Line

It is often necessary to establish a long straight line where it is impossible to see both ends from any one point.   With the instrument at one end, a new

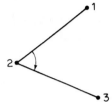

1	1D	67° – 12' – 20"
2	2R	134° – 25' – 00"
3	Avg.	67° – 12' – 30"

Point 1 = B.S.
Point 2 = Transit location
Point 3 = F.S.
  1D   = Once, scope direct
  2R   = Twice, scope reversed

Figure 5.22   Field notes: angle doubled for increased accuracy

point is established on the line.   The instrument is set up on the new point, and the line extended from the end point through the instrument to another new point.   The instrument must then be set up on the second new point, and the line extended through the instrument again to a third new point. This is repeated as many times as is necessary to reach the opposite end.

A line can be extended more accurately by plunging the telescope than by turning a 180° angle.   Upper and lower plates must be clamped when the scope is plunged.   Plunging the scope eliminates the errors that occur when setting and reading the vernier.   Error caused by telescope misalignment or by the horizontal axle not being level can be eliminated by a procedure called *double centering*.   After one point is set by plunging the scope, the inverted telescope is turned through a horizontal angle, aligned on the B.S., and plunged again.   It is then upright.   The two sights will have equal and opposite errors.   Therefore, another point is set on line, and the corrected line passes through a point midway between the two points.   See Fig. 5.23 for illustration.

It is not necessary to go through the double centering procedure to extend a line unless a high degree of accuracy is needed or the transit is out of adjustment.   However, it should be appreciated that an instrumental error in plunging the scope is usually systematic.   It is greater with longer foresights, and the angular deflection of the line approximately doubles with each setup. In a long line or in one with many setups, the errors may be significant even in a survey of third-order accuracy.

Figure 5.23   Double centering

Extending a Line Beyond an Obstruction

METHOD 1
PARALLEL LINE

A transit may be taken around an obstruction and brought back on line by the method shown in Fig. 5.24. The instrument is set up at each point, and a 90° angle is turned. This method is satisfactory for surveys below third-order accuracy.

More accuracy is obtained by taking longer sights in the following manner. Set points *A* and *B* on line. Set offset points *A'* and *B'* at right angles at the same distance from *A* and *B*. This establishes a parallel line through *A'* and *B'*. This line is extended to *C'* and *D'*. To return to the original line, the offsets *C* and *D* are established. If *C' D'* is as long as *A' B'*, no accuracy will be lost in establishing the second parallel line. The procedure is illustrated in Fig. 5.25.

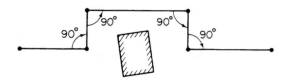

Figure 5.24 Extending a line beyond an obstruction with a low degree of accuracy

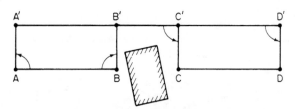

Figure 5.25 Extending a line beyond an obstruction with higher degree of accuracy

METHOD 2
RANDOM ANGLE

An obstruction can be bypassed and the line continued by the method shown in Fig. 5.26. Deflection angles of a convenient size are used, and a convenient distance *L* is chosen. The distance *BD* is twice the length of a leg of a right triangle having a hypotenuse *L* and an adjacent angle α. Distance *BD* equals $2 L \cos \alpha$. The transit is set up at each point shown in Fig. 5.26, and the next point is set at the appropriate angle and distance.

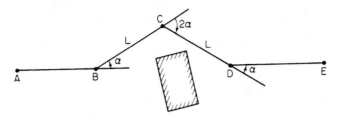

Figure 5.26   Extending a line beyond an obstruction by random angle

Bucking In

It is sometimes necessary, between two points that are not visible from each other, to establish a line that can be seen from a point between them. The instrument is set up as close to the line as the instrument person can align himself or herself by eye. The farther point is sighted, and the telescope is plunged. The line of sight will then be offset from the nearer point. The instrument must be moved a fraction of the offset distance to be on line. The offset distance may be measured and called to the instrument person, or the instrument person may estimate it. The transit is then moved toward the line by an amount estimated to be the correct fraction. The process is repeated until the instrument is on line. The final adjustment can be made by double centering if the greatest possible accuracy is desired. See Fig. 5.27.

Establishing a Point of Intersection

It is sometimes necessary to establish the point of intersection of two lines when the directions of the lines are known but the distances to the intersection point are not known. One line is extended as already described,

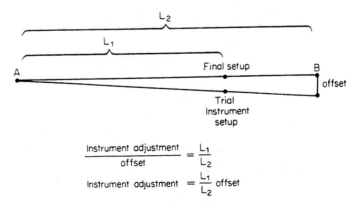

$$\frac{\text{Instrument adjustment}}{\text{offset}} = \frac{L_1}{L_2}$$

$$\text{Instrument adjustment} = \frac{L_1}{L_2} \text{ offset}$$

Figure 5.27   Bucking in

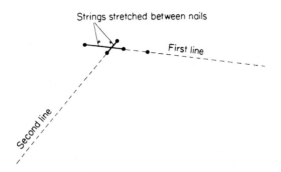

Figure 5.28 Establishing point of intersection of two lines

by double centering if necessary. Points are set on line in the vicinity of the intersection. Judgment is required to do this efficiently. The points can be spaced according to the required accuracy, but not more than a few feet apart. There should be at least one point on each side of the intersection. Two points may be enough to accomplish this.

The other line is then extended, and two points are set on line, one on each side of the first line. A string is stretched between points on each line so that the strings intersect at the point of intersection of the lines. See Fig. 5.28 for illustration. This is a practical application of locating a point by directions from two other points as covered in Chapter 2. It is subject to the inaccuracies depicted in Fig. 2.1, Method 2. A right-angle intersection will result in the least probable error. If the intersecting angle is too sharp, this method should be avoided.

5.10 SIGNALS

Commonly used signals are as follows:

"Right" or "Left" when setting a point or giving line. Extend the arm in the direction of desired movement making a long slow motion for a large distance and a short quick motion for a small distance. A handkerchief may be held in the hand for better visibility over long distances.

"Foresight" when the instrument person wants a foresight or another member wants the instrument person to take or give a foresight. Extend one arm vertically over the head as if holding the plumb bob string high over a point.

5.11 NOTEKEEPING

Notes must show the following:

1. Location of the angle (vertex and two sides).

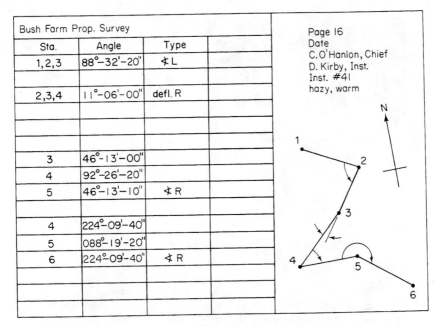

Bush Farm Prop. Survey			
Sta.	Angle	Type	
1,2,3	88°-32'-20"	∡ L	
2,3,4	11°-06'-00"	defl. R	
3	46°-13'-00"		
4	92°-26'-20"		
5	46°-13'-10"	∡ R	
4	224°-09'-40"		
5	088°-19'-20"		
6	224°-09'-40"	∡ R	

Page 16
Date
C. O'Hanlon, Chief
D. Kirby, Inst.
Inst. #41
hazy, warm

Angles 1,2,3 and 2,3,4 are turned once.
Angles 3,4,5 and 4,5,6 are doubled without plunging scope.

Figure 5.29 Complete angle notes

2. Type and direction of angle (angle right, angle left, deflection angle right, deflection angle left).
3. Method used (single, double direct, double direct and reversed).
4. Size of angle.

All this information is needed if another person is to understand what was done in the field. A sketch is helpful for this purpose and also for keeping the note keeper oriented in the field. Notekeeping examples are shown in Fig. 5.29 to illustrate the method.

5.12 THE THEODOLITE

A *theodolite* is an instrument designed for the same purposes as a transit— to measure vertical and horizontal angles and to extend straight lines. The appearance of a theodolite distinguishes it from a transit. Theodolites are smaller, with short telescopes and no exposed verniers, compasses, clamps, or tangent screws. There is only one horizontal motion so that angles cannot

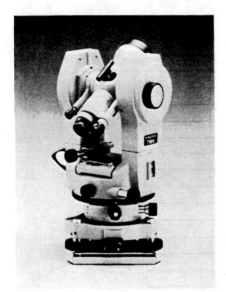

Figure 5.30   Theodolite
(*Courtesy The Lietz Company*)

be repeated.   These are called *pointing instruments*, and the American style transit is a *repeating instrument*.   Optical devices allow angles to be read as accurately with a single turning as they can be read by repetition with a transit; and with some models, they can be read more accurately.   Some instruments with the characteristics of theodolites have upper and lower plates so that angles can be repeated.   These are called *theodolites* by some manufacturers and *transits* by others.   Thus, the term *theodolite* is not fully agreed upon.

Electronic digital theodolites read and record horizontal and vertical angles automatically.   Results are displayed digitally and can be copied into the field notes, and are also stored in the instrument and can be put directly from the theodolite into a computer system for further processing.

Characteristics of theodolites vary so much that they are not covered in detail here.   Manufacturers' literature is available for each type.   The transit described in this chapter has its parts exposed so that functions of the parts can be visualized and understood while the transit is being used.   This is not true of theodolites.   If the student learns the fundamentals of surveying using an American style transit, he or she will understand principles more completely and should have little difficulty learning to use any theodolite later. See Fig. 5.30 for illustration.

PROBLEMS

1. Read the angles of Fig. 5.8 to right and to left.
2. Insert the average angles in the field records of doubled angles.

(a)	Sta.	Angle		(b)	Sta.	Angle
	1	84°–11′–20″			6	63°–19′–40″
	2	168°–23′–00″			7	126°–39′–00″
	3				8	
	2	192°–38′–40″			7	208°–41′–15″
	3	25°–17′–40″			8	57°–22′–15″
	4				9	
	3	18°–56′–00″			8	35°–18′–40″
	4	37°–51′–00″			9	70°–37′–20″
	5				10	
	4	295°–41′–20″			9	187°–56′–30″
	5	231°–22′–20″			10	15°–52′–30″
	6				11	

3. Use the following field data to prepare field notes including sketches:

	Inst.@	B.S.	F.S.	Angle	No. of Times Turned
(a)	2	1	3	96°–30′ ∢ R	1
	17	16	18	17°–19′ defl. ∢ L	1
	C	B	D	9°–11′ defl. ∢ R	1
	3	2	4	136°–35′ ∢ L	1
(b)	2	1	3	7°–14′–30″ ∢ R 14°–29′–15″	2
	2	1	2A	72°–15′–15″ ∢ L 144°–30′–15″	2
	D	C	E	21°–36′–20″ defl. ∢ R 43°–12′–20″	2
	D	C	D1	6°–13′–40″ defl. ∢ L 12°–27′–00″	2

4. A bearing turned from magnetic north is N 37°30′ E. What is the true bearing if the declination is 1°15′ E?

5. A bearing turned from magnetic north is S 46°45′ E. What is the true bearing if the declination is 2°30′ W?

6. Magnetic north is 3° to the left of true north. What is the declination?

7. A bearing turned from magnetic north is N 18°–19′ W. What is the true bearing if the declination is 0°–45′ W?

8. A bearing turned from magnetic north is S 72°–40′ W. What is the true bearing if the declination is 0°–15′ W?

9. Two stakes are aligned on a magnetic north line. If the declination is 1°–30′ E, which way is an angle turned if the instrument is at the north stake and the south stake is to be moved to a true N–S line?

10. Declination is 5°–45′ E. What angle is turned from magnetic north to set a point at a true bearing of S 55°–10′–30″ E?

11. Declination is 12°–15′ W. What angle is turned from magnetic south to set a point at a true bearing of S 36°–10′–00″ W?

12. Declination is 13° E. What angle is turned from magnetic south to set a point at a true bearing of N 25°–18'–30" W?

13. Each degree on a circle is divided into 4 parts. The vernier has 15 parts. What is the least reading of the vernier?

14. Each degree on a circle is divided into 2 parts. The vernier has 60 spaces. What is the least reading of the vernier?

15. Each degree on the circle is divided into 3 parts. The vernier has 60 spaces. What is the least reading?

16. Each degree has 6 parts. The vernier has 20 parts. What is the least reading?

17. Each degree has 3 spaces. The vernier has 80 spaces. What is the least reading?

18. An angle turned to the left is 106°–14'–20". What is the value of that angle turned to the right?

19. If an angle turned to the right is 48°–06'–45", what is the value of that angle turned to the left?

20. An angle turned to the right is 136°–14'–10". What is the value if measured as a deflection angle to the left?

21. An angle turned to the left is 173°–10'–40". What is it if measured as a deflection angle to the right?

22. If a deflection angle to the right is 11°–37'–15", what is the same angle if turned directly to the left?

23. If a deflection angle to the left is 6°–48'–05", what would the angle be if measured directly to the left?

24. If a deflection angle to the left is 10°–18'–17", what would it be if measured as a deflection angle to the right?

25. If an angle is measured to the right as 97°–24'–30", what would it be if measured as a deflection angle left?

26. The vertical vernier marks +6' when the instrument is leveled. A point is sighted at a vertical angle of 5°–13'. What is the corrected angle?

6

THE TRAVERSE

INSTRUCTIONAL OBJECTIVES

1. *Given angles and distances verbally as they would be read in the field, the student should be able to record complete traverse notes including a sketch.*

2. *Given complete field notes for a traverse, the student should be able to:*
   a. *Plot the traverse to scale.*
   b. *Determine angular error and adjust the angles.*
   c. *Determine bearings of all courses based on the bearing of one course in the notes.*
   d. *Determine latitudes and departures for each course.*
   e. *Determine accuracy of the survey.*
   f. *Determine corrections for each station.*
   g. *Adjust the traverse.*

3. *Given coordinates of two stations, the student should be able to determine bearing and distance of one from the other by inversing.*

4. *Given coordinates of the corners of a polygon, the student should be able to determine the area enclosed within the polygon by double meridian distances.*

In both preliminary surveys and construction surveys, an accurate framework is needed that allows the surveyor to locate objects from convenient points on the framework and to relate them to each other quickly, without mistakes and without accumulating errors. Not all objects that must eventually be located can be located at the time of the first survey.   Many will be needed later with short notice.

Therefore, semipermanent control points are established throughout the area of the survey as a first step in all but very minor surveying projects.   As new points must be located, they are located in relation to the control points.

6.1 THE TRAVERSE AS A MEANS OF HORIZONTAL CONTROL

A *control survey* consists of points established with high accuracy so that other objects can be located by reference to these points.   The control survey must always be of higher accuracy than is needed for the secondary points it controls.   This is necessarily so because the secondary points are established with some error in addition to the error of the control points and are thus less accurate.   Only horizontal control is considered in this chapter.

The *traverse* consists of a series of accurately positioned points called *stations*, each of which is located by direction and distance from adjacent stations.   Stations are connected by lines called *courses*.   Each station is marked by a *hub*, which is a wood stake with a nail in the top, or by some other semipermanent marker.

A *loop traverse* closes on, or returns to, the first station, thus forming a polygon.   A *connecting traverse* begins at a station of known location and closes on, or ends at, another station of known location.   Either of these is a *closed traverse*.   A closed traverse can be checked for accuracy and can be

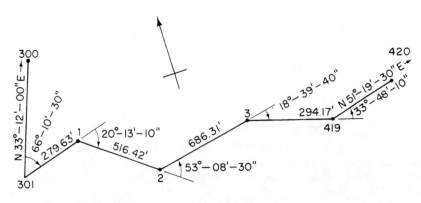

Coordinates of 301 from adjusted traverse	Coordinates of 419 from adjusted traverse
N 3470.13 E 8062.45	N 3468.43 E 9709.91

Figure 6.1   Traverse as established in field—connecting traverse

mathematically adjusted.   A traverse that does not close is called an *open traverse*.   An open traverse cannot be checked for mistakes or excessive error, nor can it be adjusted.   It is never used on important work.

Once a traverse is established, positions of existing objects can be determined by direction and distance from a traverse station, or key points for proposed construction can be set by direction and distance from a traverse station.   Figure 6.1 shows a connecting traverse as established in the field, and Fig. 6.13 shows a loop traverse.

6.2 FIELD WORK

Field work with transit and tape is described here.   If theodolite and electronic distance measuring are used or total station is used, procedures are similar.

For a connecting traverse such as shown in Fig. 6.1, two points and two directions of the traverse are already established.   The transit must always be set up on a point of known location.   The first B.S. can be on another station or on magnetic or true north.   In Fig. 6.1, the transit is first set up on sta. 301, and a B.S. is taken on sta. 300.   Field notes are in Fig. 6.2.

While the instrument person and others are setting up the transit and taking line for a B.S., the head tape person drives a stake into the ground and drives a nail or tack into the top for the forward station.   The tape person gives line on the station, and the first angle is measured.   The angles of Fig. 6.2 are doubled to increase accuracy, so the telescope is reversed for the second measurement.   Procedures for taking and giving line are described in Section 5.3.

The two tape persons then measure the distance ahead to the forward station (sta. 1) while the instrument person keeps them on line.   They need not be on line with great accuracy as explained in Chapter 3.   The distance is normally measured forward from the transit to the next station, and this need not be specified in the notes.   It is understood unless noted otherwise.

When intermediate points are needed to measure a course, the head tape person may put a nail into the ground on line and measure to it, or he may set a nail on line every 100 ft.   The field notes in Fig. 6.2 show that taping is done in 100-ft increments.   The field notes in Fig. 6.12 show that the other method is used for the loop traverse.

After the distance is measured and recorded, the instrument person sets up on the forward station while the head tape person moves ahead to establish the next station.   Experience is required to lay out a traverse so that the stations are in convenient locations for their purpose and so that there is not an excessive number of them.   The head tape person is the key operator, controlling the location of the stations and the speed of the operation.   The party chief usually is the head tape person or note keeper in a four-person

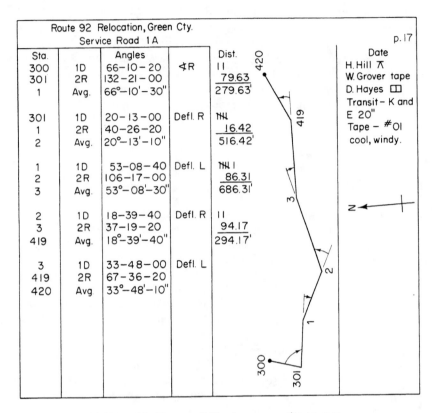

Figure 6.2 Traverse field notes—connecting traverse

party. In a three-person party, the chief is usually the head tape person and note keeper.

The head tape person continues to move ahead, establishing new stations, while the instrument person continues to set up the instrument one station behind and while another member clears the course of any brush or other obstacles to the line of sight or tape. The party proceeds until the traverse is closed by measuring distance 3-419 and measuring angle 3, 419, 420.

Often, the instrument person cannot sight the adjacent hubs. With a four-person party, one person is assigned to give line for backsights, and the head tape person gives line for foresights. With fewer people, it is not efficient for one to stay behind for the B.S. The instrument person, after measuring the angle, gives line to the rear tape person, who sets a nail on the F.S. line a short distance from the transit where it can be seen and used as a B.S. when the transit is moved to the next station. This nail is accurately set because it is set with a short F.S. from a long B.S. This is called *setting a backsight.* Another method is to use tall stakes for all stations with projecting nails that can be seen by the instrument person from the next station.

For a loop traverse, three stations must be established before the first angle can be measured. See the first angle of the field notes in Fig. 6.12. The party chief designates the position for the first transit setup, a stake is driven there, and a nail is driven into the stake. While the instrument person is setting up the transit over the nail, the party chief designates locations for a back station and a forward station. The rear tape person puts in a hub for the back station and gives line on it. The head tape person puts in a hub for the forward station and gives line. The angle is measured and recorded. The angles of Fig. 6.12 are doubled, and the telescope is not reversed for the second measurement. As discussed in Chapter 5, the scope is sometimes not reversed when the angle is doubled only as a precaution against mistakes.

6.3 TAPING SLOPE DISTANCES

Distances are often taped on a slope while running a traverse. The party chief decides whether to tape short horizontal distances on a long slope or to measure a slope distance in one operation and to convert it to a level distance.

Methods of converting a slope distance to a horizontal distance are discussed in Chapter 3. Ways of measuring a slope distance in the field are discussed here.

METHOD 1

The transit telescope is set at a vertical angle so that the line of sight passes over the station ahead. The tape is held over the back station at the center of the horizontal axle of the transit. Thus, it is at the elevation of the line of sight but is offset several inches. The slight offset causes no inaccuracy. The tape is held over the forward station at a height on the line of sight as directed by the instrument person. The instrument person directs the head tape person up or down until the tape in the head tape person's hand is at the cross hairs. The head tape person adjusts the plumb bob string as needed. If the distance is long, it can be measured in steps provided that both ends of the tape can be kept on the line of sight by the instrument person. Taped distances and vertical angles are noted in the field book. Conversion to horizontal distances is made by using a table, such as Table IV in the Appendix, or by multiplying the slope distance by the cos of the vertical angle. See Fig. 6.3 for illustration of the field method and Fig. 6.4 for field notes.

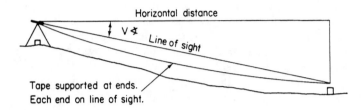

Method 1   Distance measured along line of sight

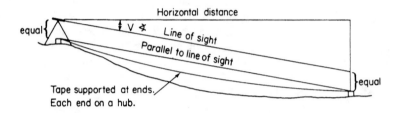

Method 2   Distance measured parallel with line of sight

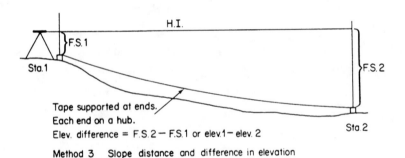

Method 3   Slope distance and difference in elevation

Figure 6.3   Methods of taping slope distances

METHOD 2

The height from the top of the hub to the center of the transit horizontal axle is measured with a level rod.   The level rod is then held on the forward hub, and the transit cross hairs are trained on the same height.   The line of sight is thus parallel with a line from the top of one hub to the top of the other hub, making a vertical angle in the transit the same as that from one hub top to the other.

The vertical angle is recorded.   The distance is measured from hub to hub, holding the tape on the hub tops.   It is thus measured at the slope of the recorded vertical angle.   The entire length must be measured in one step.

Method 1 and 2

Sta.		H ⌖		V ⌖	Dist.	Corr. Dist.	
4	1	63°-27'-30"	⌖R	4°-12'	134.86'	-0.36'	Fm. Table **IV**
5	2	126°-54'-30"				134.50'	
6	Avg.	63°-27'-15"					

Method 3

Sta.		H ⌖	Dist.	Corr.	Corr. dist.
5	1	174°-18'-30"	192.32'	-0.06'	192.26'
6	2	348°-37'-30"			
7	Avg.	174°-18'-45"			

Sta.	B.S.(+)	H.I.	F.S.(−)	Rod (−)	Elev.
B.M.	4.96	104.96			100.00
6				4.34	100.62
7				8.92	96.04
B.M.			4.96		100.00

$$C = \frac{d^2}{2L} = \frac{(100.62 - 96.04)^2}{2 \times 192.32} = 0.06$$

Figure 6.4   Field notes for slope distances

Conversion to horizontal distance is the same as for Method 1.   See Figs. 6.3 and 6.4.

METHOD 3

Each distance is measured with the tape held on hub tops at both ends.   The tape may be held at a predetermined distance above the hub tops so that it measures a line parallel with a line from hub top to hub top.   The difference in elevation between hub tops is determined from a level circuit including all necessary hub tops.   Hub elevations may be obtained from rod shots.   The horizontal distance is determined by using the Pythagorean identities or by subtracting the correction $C_s = d^2/2L$ (described in Chapter 3).   See Figs. 6.3 and 6.4.

6.4 TOTAL-STATION INSTRUMENTS

A *total-station instrument* is a theodolite and electronic distance measuring device in one unit and performs the functions of both.   Theodolites are discussed in Section 5.12 and electronic distance measuring in Section 3.3.

Figure 6.5 Total Station (*Courtesy The Lietz Company*)

Angles are measured or laid off, and distance is measured at any slope and converted to horizontal and vertical components.

All information is displayed digitally and stored for later input to a computer system for further processing. Field notes can be recorded but are not needed for computer processing.

If coordinates of the station and the bearing of the backsight are keyed into the total-station instrument, it can compute and display coordinates of the next point. This instrument provides the most efficient method of completing traverse field work. A total-station instrument is shown in Fig. 6.5.

6.5 ERROR OF CLOSURE

Figures 6.1 and 6.14 show traverses as established in the field. Since all measurements include some error, angles and distances are not exactly as measured. Even though the traverses are closed on points of known location in the field, if an accurate calculation is made using angles and distances from the field, the last course will not end exactly on the closing station. In other words, the traverse does not close. It closes physically in the field but, because of measuring errors, does not close mathematically. This discrepancy is the *error of closure*. It can be determined mathematically.

The student should review error and accuracy from Chapter 2 and also bearings and coordinates from Chapter 1.

For the sake of consistency, the probable error due to angular inaccuracies should be about the same as the probable error due to linear inaccuracies.

Taping with ordinary care should produce an accuracy of 1:5,000. The use of a new tape with a spring tension handle and temperature corrections at frequent intervals should produce an accuracy of 1:10,000. To correspond approximately to this accuracy, a transit should read to 1' and 30" respectively. Many instruments read to 30" or 20", and it is customary to double angles as a check for error even if the additional accuracy is not needed. Therefore, the angular accuracy usually exceeds the linear accuracy with no additional effort.

6.6 ADJUSTING A TRAVERSE

The procedure for computing error of closure and distributing the correction is demonstrated for the traverses shown in Figs. 6.1 and 6.14. The procedure is called *adjusting a traverse.*

Traverse adjustment is a classic example of the engineering approach to problem solving. The form is standardized and is so well designed that it could be studied for its format. It removes the chance for undetected mistakes and reduces a complex problem to simple operations.

The work is tabulated so that calculations are in a logical form, easy to compute with calculator, and easy to check for mistakes. Built-in checks are provided at various points, and if the end result does not equal a predetermined quantity, a mistake has been made. The mistake must be found and corrected. Its correction requires a minimum of revised calculations.

Some technical problems cannot be solved as neatly with so many check points along the way. However, the principles of tabulation and checking by alternative solutions can and should be applied to many problems in other fields.

The example in Fig. 6.1 is a connecting traverse beginning at a station in a previously adjusted traverse and ending at another station in a previously adjusted traverse. It represents an auxiliary traverse to control design of a short road between sections of highway each controlled by its own traverse. The two bearings shown are from a map of the original traverses after adjustment.

The original traverses are established with accuracy the same as or greater than the auxiliary traverse, and they control the auxiliary. Therefore, the auxiliary traverse can be adjusted mathematically to conform to the originals, but no part of the original ones should be adjusted to conform to the auxiliary.

Field work must include angles joining the new traverse to two courses of the controlling traverses; if not, there will be no way to adjust angles. Distances within the original traverses are not needed. Step-by-step adjustment of the traverse in Fig. 6.1 follows:

1. Plot the traverse to scale. This is necessary in order to visualize computations and to check for any obvious mistake that must be corrected before proceeding with calculations. Figure 6.1 shows the traverse plotted from field notes in Fig. 6.2.

   A traverse can be plotted using a protractor, straightedge, and scale. A line is drawn to scale to represent the first course of the traverse. A protractor is placed with its center on the vertex of the first angle and zero toward the B.S., or 180° from the B.S. if it is a deflection angle. Then, the angle from the field notes is laid off on the protractor in the same direction as it was turned in the field. A mark is made on the plotting sheet. A line is drawn from the vertex through the mark with the straightedge, and it is scaled to the right length. The end of this line is the vertex of the next angle.

   Angles can be plotted with accuracy to the nearest one-half degree. The accuracy of plotted distances depends on the scale used. The procedure is a duplication in miniature of field measurements. The angle is laid off and marked. Then the distance is measured. The plotter must visualize the instrument at the vertex turning the angle the way it was turned in the field. See Fig. 6.6 for plotting method.

2. Adjust field angles to make them mathematically correct. The bearings of the two original traverses are held, and the new angles are adjusted to make them conform. The angular error is found by holding the bearing from one original traverse and computing the closing bearing for the other from field angles.

   The difference between the closing bearing and the correct bearing is the total error, and an equal and opposite correction is distributed among the traverse angles as demonstrated in Fig. 6.7. Each angle is adjusted the same amount whether it is a large angle or a small one since there is equal chance for error in each of them.

   Angles are usually adjusted to the nearest second with excess seconds being distributed one at a time without overcorrecting any one part of the traverse and, when possible, favoring larger angles. For example, three seconds would be distributed one to every other angle of a 6-sided traverse, and either one to every fourth angle of a 12-sided traverse or one to each of the three largest angles as long as they are not too close together.

   The result of this distribution is an apparent accuracy to the nearest second. In order to indicate the true accuracy, the correction can be distributed in increments equal to the accuracy with which the angles were read. This is the least count of the vernier, or it is less if the angles are repeated. Adjustment is the same as for one-second increments. An example follows:

$$\text{No. of angles} = 12$$

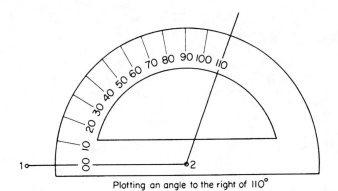

Plotting an angle to the right of 110°

Plotting a deflection angle to the right of 27°

Figure 6.6   Plotting a traverse

$$\text{Total correction} = +80''$$

$$\text{Increment} = 10''$$

Eight corrections are to be distributed to 12 angles. Therefore, two-thirds of the angles are corrected. Every third angle has no correction. Arrange the corrections so that the larger angles receive the corrections as much as possible without disturbing the pattern. If there are 13 angles, the results are the same except that there is one instance of 2 successive angles with no correction. These should be small angles if feasible.

In a particular case, the surveyor might assign the entire correction to one or two angles measured under such adverse field conditions that more error is to be expected there.

Computation and distribution of angular corrections
Hold 301–300 N 33°–12'–00" E

	Defl. R (+)		Defl. L (−)
301 – 1	66°–10'–30"		
1 – 2	20°–13'–10"	2 – 3	53°–08'–30"
3 – 319	18°–39'–40"	419 – 420	33°–48'–10"
	105°–03'–20"		86°–56'–40"

Bearing of 419–420 by field survey

$$
\begin{array}{rl}
& \text{N } 33{-}12{-}00 \text{ E} \\
+ & 105{-}03{-}20 \quad \text{to right} \\
- & 86{-}56{-}40 \quad \text{to left} \\
\end{array}
$$

Answer: N 51°–18'–40" E
Correct bearing N 51°–19'–30" E

Difference is error −50"
Correction +50"
Correction per angle $\dfrac{50"}{5} = +10"$

Field angles	Adjusted angles
+ 66°–10'–30"	+ 66°–10'–40"
+ 20°–13'–10"	+ 20°–13'–20"
− 53°–08'–30"	− 53°–08'–20"
+ 18°–39'–40"	+ 18°–39'–50"
− 33°–48'–10"	− 33°–48'–00"
	+ 105°–03'–50"
	− 86°–56'–20"
	+ N 33°–12'–00" E Bearing of 301–300
	N 51°–19'–00" E Correct bearing of 419–420

Bearing of 301–300 plus algebraic sum of adjusted
angles equals correct bearing of 419–420.
Therefore angles are correctly adjusted.

Figure 6.7 Adjustment of traverse field angles—connecting traverse

3. Determine the bearings for all courses. Starting with course 301-1, one determines the bearing for each course in succession by applying the adjusted angle to the preceding bearing until course 419-420 is reached. If the work is correct, the correct bearing will be obtained for the final course. The method is shown in Fig. 6.8. Bearings are more readily determined from deflection angles than from right or left angles, and deflection angles may be preferred for this reason.

4. Determine latitudes and departures from the beginning to the end of the traverse. The bearing and distance of each course are used to determine the latitude and departure (difference in coordinates) from one station to the next. The algebraic sum of the latitudes and depar-

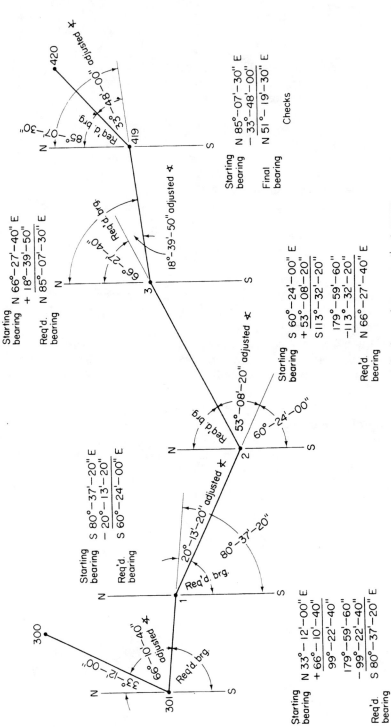

Figure 6.8 Determining bearings from deflection angles—connecting traverse

149

tures added algebraically to the coordinates of station 301 should, if there is no error, equal the coordinates of station 419.

The difference between what it does equal and what it should equal is the error of closure. The process of adding latitudes and departures algebraically is shown graphically in Fig. 6.9 with the error of closure shown in detail.

Calculations necessary to compute latitudes and departures are shown on the left side of the computation sheet in Fig. 6.10. The error in departures is greater than the error in latitudes; this is expected because these departures depend primarily on taped distances that are less accurate than the angles that primarily control latitudes in this case.

Inspection of Fig. 6.1 shows that excessive error in the latitudes must be caused by inaccurate angular measurement and that excessive error in the departures must be caused by inaccurate distance measurement. The bearings of courses in Fig. 6.10 verify this. They all run roughly east-west. When excessive error is found in a traverse, inspection sometimes indicates its source and, thereby, the field work that must be redone to correct it.

5. Compute the accuracy of the survey from the results of the latitudes and departures. If the accuracy is unacceptable, there is no use continuing the calculations until the reason is determined and the error is rectified. Usually, this requires checking work in the field. The method of computing accuracy is shown in Fig. 6.10.

6. Compute corrections to all coordinate positions using a mathematical process that distributes the corrections according to some reasonable plan. The total correction must be equal to the error of closure with opposite sign.

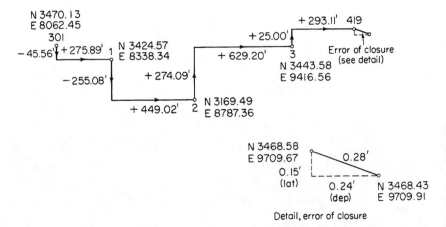

Figure 6.9 Latitudes and departures for each course—connecting traverse

	Length	Brg.	cos	sin	Lats.	Deps.	Corrections		Coordinates	
							Lat.	Dep.	N	E
301									3470.13	8062.45
	279.63	S80°-37'-20"E	.1629433	.9866354	-45.56	+275.89	-0.02	+0.04	-45.58	+275.93
1									3424.55	8338.38
	516.42	S60°-24'-00"E	.4939419	.8694949	-255.08	+449.02	-0.04	+0.07	-255.12	+449.09
2									3169.43	8787.47
	686.31	N66°-27'-40"E	.3993714	.9167892	+274.09	+629.20	-0.06	+0.09	+274.03	+629.29
3									3443.46	9416.76
	294.17	N85°-07'-30"E	.0849822	.9963825	+25.00	+293.11	-0.03	+0.04	+24.97	+293.15
419									3468.43	9709.91
							-0.15	+0.24		

Total 1776.53

Total of field differences*   -1.55   +1647.22
Theoretical differences**   -1.70   +1647.46
Errors   +0.15   -0.24
Corrections   -0.15   +0.24

Error of closure:

$$\sqrt{.15^2 + .24^2} = 0.28 \text{ ft}$$

Accuracy

$$\frac{0.28}{1776.53} = \frac{1}{6340}$$

*Algebraic sums of lats. and deps.

**Theoretical differences from sta. 301 to sta. 419

	Lat		Dep
301	3470.13	419	9709.91
419	3468.43	301	8062.45
	-1.70		1647.46

Figure 6.10   Calculation of accuracy and traverse adjustment—connecting traverse

a. The *compass rule* assigns corrections to the coordinate position of each station in proportion to the length of the course leading from the previous station to that station. In a connecting traverse, each station is mathematically moved except the starting and closing stations.

The first station is moved in the two coordinate directions in amounts determined by multiplying the latitude and the departure of the total correction by the length of the first course divided by the total length of traverse. The rest of the traverse moves with it so that all following stations are adjusted by the same amount.

The second station is then moved an additional amount in the two coordinate directions according to the length of the second course. All succeeding stations move the same amount.

This process continues, each succeeding station moving farther from its original position than the previous station until the end of the final course moves the length of the total correction and coincides with the final station that does not move.

b. The *transit rule* assigns corrections to the coordinate position of each station in proportion to the length of latitude and departure of the course leading from the previous station to that station. The procedure is similar to the procedure using the compass rule, but the latitude corrections depend on length of latitude for the preceding course, and departure corrections depend on length of departure for the preceding course instead of both depending on length of preceding course.

Corrections for the traverse are worked out by both methods in Fig. 6.11. Graphic application of the corrections is shown in Fig. 6.12.

The lengths used in Fig. 6.11 to compute corrections need not be carried out to decimal places. It is done here so that the student can easily see where each number comes from. Corrections are carried only to two significant places. It is advisable to carry each one to three decimal places as a preliminary step so that the final corrections can be distributed to the nearest hundredth to equal the total correction.

Corrections shown in Fig. 6.10 are the ones computed by the compass rule. This method is more commonly used and is mathematically more correct. The transit rule theoretically changes lengths with little effect on angles. This is logical because angles are more accurate than distances in a transit and tape survey. However, some angles are changed excessively under certain conditions. Results depend on the orientation of the traverse with the north line and are not consistent.

Corrections are sometimes made to coordinates of each station solely on the basis of the difficulty of the measuring conditions for the course preceding that station. This method is as valid as any other when performed carefully by an experienced surveyor. The *method of*

Corrections by compass rule

Course	Lat. calcs.	Corr.
301-1	$\frac{279.63}{1776.53}$ x 0.15 = .024	0.02
1-2	$\frac{516.42}{1776.53}$ x 0.15 = .044	0.04
2-3	$\frac{686.31}{1776.53}$ x 0.15 = .058	0.06
3-419	$\frac{294.17}{1776.53}$ x 0.15 = .025	0.03
Total		0.15

Course	Dep. calcs.	Corr.
301-1	$\frac{279.63}{1776.53}$ x 0.24 = .038	0.04
1-2	$\frac{516.42}{1776.53}$ x 0.24 = .070	0.07
2-3	$\frac{686.31}{1776.53}$ x 0.24 = .093	0.09
3-419	$\frac{294.17}{1776.53}$ x 0.24 = .040	0.04
Total		0.24

Denominator is total distance along traverse for lat. and dep. corrections.

Corrections by transit rule

Course	Lat. calcs.	Corr.
301-1	$\frac{45.56}{599.73}$ x 0.15 = .011	0.01
1-2	$\frac{255.08}{599.73}$ x 0.15 = .064	0.06
2-3	$\frac{274.09}{599.73}$ x 0.15 = .069	0.07
3-419	$\frac{25.00}{599.73}$ x 0.15 = .006	0.01
Total		0.15

Course	Dep. calcs.	Corr.
301-1	$\frac{275.89}{1647.22}$ x 0.24 = .040	0.04
1-2	$\frac{449.02}{1647.22}$ x 0.24 = .065	0.07
2-3	$\frac{629.20}{1647.22}$ x 0.24 = .092	0.09
3-419	$\frac{293.11}{1647.22}$ x 0.24 = .043	0.04
Total		0.24

Denominator is sum of lats.   45.56   Denominator is sum of deps.   275.89
disregarding signs   255.08   disregarding signs   449.02
                                  274.09   629.20
                                   25.00   293.11
                                  599.73   1647.22

Figure 6.11   Computation of corrections—connecting traverse

least squares is a mathematically exact method suitable for computer use.   It is the most satisfactory mathematically.

The *Crandall method* is a method suitable for use where the method of linear measurements is much less accurate than the method of angular measurements.   It is more reliable than the transit method, but the computations are time-consuming and are not usually performed except by computer.

7. Adjust the traverse by adding the corrections to the coordinates of each station.   In practice, the corrections are added at the same time as the latitudes and departures.   See Fig. 6.10 for the procedure.

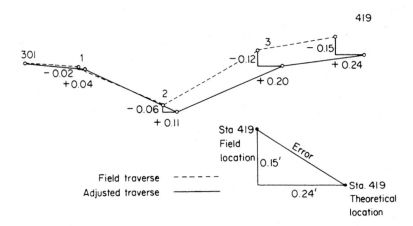

Figure 6.12   Applying corrections to traverse—connecting traverse

The adjustment of the loop traverse in Fig. 6.14 is also shown. The work is similar and some steps are repetitious. They are included so that each example—the connecting traverse and the loop traverse—will stand by itself.

Field work must include every angle and course of the loop traverse. This is obvious when looking at the plot but is an oversight easily made in the field when the last station is sometimes forgotten because it has already been used for a B.S. Field notes and the traverse as established in the field are shown in Figs. 6.13 and 6.14.

Step-by-step adjustment of the loop traverse follows:

1. Plot the traverse to scale. This is necessary in order to visualize computations and to check for any obvious mistake that must be corrected before proceeding with calculations.

2. Adjust field angles to make them mathematically correct. The sum of the interior angles of a closed traverse equals $(N - 2)$ 180° where N is the number of angles. The algebraic total of deflection angles left and right around a closed traverse is zero. Either rule can be used to determine the total angular error. The total correction (equal to the total error and opposite in sign) is distributed as equally as can be among all the angles of the traverse since there is equal chance for error in each of them. See Fig. 6.15 for procedure.

   Often, the angular error is computed in the field. If a large error is discovered, the source might be recalled while the work is still fresh in mind. If not, all angles must be remeasured until the excessive error is found. The remeasuring can be started immediately rather than requiring a return trip to the field.

McNamara Property, Williamstown
Prelim. Survey Traverse   page 46

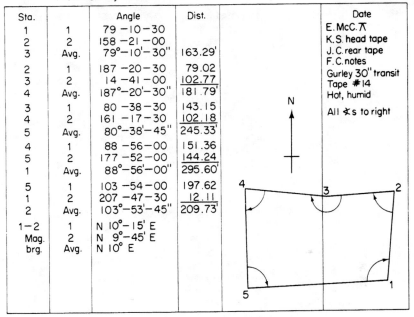

Sta.		Angle	Dist.		Date
1	1	79 −10−30			E. McC. 人
2	2	158 −21 −00			K.S. head tape
3	Avg.	79°−10'−30"	163.29'		J.C. rear tape
					F.C. notes
2	1	187 −20−30	79.02		Gurley 30" transit
3	2	14 −41 −00	102.77		Tape #14
4	Avg.	187°−20'−30"	181.79'		Hot, humid
3	1	80 −38−30	143.15		All ∡s to right
4	2	161 −17−30	102.18		
5	Avg.	80°−38'−45"	245.33'		
4	1	88 −56−00	151.36		
5	2	177 −52−00	144.24		
1	Avg.	88°−56'−00"	295.60'		
5	1	103 −54−00	197.62		
1	2	207 −47−30	12.11		
2	Avg.	103°−53'−45"	209.73'		
1−2	1	N 10°−15' E			
Mag.	2	N 9°−45' E			
brg.	Avg.	N 10° E			

Figure 6.13   Traverse field notes—loop traverse

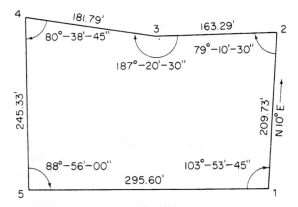

Figure 6.14   Traverse as established in field—loop traverse

Computation and Distribution of Angular Corrections

Unadjusted Interior Angles

79°10′30″
187°20′30″
80°38′45″
88°56′00″
103°53′45″

Total Unadjusted ∢s = 539°59′30″
(N − 2)180 = 540°00′00″

Angular Error   −30″
Angular Correction +30″
No. of Angles   5
Correction per ∢ $\dfrac{+30″}{5} = +6″$

Adjusted Interior Angles

79°10′36″
187°20′36″
80°38′51″
88°56′06″
103°53′51″

Total Adjusted ∢s   540°00′00″

Total shows angles are correctly adjusted.

Figure 6.15   Adjustment of traverse field angles—loop traverse

3. Determine the bearings for all courses. The bearing of one course must be determined either by using the transit compass, by sighting the sun or a star, by using a map, or by assuming a bearing. A magnetic bearing is shown for course 1–2 in the field notes in Fig. 6.13. Bearings of other courses are calculated in succession around the traverse starting with that bearing and applying the adjusted angles until the bearing of the starting course is determined. If the work is correct, the final bearing of the starting course will be the same as it was at the beginning. The method is shown in Fig. 6.16.

4. Determine latitudes and departures from the beginning to the end of the traverse. The bearing and distance of each course are used to determine the difference in coordinates from one station to the next. The algebraic sums of these differences added to the starting coordinates should equal the ending coordinates if there are no errors. A loop traverse ends where it starts, so the algebraic total of latitudes and departures should be zero. Therefore, the algebraic sums of latitudes and departures around the traverse represent the error of closure.

     Station 1 of the traverse of Fig. 6.14 is assigned coordinates of N1000.00, E1000.00 so that we may determine coordinates of all stations

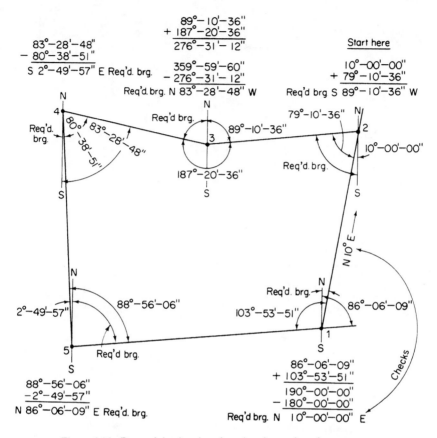

Figure 6.16 Determining bearings from interior angles—loop traverse

and return to station 1 without being outside the first quadrant, which would involve negative numbers. The process of adding latitudes and departures algebraically is shown graphically in Fig. 6.17 with the error of closure shown in detail. The calculations necessary to compute latitudes and departures are shown on the left side of the computation sheet in Fig. 6.18.

5. Compute the accuracy of the survey from the results of the latitudes and departures. If the accuracy is unacceptable, there is no use continuing the calculations until the reason is determined and the error is rectified. The method of computing accuracy is shown in Fig. 6.18.

6. Using an acceptable method, compute corrections. In a loop traverse, each station is moved except the first station, which is also the final station. The procedure is the same as for a connecting traverse except that the courses are adjusted to close on the starting point. Corrections

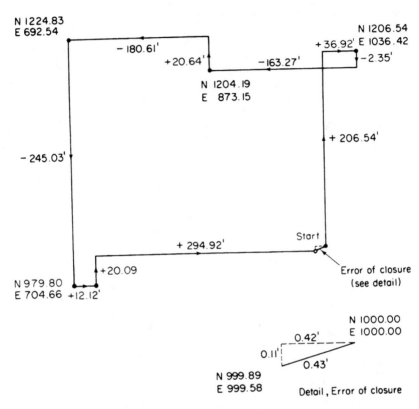

Figure 6.17   Latitudes and departures for each course—loop traverse

shown in Fig. 6.18 are computed by the compass rule. Corrections are worked out by transit rule and compass rule in Fig. 6.19.

7. Adjust coordinates by adding or subtracting corrections, increasing corrections as you proceed from station to station. This is done in the last two columns in Fig. 6.18 in which latitudes and departures are combined with corrections and are applied to each station in succession, returning to station 1 as a check.

Two points should be remembered:

1. If systematic errors are made throughout a loop traverse, they will not cause an excessive error and, therefore, will not be discovered by computing error of closure. For example, if a tape is consistently pulled with too little tension, all readings will be too long in the same ratio for each measurement. The result will be a traverse that appears larger in the field notes than it actually is. However, north error from this source

| Sta | Length | Brg. | cos | sin | Lats. | Deps. | Corrections | | Coordinates | |
							Lat.	Dep.	N	E
1									1000.00*	1000.00*
	209.73	N 10°-00'-00"E	.9848078	.1736482	+206.54	+36.42	+0.02	+0.08	+206.56	+36.50
2									1206.56	1036.50
	163.29	S 89°-10'-36"W	.0143694	.9998965	-2.35	-163.27	+0.02	+0.06	-2.33	-163.21
3									1204.23	873.29
	181.79	N 83°-28'-48"W	.1135500	.9935323	+20.64	-180.61	+0.02	+0.07	+20.66	-180.54
4									1224.89	692.75
	245.33	S 2°-49'-57"E	.9987782	.0494163	-245.03	+12.12	+0.02	+0.10	-245.01	+12.22
5									979.88	704.97
	295.60	N 86°-06'-09"E	.0679718	.9976873	+20.09	+294.92	+0.03	+0.11	+20.12	+295.03
1									1000.00	1000.00

Total 1095.74

+ Total	247.27	343.46
− Total	247.38	343.88
Errors	−0.11	−0.42
Corrections	+0.11	+0.42

Error of closure

$$\sqrt{.11^2 + .42^2} = .43 \text{ ft}$$

Accuracy

$$\frac{43}{1095.74} = \frac{1}{2550}$$

*Coordinates are assumed for sta.1

Figure 6.18 Calculation of accuracy and transverse adjustment—loop traverse

Corrections by compass rule

Course	Lat. calcs.	Corr.	Course	Dep. calcs.	Corr.
1-2	$\dfrac{209.73}{1095.74} \times 0.11 = .021$	0.02	1-2	$\dfrac{209.73}{1095.74} \times 0.42 = .080$	0.08
2-3	$\dfrac{163.29}{1095.74} \times 0.11 = .016$	0.02	2-3	$\dfrac{163.29}{1095.74} \times 0.42 = .062$	0.06
3-4	$\dfrac{181.79}{1095.74} \times 0.11 = .018$	0.02	3-4	$\dfrac{181.79}{1095.74} \times 0.42 = .069$	0.07
4-5	$\dfrac{245.33}{1095.74} \times 0.11 = .025$	0.02	4-5	$\dfrac{245.33}{1095.74} \times 0.42 = .093$	0.10
5-1	$\dfrac{295.60}{1095.74} \times 0.11 = .030$	0.03	5-1	$\dfrac{295.60}{1095.74} \times 0.42 = .113$	0.11
Total		0.11	Total		0.42

Denominator is total distance around traverse for lat. and dep. corrections

Corrections by transit rule

Course	Lat. calcs.	Corr.	Course	Dep. calcs.	Corr.
1-2	$\dfrac{206.54}{494.65} \times 0.11 = .046$	0.04	1-2	$\dfrac{36.42}{687.34} \times 0.42 = .022$	0.02
2-3	$\dfrac{2.35}{494.65} \times 0.11 = .000$	0.00	2-3	$\dfrac{163.27}{687.34} \times 0.42 = .100$	0.10
3-4	$\dfrac{20.64}{494.65} \times 0.11 = .005$	0.01	3-4	$\dfrac{180.61}{687.34} \times 0.42 = .110$	0.11
4-5	$\dfrac{245.03}{494.65} \times 0.11 = .054$	0.05	4-5	$\dfrac{12.12}{687.34} \times 0.42 = .007$	0.01
5-1	$\dfrac{20.09}{494.65} \times 0.11 = .004$	0.01	5-1	$\dfrac{294.92}{687.34} \times 0.42 = .181$	0.18
Total		0.11	Total		0.42

Denominator is sum of lats.	206.54	Denominator is sum of deps.	36.42
disregarding signs.	2.35	disregarding signs.	163.27
	20.64		180.61
	245.03		12.12
	20.09		294.92
	494.65		687.34

Figure 6.19 Computation of corrections—loop traverse

will equal south error and east error will equal west error so that closure will be as accurate as without the systematic error. Thus, there may be no way to expose an excessive systematic error.

2. Sometimes, an accuracy is calculated that is much higher than expected from the equipment and field methods used. This is a false accuracy caused by lucky cancelling of some errors by others. The fact that the

final station determined mathematically is close to the final station in the field does not mean that all other stations are located that accurately.

For example, several plus errors in succession in the field could cause a large error in the third or fourth station.   Several minus errors following these could balance the plus errors so that the error of closure is smaller than the error in station 3 or 4.   If the equipment and methods used are not appropriate for the accuracy determined mathematically, the work should not be considered to be that accurate.

6.7 LOCATIONS OF POINTS NOT ON A TRAVERSE

As explained at the beginning of this chapter, the traverse is a framework to establish other locations.   An example is shown in Fig. 6.20, in which the traverse in Fig. 6.1 is shown with six critical points of the many whose locations are needed to design a connecting road between two highways.   Two points serve to establish the edge of pavement of each highway, and two points serve to locate the center line of a railroad track.   The points are all located by *sideshots*.

In Fig. 6.21, a set of field notes for the connecting traverse is shown including sideshots to points 11, 12, 21, 22, 31, and 32.   The system used here to differentiate between traverse stations and other points is to assign

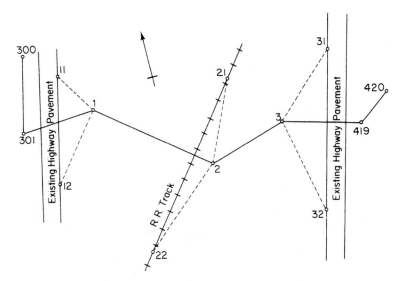

Figure 6.20   Connecting traverse used to locate design information

Route 92 relocation, Green City,
Service road 1A.

Sta.		Angles		Dist.
300	1D	66-10-20		II
301	2R	132-21-00	∡R	79.63
1	Avg.	66°-10'-30"		279.63'
301	1D	20-13-00		₶
1	2R	40-26-20	Defl.R	16.42
2	Avg.	20°-13'-10"		516.42'
301	1D	63-11-00		
1	2R	126-21-40	∡R	
11	Avg.	63°-10'-50"		46.35'
301	1D	52-16-00		
1	2R	104-32-00	∡L	
12	Avg.	52°-16'-00"		98.21'
1	1D	53-08-40		₶ I
2	2R	106-17-00	Defl.L	86.31
3	Avg.	53°-08'-30"		686.31'
1	1D	84-10-00		
2	2R	168-20-00	∡R	
21	Avg.	84°-10'-00"		105.62'
1	1D	88-25-00		I
2	2R	176-50-00	∡L	94.22
22	Avg.	88°-25'-00"		194.22'
2	1D	18-39-40		II
3	2R	37-19-20	Defl.R	94.17
419	Avg.	18°-39'-40"		294.17'
2	1D	142-23-20		
3	2R	284-46-40	∡R	
31	Avg.	142°-23'-20"		85.75'
2	1D	91-57-40		
3	2R	183-55-00	∡L	
32	Avg.	91°-57'-30"		80.76'
3	1D	33-48-00		
419	2R	67-36-20	Defl.L	
420	Avg.	33°-48'-10"		

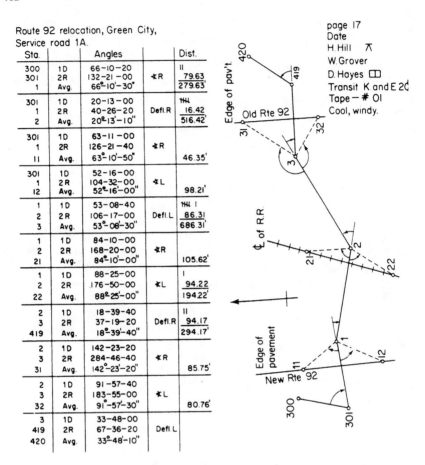

page 17
Date
H. Hill   ⅄
W. Grover
D. Hayes   ▭
Transit K and E 2C
Tape — # 01
Cool, windy.

Figure 6.21 Field notes—connecting traverse with sideshots

two-digit numbers to sideshots with the first digit being the number of the station from which the sideshot is taken. This or a similar system should be used for orderly notekeeping.

The locations of points 11, 12, 21, 22, 31, and 32 are more useful in coordinate form. Coordinates can be computed by applying the sideshot angles and distances from the field notes to the previously computed coordinates of the appropriate stations.

First, sideshot angles are converted to bearings using new traverse bearings determined from adjusted station coordinates. Then, bearings and distances are converted to latitudes and departures. Adding these algebraically to station coordinates gives the coordinates of the six points. The process involves the same steps that were originally used to determine coordinates of the stations except that there is no way to adjust these new points. Figure 6.22 illustrates the procedure for points 21 and 22.

The two points, 21 and 22, are now located in the coordinate system. It is necessary to find the direction of the track so that the angle for the road crossing can be decided. Whether the road crosses by bridge, by underpass,

Compute bearing for course 2−1 using adjusted station coordinates.
This is the backsight for sideshots to 21 and 22.

Course	From Fig 6-9		tan brg. ∢ dep./lat.	Adjusted bearing	
	lat.	dep.			
2 − 1	+255.12	−449.09	1.7603088	N 60°−24'−00" W	Bearing does not change in this case

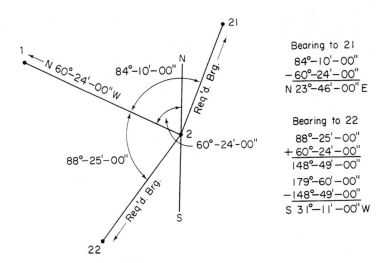

Bearing to 21

84°−10'−00"
−60°−24'−00"
N 23°−46'−00" E

Bearing to 22

88°−25'−00"
+60°−24'−00"
148°−49'−00"

179°−60'−00"
−148°−49'−00"
S 31°−11'−00" W

	Length	Brg.	cos	sin	Lats.	Deps.	Coordinates	
							N	E
2							3169.43	8787.47
	105.62'	N 23°−46'−00"E	.9151943	.4030129	+96.66	+42.57		
21							3266.09	8830.04
2							3169.43	8787.47
	194.22'	S 31°−11'−00" W	.8555149	.5177782	−166.16	−100.56		
22							3003.27	8686.91

Figure 6.22 Computing coordinates from sideshots

or at grade, this angle is critical for design.   The direction of the road is determined by the crossing angle selected.

Figure 6.23 shows how to find bearing and length of the track between the two points.   This process is called *inversing* because it is the opposite or inverse of the process of determining coordinates.   The process is described in Chapter 1 under "Coordinates," although it is not called inversing there.

$$\text{The tan of the bearing angle is } \frac{\text{dep}}{\text{lat}}$$

The cos of the bearing angle is $\dfrac{\text{lat}}{\text{distance}}$, and the sin of the bearing angle is $\dfrac{\text{dep}}{\text{distance}}$. These three relationships are seen by studying Fig. 6.23.

The steps in inversing are as follows:

1. Calculate lat and dep.
2. Calculate tan of bearing angle.

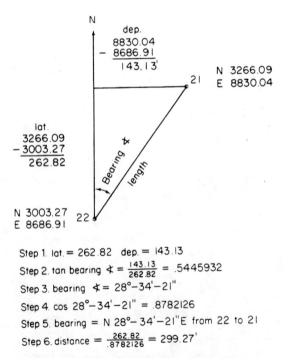

Step 1. lat. = 262.82   dep. = 143.13

Step 2. tan bearing ∡ = $\frac{143.13}{262.82}$ = .5445932

Step 3. bearing ∡ = 28°–34'–21"

Step 4. cos 28°–34'–21" = .8782126

Step 5. bearing = N 28°– 34'–21"E from 22 to 21

Step 6. distance = $\frac{262.82}{.8782126}$ = 299.27'

Figure 6.23   Inversing to determine bearing and distance of a line

3. Determine bearing angle.

4. Determine sin or cos of bearing angle.

5. Determine compass points from the signs of lat and dep.

6. Determine distance from the formula: $\cos \text{ bearing angle} = \dfrac{\text{lat}}{\text{distance}}$; or

$\sin \text{ bearing angle} = \dfrac{\text{dep}}{\text{distance}}$. The use of the function (cos or sin) with the larger value results in greater accuracy.

Traverses are frequently used to determine dimensions of property. In Fig. 6.24, the traverse in Fig. 6.14 is shown as it is used to locate property corners. In this example, the property corners are marked by iron pipes, and the owner wants to know the dimensions of the property and the area enclosed by its boundaries.

A station is located at each property corner if this is convenient. In the example, because trees or bushes are in the way and excessive cutting would be required, only two traverse stations are on property corners. Similarly, the points located for design in Fig. 6.20 would have been stations in the traverse if that had been convenient.

The traverse is already adjusted, which provides coordinates for P.C. 1 and P.C. 4. The coordinates for P.C. 2 and P.C. 3 are computed. Bearings and distances of the four sides of the property are obtained by inversing. The necessary calculations are performed in Fig. 6.25.

A property map may show sides of the boundary labeled with bearings and distances, or it may show lengths of sides and sizes of angles. The two methods are illustrated in Fig. 6.26.

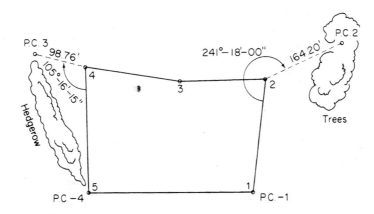

Figure 6.24 Loop traverse used to locate property corners

Compute bearings for courses 2−1 and 4−5 using adjusted station coordinates. Both are backsights for side shots to property corners.

Course	From Fig 6−17		tan brg ✗ Dep./Lat.	Adjusted bearing
	Lat.	Dep.		
2−1	− 206.56	− 36.50	.1767041	S 10°−01'−15" W
4−5	− 245.02	+ 12.22	.049855	S 2°−51'−19" E

Coordinates

Sta.	Length	Brg.	cos	sin	Lat.	Dep.	N	E
2							1206.56	1036.50
	164.20	N 71°−19'−15" E	.3202685	.9473267	+52.59	+155.55	52.59	155.55
P.C.2							1259.15	1192.05
4							1224.89	692.75
	98.76	N 77°−35'−04" W	.2150004	.9766139	+21.23	−96.45	21.23	96.45
P.C.3							1246.12	596.30

Sta.	Lat.	Dep.	Dep./Lat. = tan brg ✗	Brg.	cos or sin	Distance *
P.C.1	1000.00	1000.00				
	+259.15	+192.05	+192.05 / +259.15	.7410765 N 36°−32'−29" E	cos .8034270	322.56'
P.C.2	1259.15	1192.05				
	−13.03	−595.75	−595.75 / −13.03	45.721412 S 88°−44'−49" W	sin .9997608	595.89'
P.C.3	1246.12	596.30				
	−266.24	+108.67	+108.67 / −266.24	.4081655 S 22°−12'−13" E	cos .9258468	287.57'
P.C.4	979.88	704.97				
	+20.12	+295.03	+295.03 / +20.12	14.663519 N 86°−05'−55" E	sin .9976827	295.72'
P.C.1	1000.00	1000.00				

Check

$$* \text{Distance} = \frac{\text{Lat.}}{\cos \beta} \text{ or } \frac{\text{Dep.}}{\sin \beta}$$

Use the larger of Lat. or Dep.

Figure 6.25   Computing bearing and length of property boundary from sideshots

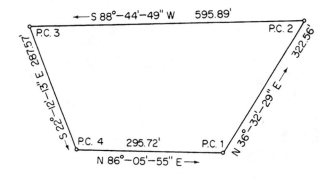

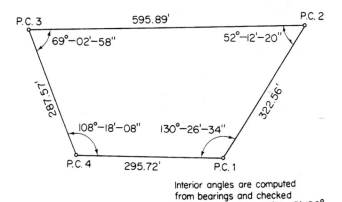

Interior angles are computed
from bearings and checked
to see that they equal (N − 2) 180°

Figure 6.26   Typical property maps

6.8 AREA DETERMINATION

Any area enclosed by straight lines can be found by using *double meridian distances*. A north-south base line is constructed through the westernmost corner of the area. Perpendiculars are constructed from the base line to the other corners of the area boundary. See Fig. 6.27.

The area boundary lines, together with the base line and its perpendiculars, form trapezoids and triangles. The two lengths of each trapezoid and the length of each triangle are in a east-west direction, and the widths of all of them are in a north-south direction. The north-south lines are latitudes of boundary lines, and the east-west lines are departures or the sum of several departures.

The correct combination of trapezoid areas added together, with triangles and other trapezoids subtracted from them, leaves the desired area as

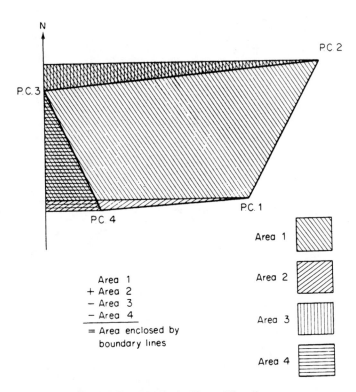

Figure 6.27   Area by double meridian distances

a remainder.   Study of Fig. 6.27 shows how this is done with the area under discussion.   This method works with areas of any number of sides.   However, a systematic tabulation must be used when there are many sides.

The area of a trapezoid is equal to the average length of the two parallel sides multiplied by the width or distance between them.   The area of a triangle is equal to one-half the length multiplied by the width.   The formulas follow:

$$\text{Area of trapezoid} = \frac{\text{dep side 1} + \text{dep side 2}}{2} \times \text{lat}$$

$$\text{Area of triangle} = \frac{\text{dep}}{2} \times \text{lat}$$

In the double meridian distance method, latitudes and departures of each boundary line are tabulated, starting at the most westerly corner and proceeding counterclockwise.   The latitudes and departures are considered plus or minus according to their direction.

The departures are manipulated in such a way that they result in a figure called the *double meridian distance*.   The double meridian distance is twice

Course	Lat.	Dep.	DMD	Double areas
3 – 4	– 266.24	+ 108.67	+ 108.67	– 28,932.30
4 – 1	+ 20.12	+ 295.03	+ 108.67 + 108.67 + 295.03 + 512.37	+ 10,308.88
1 – 2	+ 259.15	+ 192.05	+ 512.37 + 295.03 + 192.05 + 999.45	+ 259,007.47
2 – 3	– 13.03	– 595.75	+ 999.45 + 192.05 – 595.75 + 595.75 Check	– 7,762.62 Check
Check sums	0.00	0.00		

$$\text{Total area} = \frac{232,621.43}{2} = 116,310.71 \text{ sq. ft.}$$

Figure 6.28 Computing area by double meridian distances

the average of the two lengths for trapezoids and is the length for triangles. Each double meridian distance multiplied by half the latitude or width equals the area of a trapezoid or a triangle. All the areas are added algebraically. This results in adding large trapezoids as we proceed north up the east side of the area and in deducting triangular and trapezoid parts of those areas as we proceed south down the west side.

The method of determining area by double meridian distance (DMD) by using the tabular form is as follows:

1. Begin with the course that has the most westerly coordinate at its starting point. Proceed counterclockwise.
2. Enter latitude and departure for each course consecutively. The value is plus if the course goes north or east, and minus if the course goes south or west.
3. Determine DMD by using the following formulas:
   a. DMD of first course equals departure of first course. Begin at most westerly point.
   b. DMD of other courses equals DMD of previous course plus departure of previous course plus departure of the course itself.
4. Determine double areas by multiplying each DMD by the latitude.

5. Total the double areas, deducting minus areas, and divide the total by two to obtain the total area.

As a check, the DMD of the last course should be numerically equal to its departure with opposite sign.

The process results in adding the distance from the north-south line of one end of each course to the distance from the north-south line of the other end of the course and multiplying the sum by the distance along the north-south line. The result is that the two parallel sides of each trapezoid and triangle are added and their sum is multiplied by the width if a triangle is considered a trapezoid with one of the parallel sides equal to zero. This equals twice the area of each trapezoid and triangle since the sum of the parallel sides is not divided by two. The algebraic total is thus twice the area and must be divided by two.

PROBLEMS

1. From the following loop traverse data, prepare field notes, plot traverses to scale, adjust angles, determine bearings, determine accuracy, and adjust the traverses by the compass rule. Assign a bearing of N10°00′00″ E to course 1–2 and coordinates of 1000.00, 1000.00 to station 1. Accurate final coordinates may vary slightly when rounded to two decimal places.

1	104°−29′−40″ 208°−59′−20″	199.72′
2	77°−47′−40″ 155°−35′−20″	157.73′
3	188°−50′−20″ 17°−40′−20″	176.69′
4	79°−56′−40″ 159°−53′−20″	233.85′
5	88°−55′−00″ 177°−50′−20″	285.64′

(a)

1	105°−52′−00″ 211°−44′−20″	179.03′
2	73°−54′−40″ 147°−49′−20″	146.97′
3	193°−28′−40″ 26°−57′−20″	166.87′
4	77°−46′−40″ 155°−33′−20″	209.85′
5	88°−57′−40″ 177°−55′−20″	264.30′

(b)

1	103°−53′−50″ 207°−47′−40″	209.73′
2	79°−10′−40″ 158°−21′−10″	163.29′
3	7°−20′−40″ 14°−41′−10″	181.79′
4	80°−38′−50″ 161°−17′−40″	245.28′
5	88°−56′−00″ 177°−52′−10″	295.90′

(c)

2. Given the following coordinates, determine bearings and distances from A to B.

A	B
(a) N 900.00, E 400.00	N 1000.00, E 918.20
(b) N 900.00, E 1281.80	N 1000.00, E 1000.00
(c) N 1000.00, E 900.00	N 900.00, E 600.00
(d) N 339.97, E 408.89	N 200.01, E 1269.72
(e) N 121.34, E 187.56	N 790.07, E 715.35
(f) N 238.76, E 654.91	N 491.16, E 17.48

3. Use the unadjusted field data shown in the accompanying sketch.

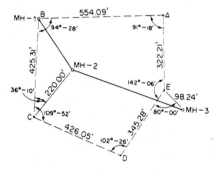

(a) Adjust the traverse by the compass rule. Station A has coordinates of N 1000.00, E 1000.00, and the true bearing of B–C is S 3°11′00″ E. If B–C is assigned a bearing of S 3°11′00″ E before adjustment, the bearing will be slightly different after adjustment and must be changed to S 3°11′00″ E. To find the true bearing of any line whose location is determined from the adjusted traverse, the line must be rotated the same as B–C.

(b) Determine coordinates of manholes.

(c) Determine bearing and distance from MH–1 to MH–2 and from MH–2 to MH–3. Rotate the bearings to orient them to true north.

4. Find the areas by double meridian distances within polygons whose corners have the following coordinates. Corners are listed in counterclockwise order.

(a) 1) 1176.07, 1000.00	**(b)** 1) 1000.00, 1000.00
2) 1177.39, 831.35	2) 1200.97, 1153.56
3) 1199.10, 645.50	3) 1189.77, 1070.87
4) 941.93, 655.96	4) 1220.42, 981.89
5) 959.53, 961.84	5) 971.86, 1097.44
(c) 1) 1000.00, 1000.00	**(d)** 1) 1000.00, 1000.00
2) 1206.55, 1036.44	2) 1176.29, 1031.08
3) 1204.21, 873.19	3) 1160.68, 884.93
4) 1224.85, 692.60	4) 1182.13, 719.44
5) 979.88, 704.75	5) 973.00, 737.10
(e) 1) 1000.00, 1000.00	**(f)** 1) 1000.00, 1000.00
2) 1196.69, 1034.63	2) 1113.99, 974.15
3) 1190.62, 876.98	3) 1044.27, 768.54
4) 1211.04, 701.43	4) 955.71, 891.01
5) 977.60, 715.31	5) 1092.71, 802.06

5. Given the following coordinates for point *A* and bearings and distances to point *B*, determine coordinates of point *B*.

	A	Bearing	Distance
(a)	900.00, 800.00	N 36°21′00″ E	261.73′
(b)	1000.00, 1000.00	N 14°18′20″ W	118.13′
(c)	3247.21, 2165.38	N 82°00′45″ W	196.35′
(d)	2173.48, 2110.90	S 46°10′00″ E	218.31′
(e)	1876.32, 2017.16	S 76°17′11″ W	422.67′
(f)	418.76, 452.37	S 18°49′42″ E	311.84′

7

STADIA SURVEYING AND MAPPING

INSTRUCTIONAL OBJECTIVES

1. *Given a transit already set up over a traverse station, one additional traverse station, and the assistance of a rod person, the student should be able to obtain proper data to locate an object in plan and elevation relative to the traverse stations.*

2. *Given stadia field data as they would be read in the field, the student should be able to set up field notes and to enter the data correctly.*

3. *Given stadia field data, the student should be able to reduce them to obtain horizontal distances and elevations.*

4. *Given stadia field data that have been reduced, the student should be able to plot a planimetric map or traverse.*

5. *Given field data from other types of map surveys, the student should be able to plot a map.*

6. *The student should be able to demonstrate how to obtain field data with only a tape.*

7. *Given a map with key elevations plotted on it, the student should be able to prepare contour lines at a required contour interval.*

The stadia method may be used for measuring horizontal distances and for determining elevations. It is not as accurate as taping distances or determining elevations with an engineer's level, but it is faster. The stadia method is sometimes used in traverse work and sometimes for leveling, but its chief use is to obtain field information for mapping.

7.1 STADIA PRINCIPLES

The distance between two straight lines diverging from a common point (vertex) increases in proportion to the distance from the common point. This principle is illustrated in Fig. 7.1, and it is demonstrated that the vertical distance between the two lines can be used to indicate the horizontal distance from the common point. Each vertical distance, if multiplied by a constant, equals the corresponding horizontal distance from the vertex. The constant is the ratio $\dfrac{H_1}{V_1}$.

In the transit telescope, two *stadia hairs* are aligned horizontally at equal distances, one above and one below the horizontal cross hair. The *stadia intercept* or distance between stadia hairs is 1/100 of the horizontal distance between vertex and stadia hairs. When the instrument person looks through the telescope, the stadia hairs are seen imposed on the image. The greater the distance to the object sighted, the farther apart the stadia hairs are on the image. If a level rod is vertical and the telescope is horizontal, the length of rod seen between stadia hairs is 1/100 of the horizontal distance to the rod from the vertex. Distance can thus be measured by multiplying the stadia intercept by 100. Figure 7.2 illustrates the relationship.

The simple diagram in Fig. 7.2 does not show the optical properties of the telescope. These were illustrated in Fig. 4.3. However, this simplification provides a means of visualizing the relationship between stadia intercept and horizontal distance. The actual relationship involves exactly the same principle. The vertex is located within one in. or two in. of the instru-

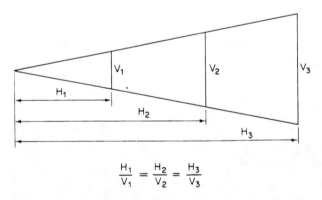

$$\frac{H_1}{V_1} = \frac{H_2}{V_2} = \frac{H_3}{V_3}$$

Any horizontal distance equals the corresponding vertical distance multiplied by the ratio $\dfrac{H_1}{V_1}$ $H = V \times \dfrac{H_1}{V_1}$

Figure 7.1 Stadia principle

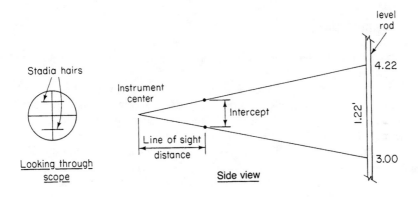

Intercept equals $\frac{1}{100}$ of line of sight distance within the transit and this ratio holds true for extensions beyond the transit. The rod is 122 ft from the instrument center.

$$1.22 \times \frac{100}{1} = 122$$

Figure 7.2   Simplified relationship between transit and level rod

ment center for internal-focusing transits and approximately one ft from the instrument center toward the object for external-focusing transits.

The discrepancy is ignored for internal-focusing instruments, and the vertex is assumed to be over the plumb bob. When using an external-focusing instrument, one ft should be added to the measured distance. External-focusing transits can be recognized by movement in and out of the objective side when the instrument is being focused.

Horizontal Sights

The stadia intercept read on a level rod with a horizontal line of sight is 1/100 of the horizontal distance. Thus, the distance from the instrument to the rod can be calculated mentally from the stadia intercept. The direction to the rod can be determined by horizontal angle from a backsight of known direction. The elevation of the bottom of the rod can be determined by differential leveling procedures using the horizontal cross hair, not the stadia hairs.

Reduced to mathematical formulas, horizontal distance to rod and elevation at bottom of rod are:

$$H = 100\ S$$

and

$$\text{Elev.} = \text{H.I.} - \text{F.S.}$$

Inclined Sights

The ratio illustrated in Fig. 7.1 applies when rod and line of sight are perpendicular to each other.

If the line of sight is inclined, the intercept on a vertical rod will be greater than 1/100 of the distance between vertex and rod. The intercept as read can be converted to the slope distance by reducing it to the value of a perpendicular intercept and multiplying by 100.

The intercept as read is reduced to the proper length by multiplying it by the cos of the vertical angle. See Fig. 7.3 for illustration. The use of the cos function does not provide a mathematically exact answer, but one that is accurate enough for stadia work.

The following formulas are illustrated in Fig. 7.3:

$$S = S' \cos \alpha$$

$$D = 100 \, S$$

$$\therefore D = 100 \, S' \cos \alpha$$

The slope distance can be converted to a horizontal distance from instrument center to rod and to a vertical distance from instrument center to the intersection of the line of sight with the rod. The horizontal and vertical components of the slope distance are illustrated in Fig. 7.4.

Two formulas illustrated in Fig. 7.4 are:

$$H = D \cos \alpha$$

and

$$V = D \sin \alpha$$

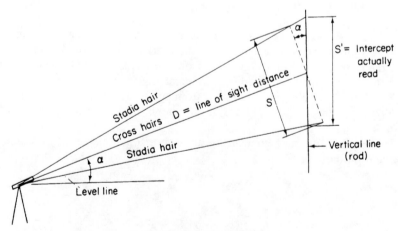

Figure 7.3 Inclined stadia sight

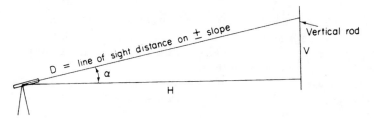

Figure 7.4 Horizontal and vertical components of inclined stadia distance

If the value 100 s' cos α is substituted for D as illustrated in Fig. 7.3, the two formulas become:

$$H = 100 \, S' \cos^2 \alpha$$

and

$$V = 100 \, S' \cos \alpha \sin \alpha$$

These formulas reduce field observations to horizontal and vertical components. Table V in the Appendix, prepared from these formulas, can be used.

7.2 STADIA FIELD METHODS

Stadia work is usually performed by a two or three person party. An instrument person and a rod person can perform the work with either one keeping notes. In a party of three, the third person keeps notes. One instrument person and one note keeper can keep two rod persons busy in some situations so that a party of four is sometimes economical. The party chief is usually a rod person or the note keeper with the additional duty of directing the rod persons.

When an object is to be located by stadia in relation to the transit, the horizontal and vertical location of the instrument center must be determined. The transit is often set up over a station of known horizontal and vertical location, such as a station hub for which elevation is determined by differential leveling. The H.I. (height of the instrument) is found by holding the level rod on the hub top and reading the vertical distance to the center of the transit horizontal axle. This distance is called $h.i.$ The elevation of the hub plus the h.i. equals the H.I. The instrument is thus located horizontally and vertically. Note that H.I. is an elevation and that h.i. is a vertical distance.

The location of an object is determined by horizontal angle from a backsight, by horizontal distance from transit to the object, and by difference in elevation above or below the instrument center. The B.S. can be a traverse station or other point or it can be true or magnetic north. If the B.S. is a visible point, direction is indicated by recording an angle from it. If it is the north direction, a bearing or azimuth is recorded. Stadia intercept and vertical angle are recorded, and horizontal and vertical distances from the instrument are determined from them.

The elevation of an object can be determined by stadia from a known elevation as shown in Fig. 7.5. The method is shown for a level line of sight and for inclined lines of sight.

An inclined line of sight is often necessary to achieve the full potential

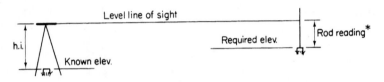

Required elev. = Known elev. + h.i. − rod

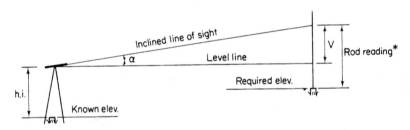

Required elev. = Known elev. + h.i. + V** − rod

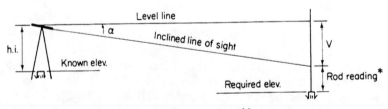

Required elev. = Known elev. + h.i. − V** − rod

* Rod is read with cross hairs, not stadia hairs

** $V = 100S' \cos \alpha \sin \alpha$ (Fig. 7 − 4 and discussion following it)

Figure 7.5   Elevation by stadia

of the stadia method.   When obtaining information for preparation of a map, the more shots a party can obtain from one instrument setup, the more efficient the operation is.   More shots are possible before moving the transit if the line of sight is raised for objects uphill and is lowered for objects downhill than if all shots are level.   However, each inclined sight takes longer than a level sight because a vertical angle must be read.

If the situation justifies taking only level sights, the instrument person checks the telescope level vial before each sight.   He or she reads the rod at the cross hairs, then raises or lowers the line of sight with the vertical tangent screw until the lower stadia hair marks the nearest full foot.   The stadia intercept can then be calculated mentally by subtracting the full foot value from the reading at the upper stadia hair.

The slight angle caused by this adjustment does not cause a significant error.   Speed is increased because of the simple mental arithmetic, and the chance of making a mistake is greatly decreased.

The rod reading at the cross hairs and the stadia intercept are recorded along with the horizontal angle, which is read after the level rod.   Figure 7.6 illustrates the procedure for reading the rod.

When sights may be either inclined or level, the instrument person adjusts the line of sight while taking each shot so that the cross hairs intersect the rod at the h.i.   This makes the line of sight parallel with a line from the station hub below the instrument to the bottom of the level rod.   This alignment simplifies calculations as demonstrated in Fig. 7.7.

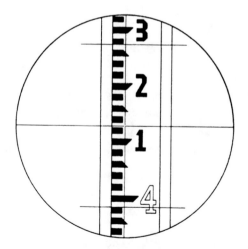

With vertical tangent screw raise telescope until
lower stadia hair is at 4.00. The upper stadia
hair will be at 4.29 and the stadia intercept
is still 0.29 but easier to determine.

Figure 7.6   Stadia sight on level rod

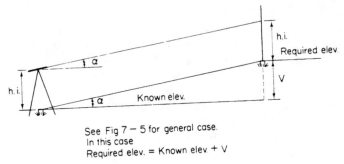

See Fig 7 — 5 for general case.
In this case
Required elev. = Known elev + V

Figure 7.7 Stadia field method for determining elevation

The instrument person raises or lowers the line of sight until the lower stadia hair marks the nearest full foot. He or she determines the stadia intercept mentally by subtracting this full foot value from the reading at the upper stadia hair. He or she then returns the cross hairs to the h.i. so that the vertical angle is accurate. The stadia intercept is recorded, and then horizontal and vertical angles are read and recorded. The rod person is waved to the next point as soon as rod readings are complete, and goes there while angles are read.

7.3 STADIA NOTEKEEPING

The notes must completely define the transit location and line of sight location both horizontally and vertically. The following information is required:

1. Transit location by station or other point.
2. Backsight direction, by station or other point, bearing, or azimuth.
3. Elevation of transit station, above appropriate datum.
4. Instrument height above station (h.i.) measured with a level rod.

The notes then locate each desired object relative to the transit and backsight. The following information is obtained in the field:

1. Stadia intercept.
2. Horizontal angle from B.S. to object.
3. Vertical angle.
   or
3. Rod reading, if all sights are level.

The following additional information is calculated in the field book:

1. Horizontal distance from transit.
2. Vertical distance above or below transit elevation.
3. Elevation of the object.

Examples of notekeeping are shown in Figs. 7.8, 7.9, and 7.10.   Figure 7.8 shows stadia notes for the connecting traverse of Fig. 6.2.   Inclined sights are used.   Stadia readings are taken from both ends of each course in order to check for a mistake.   The average of the two distances should be used.

The first line contains headings identifying three columns of field information obtained at each station and three columns of calculated information for each station.   The second line interrupts the columns and has information about the instrument location and B.S. and F.S.   New information similar to that in the second line is required at each station.   Each elevation except the first must be calculated from the previous elevation.

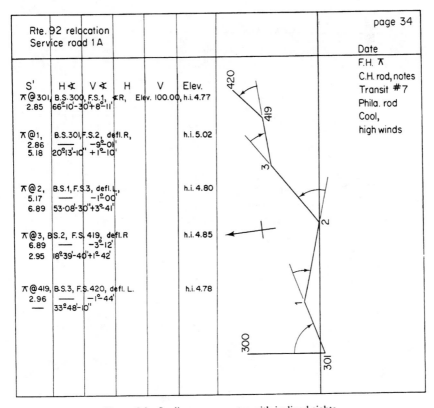

Figure 7.8 Stadia traverse notes with inclined sights

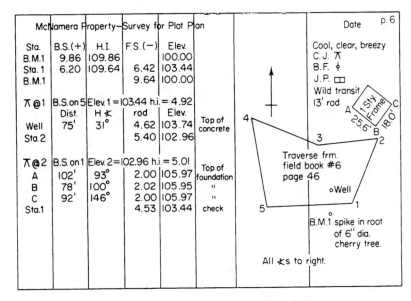

McNamera Property—Survey for Plot Plan   Date   p.6

Sta.	B.S.(+)	H.I.	F.S.(−)	Elev.	
B.M.1	9.86	109.86		100.00	
Sta. 1	6.20	109.64	6.42	103.44	
B.M.1			9.64	100.00	
⊼@1	B.S.on5	Elev.1 = 103.44 h.i. = 4.92			
	Dist.	H ✶	rod	Elev.	
Well	75'	31°	4.62	103.74	Top of concrete
Sta. 2			5.40	102.96	
⊼@2	B.S.on1	Elev.2 = 102.96 h.i. = 5.01			
A	102'	93°	2.00	105.97	Top of foundation
B	78'	100°	2.02	105.95	"
C	92'	146°	2.00	105.97	"
Sta.1			4.53	103.44	check

Cool, clear, breezy
C.J. ⊼
B.F. ◊
J.P. ▭
Wild transit
13' rod

Traverse frm. field book #6 page 46

○ Well

B.M.1 spike in root of 6" dia. cherry tree.

All ✶s to right.

Figure 7.9   Stadia mapping notes with level sights

Elevations can be determined for each station starting with the assumed elevation of 100.00 at station 301. Data for the last three columns, H, V, and elev., are not entered in these field notes because they are normally entered in the office after field work is finished. Although stadia work is not accurate enough to justify reading angles to the nearest ten seconds, it is done here to provide a check against a mistake.

Figure 7.9 shows notes for the location of two objects, house and well, from a loop traverse previously established. Because all sights are level, no vertical angles are recorded. Horizontal angles are read to the nearest degree. It is assumed that directions cannot be plotted more accurately on a map at these short distances. They can be plotted more accurately at longer distances.

The elevation of station 1 is established from a B.S. on B.M.1. Note that the transit is moved before returning to B.M.1. This completes a differential leveling circuit and safeguards against misreading the same number twice on the rod. The elevation of station 1 is used to determine the elevation of station 2 by stadia. A check is made on station 1 after work is complete.

Elevations are determined as follows:

sta. 1, top of stake elev.	103.44
h.i. @ 1	+4.92
H.I. @ 1	108.36
F.S. on 2	−5.40

Plot	plan for	Pallies Bros. Apt. bldg, Hurffville					p.32
S'	H ∢	V ∢	H	V	Elev.		Date
Π@1	B.S. on 2	elev =	117.48	h.i.=	5.23		C.B. inst
1.31	15½°	+8°–10'				Power pole N.E Elec.Co.	J. R. rod and notes
1.93	16°	+6°–03'				Close edge of pavement 24' concrete	Transit #3
1.82	21°	+10°–52'				" "	Warm, sunny.
1.68	23°	+9° – 41'				" "	
1.50	21½°	+7°–40'				Hydrant	
Π@2	B.S. on 1	elev =	120.33	h.i.=	5.19		
1.82	30°	–4°–10'				₵ creek 6' wide	
2.08	56°	–2°–16'				" 8' wide	
1.77	174½°	–7°–25'				Power pole N.E.Elec.Co.	

Notes
All ∢s to left.
All stadia shots read at h.i. on rod.
Traverse from p.11

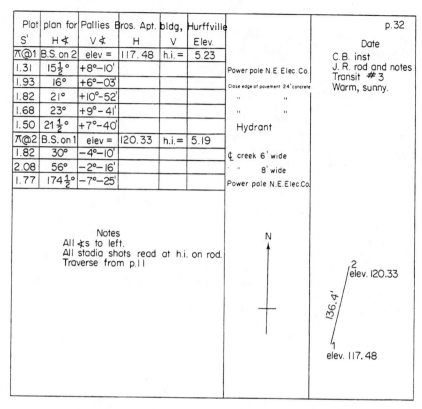

Figure 7.10   Stadia mapping notes with inclined sights

sta. 2, top of stake elev.	102.96
h.i. @ 2	+5.01
H.I. @ 2	107.97
F.S. on 1	–4.53
sta. 1, top of stake elev.	103.44

The usual method of locating a building by locating three corners and measuring the sides with a cloth or steel tape is shown with the instrument at sta. 2 and on the sketch.   Stadia intercepts are not recorded but are multiplied by 100 and recorded as distances.   Because this traverse is already complete, no traverse courses are measured by stadia.

Figure 7.10 shows notes for a stadia mapping project using, for control, two stakes with elevations previously determined.   Inclined sights are used. Horizontal angles are read to the nearest half degree because it is assumed that points can be plotted on a map to this accuracy at these longer distances.

Distance between stakes is needed because shots are taken from each stake, and points plotted from each stake must be in correct relationship.

7.4 STADIA TRAVERSE

If a traverse is to be established by stadia, the transit is set up over a station, and a horizontal angle is measured between the back station and the forward station. The angles may be read to the accuracy of the transit or to a reduced accuracy more suitable to the stadia accuracy. The distance to the forward station is obtained by reading the stadia intercept on a level rod held on the hub and reading the vertical angle. Stations are usually marked by hubs with no nails because stadia accuracy does not justify centering the instrument over a nail head.

The transit is moved to the next station, and the distance is measured to the first station by stadia. The distance for each course is measured once from each end to check for mistakes, and the two distances are averaged to improve accuracy. The angle to the next station and the distance to the next station are then obtained.

7.5 STADIA MAP SURVEY

To locate an object for mapping, it can be located in relation to a control traverse. The traverse and sideshots for map information may be run together. Horizontal angles are usually read only to the nearest degree or half degree for sideshots. Maps of several acres or less are made from stadia field data. However, field data for most larger mapping projects are obtained by aerial photography.

Two stakes driven into the ground at random provide sufficient framework for a stadia map that need not be related to any other area. In fact, one stake under the instrument is sufficient if direction to the first object located is considered a backsight for all other shots. North orientation requires a compass or true bearing of the first backsight.

7.6 OTHER MAP SURVEYS

Field information for mapping can be obtained by any of the methods of Fig. 2.1. Distances can be measured by any of the methods discussed in Chapter 3. These include pacing, taping, electronic distance measuring, subtense bar, stadia, and measuring wheel. Directions can be measured with transit, theodolite, or right-angle prism. Elevations can be determined with stadia, level and rod, or electronic distance measuring. Total station equipment can be used to determine direction, distance, and elevation all in one operation.

One way to survey the area in front of a building where elevations are not needed is to tape the distance between the two front corners and then locate each object by taped distances to it from each of the corners.   Another way is to use the front of the building as a base line and locate each object by distance along the front wall from one corner and the distance outward perpendicular to the wall.   If the building is already plotted on a map and the purpose of the survey is to add new development to the map, orientation with a north line is not needed.   New development is automatically in its correct relationship to the building.

A survey of the area at the intersection of two streets could be controlled by setting up two base lines, one on the center line of each street pavement and by measuring base line distances from the intersection of the two center lines and offset distances to right and left.   The survey could instead be controlled by a single base line on one of the streets either at the center line of pavement or at the face of one of the curbs.   These controls are adaptations of the coordinate system and of stationing and offsets discussed in Chapter 1.   A true or magnetic bearing of one of the streets might be needed if not available on the city map.   If elevations are needed, a level run with rod shots is necessary.

There are no widely recognized standards for arranging field notes. Sketches of the control and tabulated angles and distances to the objects are needed.   A few objects may be included in the sketch as a check on the final map.   However, it is not necessary to show all objects because the tabulated data indicate where they belong on the map.   See the questions at the end of this chapter for examples of field notes.

To survey a playground in order to regrade it for better drainage, a grid could be set up over the entire area and elevations determined with level and level rod.   See Fig. 7.18.

Any one of these surveys could be completed by stadia or total station with locations and elevations determined in one operation.   It might be possible to provide north orientation by setting up the instrument on the extension of the building front or side or on curb line or pavement center line if their bearings are given.

A map can be plotted from field information obtained by any of the methods of Fig. 2.1.   Plotting involves laying off the field measurements with a scale or compass for distances and a protractor or azimuth circle for direction.

7.7 MAPPING

A *map* is a drawing of part of the earth's surface.   Natural and man-made features may be shown.   Because the map must be much smaller than the actual surface it represents, it cannot show all the features that can be seen at the site, and those features that are shown must be shown by use of *symbols*.

Commonly used symbols are shown in Fig. 7.11. However, there is some variation in symbol usage.

The features to be shown will depend on the purpose of the map. Unnecessary features will clutter the map and make it difficult to see what should be seen. For example, a map prepared as a guide for new arrivals at a college campus does not require information on underground utilities. A property map must show property boundaries, but the slope of the ground is not necessary. A *plot plan* to be used to design a building must show property boundaries, ground slopes, and underground utilities so that the building can be designed intelligently.

Information to be shown on the map must be decided before the field party begins work. This saves time that might be spent obtaining unnecessary information and assures that necessary information is obtained. Stadia notes for mapping using a previously established traverse are shown in Fig. 7.9.

The scale of the map is selected to show all necessary information without crowding. *Scale* means ratio between the length of a horizontal line on the map and the length of the same line on the ground. Scale is indicated by a *representative fraction*, such as $\frac{1}{2400}$, or an *equivalent*, such as 1 in. =

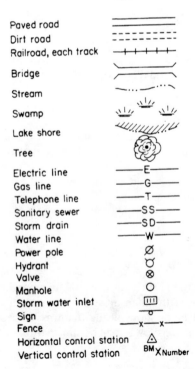

Paved road	
Dirt road	
Railroad, each track	
Bridge	
Stream	
Swamp	
Lake shore	
Tree	
Electric line	E
Gas line	G
Telephone line	T
Sanitary sewer	SS
Storm drain	SD
Water line	W
Power pole	
Hydrant	
Valve	
Manhole	
Storm water inlet	
Sign	
Fence	x—x
Horizontal control station	
Vertical control station	BM X Number

Figure 7.11 Map symbols

200 ft. This representative fraction means that any one unit of linear measurement on the map represents 2400 of the same units on the ground. In
this case, 1 in. equals 2400 in. or 200 ft. The representative fraction $\frac{1}{2400}$
and the equivalent 1 in. = 200 ft indicate the same scale. Commonly used
scales are 1 in. = 20, 40, 50, or 100 ft.

The map is begun by plotting the control (traverse or other points) at
the map scale. A protractor and engineer's scale may be used to reproduce
the field angles and distances and to plot stations by duplicating field procedures in miniature as shown in Fig. 6.5. When each station is plotted from
the previous station, accidental plotting errors are accumulated. A traverse
plot of many courses becomes too inaccurate when plotted this way and must
be plotted by coordinates.

When plotting by coordinates, one plots each point from two base lines
as shown in Fig. 7.12. The unavoidable plotting error in each line is not
carried to any other line.

Next, the locations from the field notes are plotted on the map with
protractor and straightedge. Distances are laid off at the selected scale.
There is no further accumulation of errors because each location is plotted
in one operation. Except for very simple maps, the plotting is done on a
worksheet, and the finished map is traced from the worksheet. If the traverse
is shown at all on the finished map, it is shown lightly because it is not of
primary importance. It is a tool used in preparing the map, and it may also
be used later to control construction.

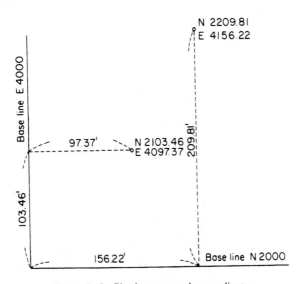

Figure 7.12 Plotting traverse by coordinates

A map that does not indicate differences in elevation of the ground surface is called a *planimetric map*. This type is sufficient for many purposes, but in some cases, the shape of the ground surface, or *topography*, must be shown. A map showing topography is called a *topographic map*.

Topography is indicated by contour lines. A *contour line* has a designated elevation and connects all points on the surface that are at that elevation. The elevation is always in whole feet. Contour lines are spaced at a uniform elevation difference called the *contour interval*. Commonly used contour intervals are 1, 2, 5, and 10 ft. The elevation of each contour line is divisible by the contour interval. Therefore, with a 2-ft contour interval, contour line elevations are even numbers and, with a 10-ft contour interval, contour line elevations are multiples of 10. Usually, every fifth or tenth line is a heavy line and is labeled with its elevation. The elevation is written uphill of the contour line, or the line is interrupted for it. A topographic map or *contour map* is shown in Fig. 7.13 with a profile to help in visualizing the land shape.

Topography is measured in the field by taking *ground shots* on the ground surface. The rod is held on the ground and is read to the nearest

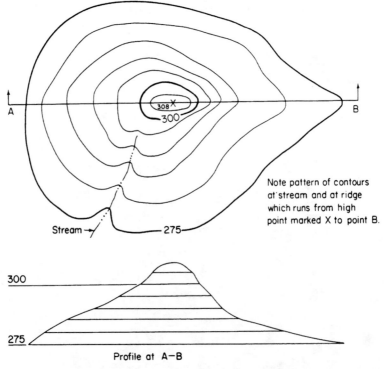

Figure 7.13 Contour map of hill with 5-ft contour interval

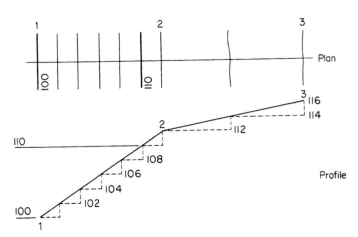

Equal vertical distances (2-ft. contour interval) on a uniform slope result
in equal horizontal spacing on a contour map.
Rod shots are needed at 1, 2, and 3 to define the slope.

Figure 7.14   Plan and profile showing contour line spacing for a nonuniform slope

0.1 ft, and the ground elevation is determined to the nearest 0.1 ft.   There
are two methods for selecting points in the field for ground shots.

One method consists of selecting key points so that the ground slopes
uniformly from each point to all adjacent points.   Then, the horizontal map
distance between points must be divided into equal parts to represent equal
elevation differences.   See Fig. 7.14 for illustration.   The key points are high
points, low points, and all points of significant slope change in any direction.
Ridge lines and valleys must be defined by ground shots.   A method of
plotting contour lines is shown in Fig. 7.15.   A plot is shown in Fig. 7.16
with ground shot points and the resulting contour lines.   In some cases,
approximate plotting by eye is accurate enough.

Experience and skill are required to select the proper points.   It is
difficult to recognize them because of the three-dimensional lay of the land,
and it is difficult to know which changes of slope are significant.   This depends
on the contour interval to be plotted and the ruggedness of the ground.

A small change in slope that would be important for mapping at a 1-
or 2-ft contour interval might not affect contour lines plotted at a 10-ft interval.
A mound or depression several feet different in elevation from the surround-
ing ground would be significant at a 1-ft contour interval and insignificant at
a 10-ft interval.

In the second method, ground shots are taken at regular intervals in a
grid pattern, and contour lines are plotted from the results.   The method is
illustrated in Fig. 7.17.   Preliminary work is time-consuming because the grid
must be laid out in the field and markers placed at the intersections.   A

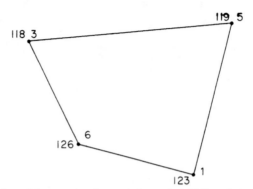

1. Plot points of known elevation and draw straight lines between them.

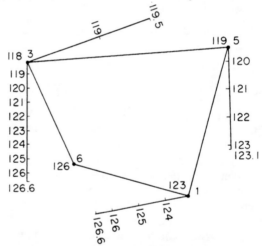

2. Construct auxiliary lines at any convenient angle and proportion them to any convenient scale to find whole foot locations. Because of the straight grades from point to point, spacing between contour lines is uniform, but the space from a plotted point to the nearest contour line is a fraction of a full space according to the elevation of the point compared to the elevation of the contour line. The purpose of the auxiliary lines is to locate points where contour lines cross the original lines.

Figure 7.15   Plotting contour lines

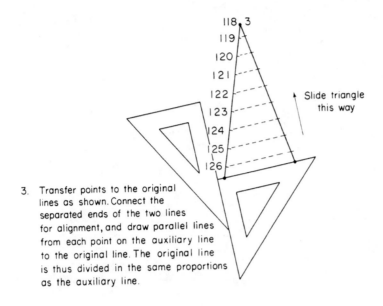

Slide triangle
this way

3. Transfer points to the original
   lines as shown. Connect the
   separated ends of the two lines
   for alignment, and draw parallel lines
   from each point on the auxiliary line
   to the original line. The original line
   is thus divided in the same proportions
   as the auxiliary line.

120

125

4. Contour lines pass through
   the points plotted on the
   original lines (not the auxiliary
   lines) and are drawn freehand
   from point to point. Faster plotting
   may be done with variations of
   this method. They are based on the
   same principal that parallel lines intercept
   proportional parts when intersected by any straight
   line.

Figure 7.15 (cont.)   Plotting contour lines

1. Key points are plotted. Decimal points indicate locations.
2. Straight lines are drawn between key points.
3. Lines are divided in correct proportion by eye.
4. Contour curves are plotted from point to point.

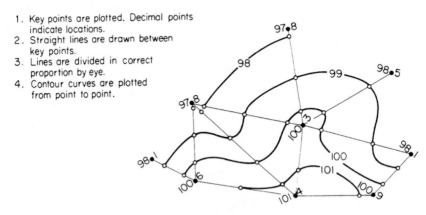

Figure 7.16   Contour lines drawn through points plotted between key points

Contour lines are plotted the same way as in Fig 7-16.

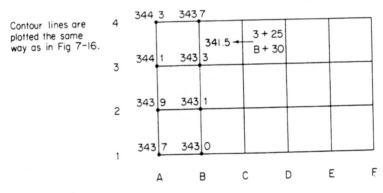

Figure 7.17   Grid layout with spot elevations partially plotted

method of laying out the grid is described in Chapter 8.   Measurements for the layout may be made with a cloth tape.   Shots are taken at each grid point, plus any other high or low points and points of significant slope change.

Generally, more shots are read this way because some of the grid locations will not be key points.   On surfaces with very slight grades and no definite breaks in slope, the grid system is the most practical method, even for experienced personnel, because of the difficulty of recognizing key points. The grid size must be selected to obtain enough shots but not an excessive number.   Because it is not necessary to turn any angles, the work is often done with an engineer's level.

The rod person proceeds from point to point in a predetermined order for ease in notekeeping.   When an extra rod shot is required, distances to it are laid off in both grid directions by laying the rod on the ground and calling the distances to the note keeper. Any object such as a tree or building corner can also be located this way. Notes for the project in Fig. 7.17 are shown in Fig. 7.18. When possible, actual lines at the site should be used as part of the grid as they are in Fig. 7.18 (property line and curb). After elevations are plotted and labeled, contour lines are plotted in the usual way.

Some rules for plotting contour lines follow:

1. Each contour line forms a loop, closing on itself within the map or outside the map.

2. No single contour line can lie between two lower contour lines or between two higher ones. The highest contour line on a ridge has a lower contour line adjacent downhill and a contour line of equal elevation adjacent to it on the other side of the ridge. The lowest contour line in a valley has a higher contour line adjacent uphill and a contour line of equal elevation adjacent to it on the other side of the valley.

3. Contour lines cannot cross. Since they represent different elevations, two cannot occupy the same space even at a single point. (The case of a vertical cliff is an exception.)

Some rules for interpreting contour maps follow:

1. Horizontal distance between contour lines is inversely proportional to

Pattison Playground Drainage Town of Parkland						Page 34	
Sta.	B.S.(+)	H.I.	F.S.(−)	Rod	Elev.		Date B. Smith ⟲ C. Jones ⟡
B.M.	3.18	350.39			347.21		A. Bakalar N.B.
1 A				6.7	343.7		Rod #2,
2 A				6.5	343.9		Level # 06
3 A				6.3	344.1		Clear, calm.
4 A				6.1	344.3		
4 B				6.7	343.7		
3+25 8+30				8.9	341.5		
3 B				7.1	343.3		
2 B				7.3	343.1		
1 B				7.4	343.0		50'
B.M.			3.17		347.22		Grid spaces

A   B   C face of curb
21st. St.
B.M.
Across 21st. St.
opposite W. prop. line of playground
concrete nail in curb

W. property line

Figure 7.18 Grid topographic mapping notes

Beech St. topo survey

Sta.	B.S.	H.I.	F.S.	Rod	Elev.	
BM	6.28	125.64			119.36	0+00 ℄ Hanson St.
0+18 18'R				4.8	120.8	
18'L				4.6	121.0	
0+50 18'R				5.5	120.1	
18'L				5.2	120.4	
30'L				2.1	123.5	
1+00 18'R				4.8	120.8	
18'L				4.1	121.5	
1+37 29'R				2.9	122.7	Spring
1+50 18'R				4.4	121.2	
18'L				4.3	121.3	
1+62 23'L						36" dia. willow
2+00 18'R				3.8	121.8	
18'L				3.7	121.9	
2+50 18'R				3.0	122.6	
18'L				2.5	123.1	
3+00 18'R				2.7	122.9	
18'L				2.0	123.6	
3+09 25.5'L						Prop. cor. marker
3+50 18'R				3.4	122.2	
18'L				3.1	122.5	
3+68 18'R				3.9	121.7	
18'L				3.6	122.0	
3+86.29				3.46	122.18	℄ Green St.
BM			6.28		119.36	

Page
Date
F. Byham π
N. Byham ♦
25' rod
Dietzgen level
cool, light drizzle

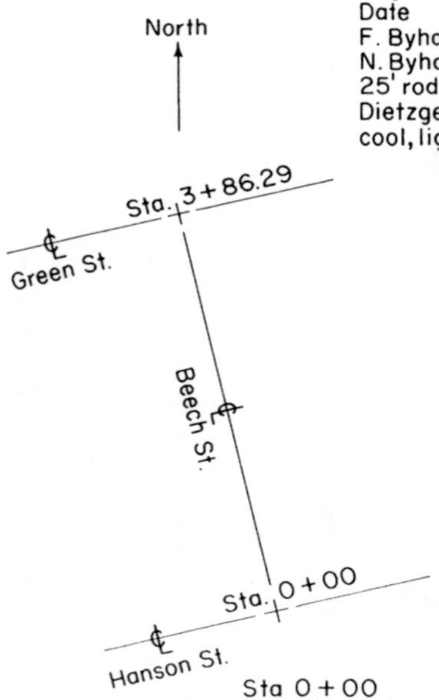

North ←

Sta. 3+86.29
Green St.
℄ Beech St.
Sta. 0+00
Hanson St.
Sta 0+00 Intersection of ℄'s used as B.M.

Figure 7.19 Station and offset topographic mapping notes

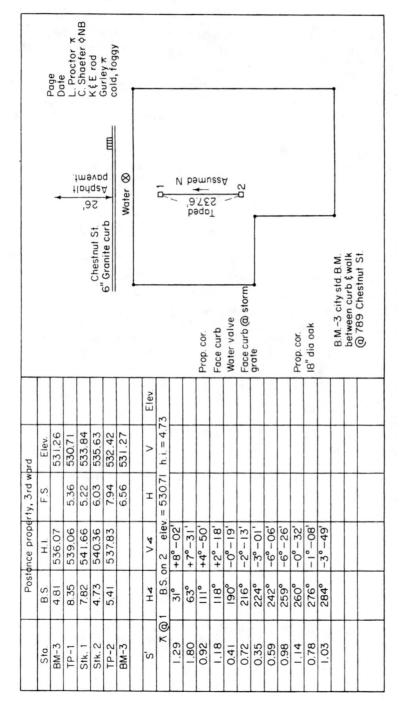

Sta	B.S.	H.I.	F.S	Elev.
BM-3	4.81	536.07		531.26
TP-1	8.35	539.06	5.36	530.71
Stk.1	7.82	541.66	5.22	533.84
Stk.2	4.73	540.36	6.03	535.63
TP-2	5.41	537.83	7.94	532.42
BM-3			6.56	531.27

Postance property, 3rd wprd

S'	H∡	V∡	H	V	Elev.
∡@1	B.S. on 2	elev. = 53071	h.i. = 4.73		
1.29	31°	+8°-02'			
1.80	63°	+7°-31'			
0.92	111°	+4°-50'			
1.18	118°	+2°-18'			
0.41	190°	-0°-19'			
0.72	216°	-2°-13'			
0.35	224°	-3°-01'			
0.59	242°	-6°-06'			
0.98	259°	-6°-26'			
1.14	260°	-0°-32'			
0.78	276°	-1°-08'			
1.03	284°	-3°-49'			

Prop. cor.
Face curb
Water valve
Face curb @ storm grate

Prop. cor.
18" dia oak

B.M.-3 city std. B.M. between curb & walk @ 789 Chestnut St.

Chestnut St.
6" Granite curb
Asphalt pavemt.
26'
Water ⊗
Assumed N
Taped 237.6'
1
2

Page
Date
L. Proctor π
C. Shaefer ♦NB
K & E rod
Gurley π
cold, foggy

Figure 7.20 Stadia topographic mapping notes with simplified control

steepness of slope.   Closely spaced contour lines represent steep ground, and widely spaced contour lines represent ground more nearly level.

2. Uniform spacing indicates uniform slope.
3. Contour lines are perpendicular to the steepest slope. Therefore, water flow is perpendicular to contour lines.
4. Straight contour lines parallel with each other represent constructed features.
5. Contour lines crossing a stream point upstream (see Fig. 7.13).
6. Contour lines crossing a ridge point downhill (see Fig. 7.13).

A long, narrow area may be mapped by station and offset, which is a variation of the grid method.   The field locations to map an unpaved street or alley in order to design pavement or other improvements could be determined this way.   Notes are shown in Fig. 7.19.

Many small projects can be mapped using one or two stakes driven into the ground at convenient locations for instrument setups and locating all objects from the one stake or from one of the two stakes.

If the instrument is to be set up at each stake, the two stakes must be located relative to each other.   Their distance must be determined.   Their direction may be a bearing or azimuth from true or magnetic north, or an assumed direction.   The elevation of stake tops may be determined with a level circuit from an established B.M. or may be assumed.   If two stakes are used, one elevation is assumed and the other determined from it.   If all shots are taken from one stake, the distance between the stakes and the elevation of the second stake are not needed.   The B.S. direction for turning angles with only one stake may be true north, magnetic north, or any assumed compass direction.

Figure 7.20 shows notes for a topographic mapping project.   The direction from 2 to 1 is assumed.   The stake-top elevations are determined from an existing B.M.   Shots with no description are ground shots for contour plotting.   All shots are taken from stake 1.

To plot the map, the stake or stakes are first plotted to scale with orientation that will cause the map to be oriented as desired.

PROBLEMS

1. Record the following field notes, reduce them, and plot maps.
    (a) A connecting traverse of three stations is run starting with the instrument set up at station 14 of a completed traverse and with a B.S. on station 13.   A level B.S. of 4.72 is shot on B.M.1, which has an elevation of 1036.47.   All horizontal angles are turned to the right.   This traverse connects station 14 with station 22 of another completed traverse.   Necessary data follow:

Sta. 14 H $\sphericalangle$ = 127° $-37'$, V $\sphericalangle$ =   3° $-04'$, S′ = 1.32, h.i. = 5.28

Sta. 101 H $\sphericalangle$ = 175° $-18'$, V $\sphericalangle$ =   4° $-29'$, S′ = 2.09, h.i. = 4.96

Sta. 102 H $\sphericalangle$ = 164° $-22'$, V $\sphericalangle$ = $-2°$ $-08'$, S′ = 2.55, h.i. = 4.59

Sta. 103 H $\sphericalangle$ = 152° $-54'$, V $\sphericalangle$ = $-5°$ $-47'$, S′ = 1.49, h.i. = 5.21

Sta. 22 H $\sphericalangle$ = 85° $-17'$, V $\sphericalangle$ = $-12°$ $-18'$, S′ = 2.38, h.i. = 5.24

(b) Sideshots of various objects are taken from point 1 with a B.S. on point 2. H.I. is obtained by taking a level B.S. of 7.62 on a B.M. with elevation 2376.44. The h.i. is 4.77. All angles are to the right. Necessary data follow:

Fence corner   H $\sphericalangle$ = 137°, V $\sphericalangle$ =   8° $-42'$, S′ = 2.37

Edge of pavement H $\sphericalangle$ = 18°, V $\sphericalangle$ = $-17°$ $-13'$, S′ = 1.90

Edge of pavement H $\sphericalangle$ = 115°, V $\sphericalangle$ =   0° $-48'$, S′ = 2.70

North end culvert H $\sphericalangle$ = 297°, V $\sphericalangle$ =   5° $-31'$, S′ = 0.21

South end culvert H $\sphericalangle$ = 331°, V $\sphericalangle$ = $-0°$ $-18'$, S′ = 1.05

(c) A connecting traverse of two stations is run, starting with the instrument set up at station 3 of a completed traverse and with a B.S. on station 2. A level B.S. of 7.96 is shot on a B.M. of elevation 229.26. This traverse connects station 3 with station 11 of another completed traverse, and sideshots are taken for mapping. All angles are to the right. Necessary data follow:

To sta. A   H $\sphericalangle$ = 92° $-16'$, V $\sphericalangle$ = 5° $-18'$,   S′ = 2.26

To $\mathcal{C}_L$ stream H $\sphericalangle$ = 18½°,   V $\sphericalangle$ = $-2°$ $-10'$, S′ = 3.11

To $\mathcal{C}_L$ stream H $\sphericalangle$ = 38½°,   V $\sphericalangle$ = $-5°$ $-06'$, S′ = 0.82

sta. A, h.i. = 5.22

To sta. B   H $\sphericalangle$ = 181° $-06'$, V $\sphericalangle$ = 2° $-59'$,   S′ = 2.56

To $\mathcal{C}_L$ stream H $\sphericalangle$ = 91°,   V $\sphericalangle$ = $-8°$ $-37'$, S′ = 1.46

sta. B, h.i. = 5.49

To sta. 11   H $\sphericalangle$ = 217° $-14'$, V $\sphericalangle$ = 3° $-57'$,   S′ = 3.03

To $\mathcal{C}_L$ stream H $\sphericalangle$ = 134°,   V $\sphericalangle$ = $-10°$ $-08'$, S′ = 1.21

sta. 11, h.i. = 5.38

To sta. 10 H $\sphericalangle$ = 78° $-43'$, V $\sphericalangle$ = 0° = 00′, S′ = 2.07

(d) Sideshots of various objects are taken from points 1 and 2. Point 1 has an elevation of 3408.76. Point 2 is 157 ft ± directly north of point 1. All angles left.

Inst @1, B.S. on 2, h.i. = 4.06

H ∢	V ∢	S′	
0°	−8° −11′	1.59′	point 2
15°	−7° −22′	1.62′	trail
92°	−4° −31′	1.53′	trail
108°	−2° −08′	1.23′	32″ diameter pine
168°	−2° −35′	2.92′	trail

Inst @2, B.S. on 1, h.i. = 3.82

199	+1° −41′	0.72	trail
215	+2° −48′	1.28	20″ diameter pine
248	+4° −52′	2.09	trail

(e) Sideshots of various objects are taken with level stadia shots from points A and B with elevations of 2063.41 and 2072.65 respectively. Point B is 203 ft N25°E of point A.

⊼ @A, B.S. on B, h.i. = 4.65 ∢s to right

H ∢	S	rod	
10°	2.80′	3.76	stonewall
47°	1.46′	2.14	stonewall
98°	0.25′	2.09	stonewall
286°	1.79′	3.92	property corner

⊼ @B, B.S. on A, h.i. = 4.52 ∢s to left

116°	1.02′	10.63	monument
205°	0.41′	9.18	property corner

2. Plot contour lines on the following maps:

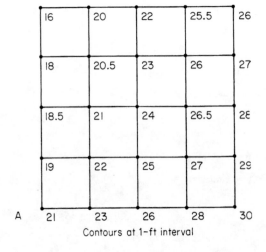

Contours at 1-ft interval

32.0	34.2	33.4	32.3	31.5
32.3	35.4	35.2	31.1	29.2
33.1	36.5	37.3	29.1	28.6
	38.9			
32.5	35.2	36.8	33.0	31.2
32.4	33.4	35.2	33.2	32.5

B

Contours at 2-ft interval

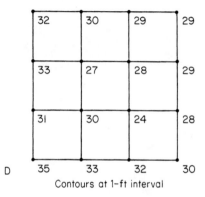

32	30	29	29
33	27	28	29
31	30	24	28
35	33	32	30

D

Contours at 1-ft interval

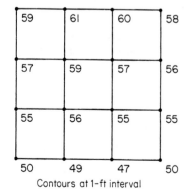

59	61	60	58
57	59	57	56
55	56	55	55
50	49	47	50

C

Contours at 1-ft interval

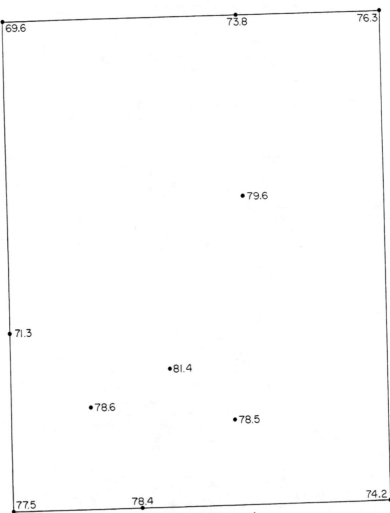

Contours at 2-ft interval

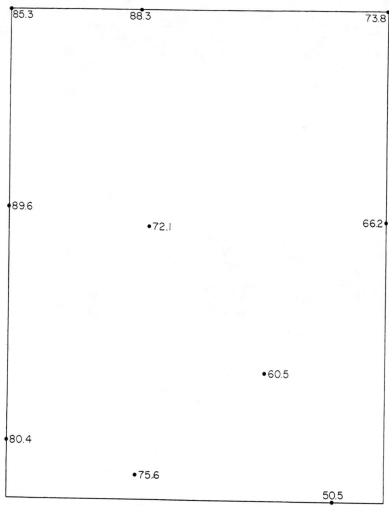

Contours at 5-ft interval

3. (a) Plot a map from the following data to a scale of 1 in. = 20 ft. Grid spaces
are 40 ft and are lettered A to C west to east and numbered 1 to 5 south to
north.

coordinates

1 + 11, A	center line stream
2, A + 16	center line stream
3, A + 29	center line stream
4, A + 33	center line stream
4 + 17, B	center line stream
5, B + 19	center line stream

| 1 + 06, B + 10 | 8″ dia apple |
| 3 + 22, B + 04 | 6″ dia plum |

(b) Plot a map from the following data to a scale of 1 in. = 40 ft. Grid spaces are 40 ft lettered A to E south to north and numbered 1 to 5 west to east.

coordinates		coordinates	
5, A + 12	fence	5, C + 17	edge of lake
4, A + 19	fence	4, C + 28	edge of lake
3, A + 26	fence	3 + 15, D	edge of lake
2 + 20, A + 30	fence	3 + 02, E	edge of lake
1 + 31, B	fence		
1, B + 11	fence		

4. The front of a building is 160 ft long and is in a north-south direction. The area to the east is surveyed by measuring distances from both corners. Plot a map to a scale of 1 in. = 50 ft from the following data:

object	N corner	S corner
near edge walk 6′ wide	45′	195′
near edge walk 6′ wide	249′	87′
18″ dia. oak	89′	105′
fire hydrant	29′	166′
storm water grate	48′	149′

5. The edge of a parking lot 200 ft long runs east-west. The area to the south is surveyed by measuring distances from both corners. Plot a map to a scale of 1 in. = 40 ft from the following data:

E corner	W corner	object
25′	213′	stream center line
42′	212′	stream center line
87′	193′	stream center line
190′	101′	stream center line
140′	150′	floodlight
76′	229′	power pole
198′	44′	power pole

6. The intersection of Baxter Ave. and Lincoln St. is surveyed using the center line of Baxter Ave. running N and S as a base line with stationing starting at the south end. Plot a map to a scale of 1 in. = 20 ft from the following data:

Sta.	offset	
0 + 00	15′ R & L	face of curb start of curve
0 + 42	15′ R & L	face of curb start of curve
0 + 67	40′ R & L	face of curb end of curve
0 + 91	40′ R & L	face of curb end of curve
1 + 16	15′ R & L	face of curb start of curve
2 + 00	15′ R & L	face of curb start of curve
1 + 95	20′ R	hydrant
0 + 97	46′ R	stop sign
0 + 96	36′ L	power pole
0 + 62	45′ L	stop sign

7. The intersection of Morgan St. and Chestnut St. is surveyed using the intersection

of center lines as station 0 + 00.   North and east are plus directions. Morgan St. runs north-south.   Plot a map to a scale of 1 in. = 20 ft from the following data:

Morgan

0 + 28	14' R & L	end of curved curb
0 + 30	18' R	power pole
0 − 28	14' R & L	end of curved curb
0 − 34	17' L	light pole
0 − 26	18' L	corner 4' high hedge
0 − 38	18' L	end 4' high hedge

Chestnut

0 + 29	13' R & L	end of curved curb
0 − 29	13' R & L	end of curved curb
0 − 39	15' R	end 4' high hedge

8. Field data are obtained with transit and tape from one instrument setup with a compass bearing for the first shot.   Plot a map to a scale of 1″ = 20′ and plot the north arrow.

∢ L	*distance*	
0°	38.8'	flag pole N 27° W
37°	19.3'	chain-link fence
92°	28.5'	corner parking lot
92°	70.5'	edge parking lot
137°	40.2'	edge parking lot
159°	20.6'	chain-link fence

9. Two stakes are set 81.0 ft apart on a NE-SW line.   Field information is obtained with transit and tape.   Plot a map to a scale of 1 in. = 40 ft from the data.   Include a north arrow.

Inst. @NE B.S. on SW ∢s R

∢	*dist.*	
31°	128'	stonewall
46°	92'	stonewall
89°	65'	stonewall
109°	48'	end of hedge
250°	49'	end of hedge

Inst. @SW B.S. on NE ∢s L

29°	131'	stonewall
48°	95'	stonewall
133°	93'	stonewall
149°	82'	Hor. control station

8

CONSTRUCTION SURVEYS—GENERAL

INSTRUCTIONAL OBJECTIVES

1. *Given outside dimensions of a building and its distance from a parallel line, desired offset distance, and a point for the transit setup, the student should be able to prepare a sketch showing all dimensions needed to stake out the building by the base line and offset method.*

2. *Given the same data, the student should be able to calculate angles and distances to stake out the building by the angle and distance method.*

3. *Given a transit setup over a point, backsight, and distance to set a construction stake, tape, hammer, stake, and nail, the student should be able to act as instrument person, rear tape person, or head tape person in setting a point for construction control.*

4. *Given a set of construction stakes in place, a bench mark, a finished grade for construction, an engineer's level, and a level rod, the student should be able to act as instrument person, rod person, or note keeper in determining the elevation of stake tops and should be able to compute cut or fill for each stake.*

5. *Given elevation of construction stake, finished grade, and desired grade rod length, the student should be able to determine the distance above or below the construction stake to build a batter board.*

6. *Given original elevations and final elevations on a grid pattern plus other necessary key points, the student should be able to compute earth volume of excavation or fill.*

Construction drawings show size and location of improvements to be built. The improvements, ranging from large bridges and buildings to fences and traffic signs, are positioned on a *plot plan* or *site plan* by directions and distances from existing objects. It is the surveyor's job to use surveying equipment and methods to provide reference marks close enough to the proposed construction so that carpenters, masons, and other trades people can build in the right location, using their own equipment and methods. The surveyor transfers ideas of architects or engineers, called *designers* in this book, from their drawings to the land in a form useful to the builder.

8.1 INTRODUCTION

The surveyor is responsible for supplying reference marks so that each individual improvement is started at the correct horizontal and vertical location on the land. Measuring from the reference marks to start construction is the responsibility of the builder, and, except in complex structures, internal measurements within each improvement are the builder's responsibility also. Much of the surveying control is through stakes hammered into the ground, and construction surveying is often called *construction stakeout*.

The one who designs a facility prepares a site plan on a copy of the surveyor's map. The purpose is to show relationships between the land and all the improvements that are to be constructed. Locations of proposed buildings, drives, parking lots, pipelines, and any other improvements are shown. Arrangements within buildings are shown on other drawings.

This overall plan provides much of the information the surveyor needs for construction stakeout. The improvements are tied down by directions and distances. The more important buildings are positioned from points on the site such as property corners or traverse stations. Less important improvements are positioned from the more important ones. The dimensions of buildings are not shown on the site plan, but dimensions are provided for many of the other improvements.

The surveyor finds additional information on the foundation plan, on elevation views that show final elevations called *final grades* or *finished grades*, and on detail sheets. Some knowledge of construction procedures is necessary in order to provide stakes in the best positions to control the work and to provide them at the right time. Construction stakes must be provided for each phase as construction progresses from start to finish, but they cannot be provided too early or other construction work will displace them.

8.2 CONSTRUCTION STAKEOUT

An example of simple construction stakeout is the placing of a stake to indicate the location for a telephone pole. Poles must be installed at definite locations to support the lines properly, but they need not be located with great accuracy.

A stake is driven into the ground at the desired center line location for the pole, and a crew later removes the stake, drills a hole centered on the stake hole, and installs the pole.

Residential construction generally does not require highly accurate control. It is common for local governments to require that houses be set back certain distances from property lines. In many cases, these *building lines* are defined by surveyor's stakes, and the builder decides where to place the house within the lines. An example is shown in Fig. 8.1.

Most work must be controlled more closely than this. Stakes must be located some distance away from the object to be built so that they will not be disturbed by construction operations and will be in their original positions for as long as needed. Usually, earth must be excavated or built up because bottom elevations of proposed construction do not coincide with the ground surface. Stakes may be set to guide the earthwork, and other stakes may be set for construction after earthmoving is completed. As an alternative, stakes may be set with an offset great enough to be clear of the earthwork. Offsets vary from 1 ft to 10 ft and are occasionally longer.

The stake indicates direction and distance horizontally and distance vertically from a point on the stake to a reference point on the object to be built. The point on the stake may be a nail or tack driven flush with

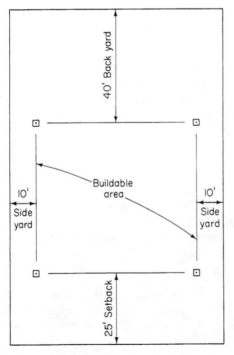

Figure 8.1 Surveyor's stakes to define building lines

the top.   Horizontal and vertical distances are laid out by the builder with a tape or rule.   Both distances are measured from the stake top unless the side of the stake is marked with a line from which the vertical distance is to be measured.   The horizontal distance is still measured from the nail in the stake top.   If there is no nail, it is measured from the mark on the side of the stake.

The equipment used to transfer line and grade from stakes to the improvement being built includes 6-ft folding rules, steel or reinforced cloth tapes, several types of levels, plumb bobs, and string lines.   The rules and tapes are usually calibrated in ft and in. to a sixteenth of an in.

A builder's level, used with a level rod or sometimes with a 6-ft folding rule as a rod, is a simplified version of the engineer's level and is used in the same way.   It has a smaller field of vision, less magnification, and a less sensitive level bubble.   It is accurate enough to transfer grades for construction over distances up to about 50 ft and costs much less than an engineer's level.

Carpenter's levels and mason's levels consist of long wooden or metal frames in which two level vials are fixed, one parallel to the long edge of the level and one perpendicular to it so that the edge can be aligned level or plumb.   A line level consists of a level vial with a hook at each end so that it can be hung from a string line to indicate whether or not the line is level.

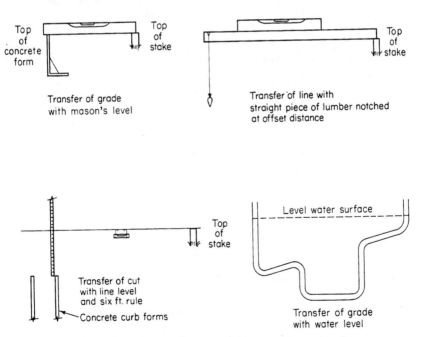

Figure 8.2   Builder's equipment for transferring line and grade

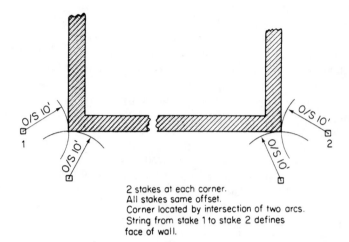

2 stakes at each corner.
All stakes same offset.
Corner located by intersection of two arcs.
String from stake 1 to stake 2 defines
face of wall.

Figure 8.3   Construction stakes for building walls

It must be placed at the middle of the line because its weight makes the line sag so that it will hang level only at the center of a level string line.   It is placed at the middle of the string line by eye.   A water level consists of a flexible transparent tube containing water.   The water surface is at the same elevation at each end of the tube.   These levels are illustrated in Fig. 8.2. The line level is useful for longer distances up to 20 ft or 30 ft.   A hand level of the kind shown in Fig. 1.1 is also used.

These levels are used to extend the offset distances from the stake in a level line, and a plumb bob is used to plumb the line either up or down to grade.   A carpenter's or mason's level can also be used to plumb to grade using the level vial perpendicular to the long axis.   Methods are illustrated in Fig. 8.2.

Key points ordinarily referenced from construction stakes are the center or four corners of column footings at their top elevation, outside corners of foundation walls at the first floor elevation, face of street curbs at the top elevation, center line or edge of pavement with center-line elevations for pavement without curbs, and face of retaining walls at the top elevation.   For a building, stakes may be set to locate each corner in such a way that strings between stakes can be used to align the walls as shown in Fig. 8.3.

8.3 ESTABLISHING CONTROL

An improvement to be built must be located with respect to the land, and various parts of any construction project must be located with respect to each other.   The relationships must be established through an overall reference system.   Several are available.

Base Line and Offset Method

A project may be staked out by locating all stakes by right angle offsets from a control line called a *base line*.   Often, this line is the one from which the designer positions the building on the plot plan.   An example is shown in Fig. 8.4 in which a building is to be located with reference to two property lines that are marked at the corners.   The building is to be constructed parallel with both property lines.   Stakes are to have 10-ft offsets.

The transit is set up over one property corner, and a line is taken by sighting the other.   Distances are measured along the property line from the southeast corner, and nails are put into the ground at proper locations to measure the offsets to the stakes.   Backsights are set at each of the property corners unless the corner markers can be seen with the transit when set up

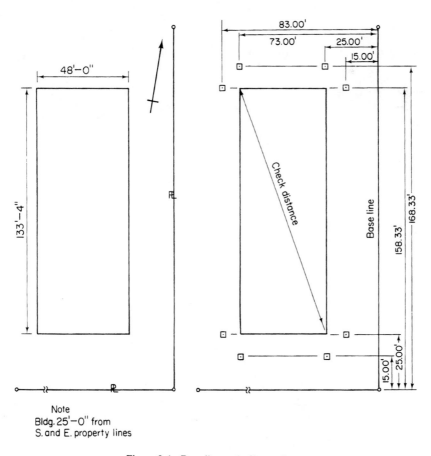

Note
Bldg. 25'−0" from
S. and E. property lines

Figure 8.4   Base line and offset stakeout

over the nails. The transit is then set up over each nail, backsight is taken on whichever property corner is farther away, and stakes are set at right angles at the correct distance.

Angle and Distance Method

The stake locations can be designated by angle and distance with the southeast corner being used as the vertex and the base line being used as a B.S. Angles and distances are computed from coordinates by inversing. The method is illustrated in Fig. 8.5.

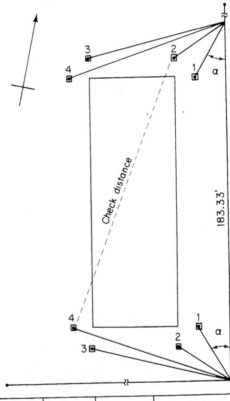

Stake	N	W	tan α = W/N	α	sin α	L = W/sin α
1	25	15				
2	15	25				
3	15	73				
4	25	83				

Figure 8.5 Angle and distance stakeout

The figure shows that four stakes are set from the SE corner, a control point is set on line at the NE end, and the other four stakes are set from that point using the same angles and distances in opposite directions. All eight stakes could be set from the SE corner, but more calculations are required and longer distances must be taped. The method shown saves field time because of shorter distances, even though an additional instrument setup with one long measurement is required.

This method permits more stakes to be put in at one instrument setting and, therefore, saves time for a field party at the cost of extra calculation time for one person in the office. The inversing can be done very quickly with a computer. Conditions of the site may limit visibility, making this method impossible, or the size of the project may require measuring much longer distances. The base line and offset method may be preferable for either reason.

It is easier to visualize what is being done when the base line and offset method is used, and this helps to prevent mistakes. Results can be checked by measuring diagonals in either case. The correct length of the diagonal may be computed before going into the field, or two diagonals may be measured to check that they are equal. The diagonals may be from nails set at the actual corner locations or from stake to stake.

Coordinate Method

Designers of complex facilities, such as a chemical processing plant, which includes buildings, large concrete tanks, and many pipes running from buildings to tanks, often provide coordinates at key construction points based on two mutually perpendicular base lines. The surveyor establishes the base lines with monuments. They should be permanent (iron rods set in a concrete base) so that they will be available for control of repairs and alterations after the plant is built.

Construction stakes are set as they are needed throughout the construction period. They can be set by base line and offset or by angle and distance by using points on a base line for the instrument setups. Figure 8.6 shows an example with coordinates of key points. The surveyor must set stakes at many other points over the construction period and must compute their coordinates and angles and distances for the stakeout.

Vertical Control

Bench marks must be set throughout the site and should be made permanent for large projects where they may be needed for several years during construction. They should be set where they can be used conveniently and are not likely to be disturbed by construction operations. A brass plate convex upward set in concrete provides a satisfactory, permanent B.M. At

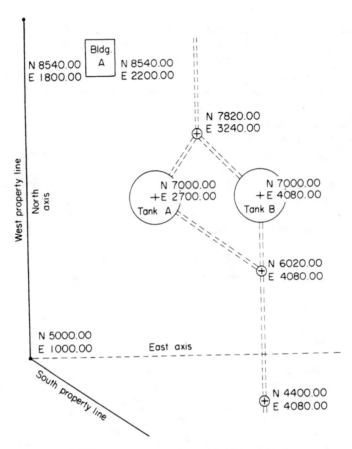

Figure 8.6 Locations of key points by coordinates

least three should be set so that if one is disturbed, agreement between the other two will indicate which of the three has been moved. When all B.M.'s are set, a level circuit is run starting and ending at the B.M. that is the origin for construction elevations. All the new B.M.'s are used as T.P.'s to establish their elevations. Level circuits are covered in Chapter 4.

8.4 FIELD METHODS

Wooden stakes are cut from lumber of various sizes and lengths. Stakes cut from 1 × 3 or 2 × 2 lumber and 18 in. long are typical. When accuracy requires it, a tack or nail is driven into the stake flush with the top. In some cases, the entire stake top provides satisfactory control. If additional stakes are to be set by measuring distances from previously set stakes, nails or tacks must be used to provide accurate measurements without excessive accumulated error.

Instructions to the builder are marked on the stakes. The construction object to which the stake refers is noted with abbreviations such as "S.E. cor" for *southeast corner* or "M.H." for *manhole*. The distance above or below the stake is noted and preceded by the letter "F" for *fill* if the finished elevation is above the stake and "C" for *cut* if the finished elevation is below the stake. For example, C-6.55 means the reference point of the object to be built is 6.55 ft below the stake. The horizontal distance is called an *offset distance* and is abbreviated o/s. For example, o/s 10 ft means that the reference point is 10 ft horizontally from the stake.

Generally, dimensions are written in ft and in. because the builder uses these units. Offsets are almost always in full ft, vertical distances are in hundredths of a ft when the surveyor determines them, and must be converted to ft and in. before writing them on the stakes. Conversion factors to convert decimals of a ft to in. and fractions are listed in Table IV in the Appendix.

Inches and fractions of an in. are converted to ft in decimal form by converting any fraction of an in. to a decimal of an in. and then dividing by 12, the number of in. to a ft. For example, $2\frac{3}{4}$ in. is converted to 2.75 in. and divided by 12 to get 0.23 ft. Two in. is converted by dividing by 12 to get 0.17 ft.

Converting ft in decimal form to inches and fractions requires multiplying by 12 to convert to inches in decimal form and then converting to a fraction with the desired denominator by multiplying the decimal by the denominator. The denominator desired depends on the accuracy needed. A larger denominator is more accurate.

For example, 0.80 ft is multiplied by 12 to indicate 9.60 in. To convert 0.60 in. to eighths, multiply by 8 and get 4.8. This is the number of eighths of an in. and must be rounded to the nearest whole number, 5. The answer is therefore $9\frac{5}{8}$ in.

Ties should be provided for stakes where the difficulty of resetting the stake justifies the time spent in setting the ties. *Ties* are marks placed at known locations in relation to an important point so that its location can be reestablished from the ties if the important point is moved. They may be located by distance from the point or by angle from a B.S. in addition to distance. Ties are usually nails driven into trees, pavement, or stakes and are located where they are unlikely to be disturbed.

Theoretically, any combination of two directions or distances from one or two points locates another point as discussed in Chapter 2. In practice, three ties are established to fix the position more surely and as a precaution against loss of one of them. The tie locations should be sketched in the field notebook as shown in Fig. 8.7.

Setting a point on top of a stake requires teamwork. A two- or three-person party is customary. The instrument person puts the transit on line

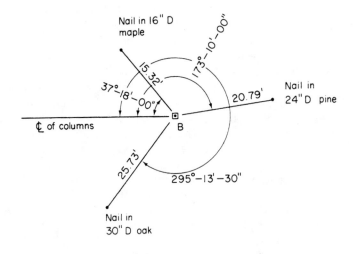

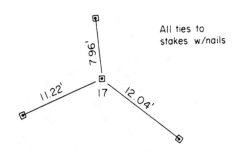

Figure 8.7 Ties in field notebook

and directs preliminary placing of the stake. The head tape person setting the stake holds the tape horizontal if possible, and holds the stake alongside the tape at the correct distance. If the tape is on a slope, the stake is held a little beyond the correct tape mark so that the stake is more nearly at the correct horizontal distance. The rear tape person holds the tape at the point under the instrument.

In a two-person party, the instrument person is also the rear tape person and can keep the tape in the correct position by holding it under foot while sighting with the transit. He or she should stand on the leather thong attached to the zero end of the tape, never on the part that is calibrated for measuring.

The stake is driven slightly into the ground with a hammer, and the distance is checked. This time, the tape should be held level by use of plumb bobs. The instrument person should watch the stake as driving begins and should signal or call to keep it on line. The head tape person calls for a distance check as often as needed and adjusts the stake top as necessary for line and distance.

He or she drives until the stake is deep enough to be solidly in position. The instrument person provides a continuous check on line.

If the stake is driven out of position, the best way to move the top horizontally is to hit the ground next to the stake. Hitting the top loosens the stake. Pounding stones into the ground next to the stake is necessary to move it without loosening in dry or sandy soil.

The tape person determines the point for the nail with plumb bob and tape while being directed on line by the instrument person. In a two-person party, the tape person marks the line with a pencil or plumb bob at two points on the stake top and draws a straight line between the marks using the tape as a straightedge. He or she then measures the distance and marks where it falls on the line. The nail is driven there. The distance may be marked at two points on the stake top, a straight line drawn between the points, and a point on line marked on the first line if this procedure is preferred.

After the stakes are placed in the desired locations, a level circuit is run with an engineer's level, and rod shots are taken on stake tops needed to control grade. The procedure is similar to that for profile leveling. Closing the circuit on another B.M. provides a check that the starting B.M. was not disturbed. Elevations are computed for stake tops, and cuts and fills are determined by the difference between stake-top elevation and finished grade of the proposed construction. Sample notes are shown in Fig. 8.8.

In order to control construction from the surveyor's stakes, it is often convenient for the builder to establish a horizontal line at a certain number of full ft above or below the finished elevation of a portion of the work. This is done by building a *batter board* of two rods or stakes stuck in the ground with a horizontal board between them at a distance above (or below) the construction stake so that the distance from top of board to finished grade is a number of whole ft.

A nail is driven into the board in a position so that a string attached to it passes directly over the nail in the stake. Figure 8.9 shows batter boards arranged above the two construction stakes from Fig. 8.8 so that the cut to the top of the first floor is 1 ft. A string line between batter boards passing over the nails in the stakes controls all elevations and defines the outside face of the wall. The top of footing is 11 ft 1 in. below the string line at all points

Sta.	B.S.(+)	H.I.	F.S. (−)	Rod	Elev.	Fin. Grade	Fill
BM−1	1.21	101.21			100.00		
Stk − 1				4.73	96.48	97.00	0.52
Stk−2				5.55	95.66	97.00	1.34
BM−2			12.34		88.87		

Note: Finished grade is first floor.

Figure 8.8 Notekeeping for grade stakes

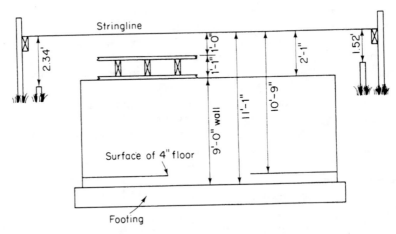

Figure 8.9 Batter boards and string line

along the line. The basement floor is 10 ft 9 in. below the string line at all points, and the top of the wall is 2 ft 1 in. below at all points. The first floor elevation is 1 ft below the string line.

A *grade rod* may be prepared with marks on it so that a mark coincides with the string when the bottom of the rod is on finished grade. A straight unmarked stick of wood 2 in. by 2 in. in cross section is suitable. A grade rod for the construction shown in Fig. 8.9 would have marks at 11 ft 1 in., 10 ft 9 in., 2 ft 1 in., and 1 ft above the bottom so that it could be used to determine all four finished grades from one string line. A level rod could be used, but the key readings would have to be marked on the rod or memorized. If finished grade is above the string line, marks are located the same way. When the bottom of the rod is at the string line, the appropriate mark coincides with the finished grade.

At times, the builder wants surveyor's stakes set at a certain number of full feet above finished grade or at finished grade. This is also accomplished by running a level circuit with rod shots on the stake tops. Instead of recording the rod shots and computing cuts and fills, the desired cuts and fills are recorded, and the rod shots necessary to obtain them are computed. Then, the stake is driven until the computed rod shot is read with the rod on top of the stake. The rod is read with the stake too high (and the rod shot too small), and then the stake is driven a little at a time and the rod read until the desired reading is obtained without driving past the correct elevation. As an alternative, the rod is slid down the side of the stake until the computed value is read, and the side of the stake is marked at that elevation. Both procedures require some trials and adjustments. It is helpful for the instrument person to signal the number of hundredths lower or higher with the number of fingers on the right hand indicating tenths and the fingers on the

Sta.	+	H.I.	−	Rod	Elev.	Fin. Grade	Cut
B.M.-1	1.21	101.21			100.00		
Stk -1				2.21	99.00	97.00	2.00
Stk -2				2.21	99.00	97.00	2.00
B.M.-2			12.34		88.87		

Note: Stakes set for same wall as in Fig. 8-8 and 8-9

Figure 8.10   Notekeeping for grade stakes with specified cut of two feet

left hand indicating hundredths.   Signals for this purpose vary greatly in different areas.   Sample field notes are shown in Fig. 8.10.

8.5 GIVING LINE AND GRADE

Some types of construction require such accuracy that the actual final alignment is guided by surveying.   Examples include steel structural members and large machinery that is completely fabricated before it is delivered to the job site.   The construction at the site must be accurate enough so that the prefabricated items will fit into place.   Allowable errors are only a few hundredths of a ft even over distances of several hundred ft.   Since the transit is set up on line and rod elevations are read for grade, this type of operation is called *giving line and grade.*

Steel Construction

Steel columns or beams are set in place on steel plates resting on a concrete base.   The steel plates are bolted to the concrete with *anchor bolts* that must be set in a pattern in the concrete to fit the holes in the plates. The distance from center to center of column or beam bearings is critical and is controlled to within a few hundredths of a ft by surveying methods.   The spacing of bolts about the center point is also critical and is controlled by ordinary measuring methods because it involves short distances.   See Fig. 8.11 for illustration.

Anchor bolts may be imbedded in fresh concrete before it solidifies. In this case, the transit is kept in place, and anchor bolts are placed with constant checking of line and distance.   Elevation of the concrete is checked at this time.   If anchor bolts are set in drill holes in hardened concrete, the centers are marked accurately on the concrete, and drill holes are located with templates from the center marks.

The elevations of the plates on which the columns or beams will rest are critical, especially in multistory buildings, since all elevations above depend on lower elevations, and excessive errors cannot be allowed to accumulate.   Plates are adjusted in elevation by using an engineer's level with the rod held on the plate.   The H.I. is determined, and the rod shot needed

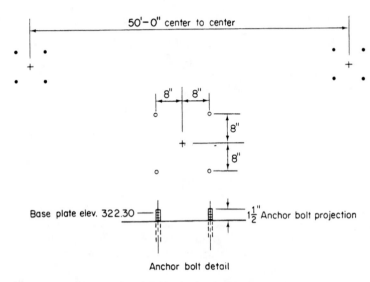

Figure 8.11   Anchor bolt layout

to put the plate at the correct elevation is computed.   The plate is set on a bed of *grout* that is built up a specified height above the concrete for a better pressure distribution.   The grout thickness is on the order of a half in.

The plate is placed over the bolts, and its elevation checked.   If it is too high, it is lowered by cutting away the grout, and if too low, it is raised with thin steel shims under the plate.   See Fig. 8.12 for illustration.   The four corners of large plates may be checked and shimmed to the correct

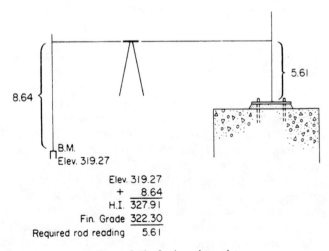

Figure 8.12   Setting a base plate

elevation. If the concrete and grout are placed as they should be, the plates will be close to grade but below it so that only a small amount of shimming is needed and no grout need be cut away.

Columns are installed plumb by aligning the top of the column with the transit on the same line it was on to align the base plate.

Laser

The laser, named for its description "light amplification by stimulated emission and radiation," is useful to control construction. Construction laser is battery-operated and produces a low-power, straight, narrow, red light beam that is seen as a small red dot on anything that interrupts its path. The light beam can be used the same way as a line of sight or string line with a level rod or plumb bob string. Construction lasers are set up similarly to a transit and are self-leveling once they are adjusted nearly level. If they are jarred out of level, they shut off the beam, level themselves, and turn on the beam.

·The operator can set the laser beam level and then hold the rod on base plates being set, reading the rod as each plate is raised until the laser dot is at the correct rod reading.

The beam can be set on line, and points can then be set on line using the beam as a guide. No operator is needed while work is done. Adapters are available to provide a narrow vertical or horizontal line. The vertical line is useful for setting and checking columns or any other construction that must be plumb, and the horizontal line is useful for controlling level construction.

Laser is also used to provide a level line for construction control throughout an area. The device shown in Fig. 8.27 generates a level, rotating laser beam using battery power. It can also direct a single stationary level beam. The device is self-leveling, mounted on a tripod or other type of platform, and is leveled the same way surveying instruments are. The beam rotates several times per second so that the result is an intermittent, level plane of light that is continuously available.

Laser tracking levels that follow specially equipped level rods are also available. These automatically follow the rod, projecting the beam onto it.

A large concrete floor must be checked constantly for correct finished grade as the concrete is being placed and finished. Ground surface being graded level must also be checked constantly as the grading progresses. An instrument person and rod person can do this work with a level and grade rod, using voice or hand signals. Using the rotating laser or tracking laser, one person can check with a grade rod as the work progresses.

Framework for a dropped ceiling can be installed around an entire room, with the installer maintaining the work level by measuring up a constant distance from the laser beam.

To determine grade rod, a level rod or other staff may be placed with its bottom at finished grade. The point at which the laser beam strikes the rod is marked. For overhead work, such as the dropped ceiling, the rod top is placed at finished elevation. Construction is controlled by finishing at such an elevation that the mark matches the laser beam when the grade rod is on the finished work.

If finished surface is not readily available, it may be determined by leveling. A B.S. is read on a B.M. by the rod person who observes the location of the laser beam on the rod. The H.I. of the beam is computed, and the rod shot necessary for finished grade is computed. Construction is then finished to a grade that gives the correct rod shot. A sample calculation follows:

786.31 B.M. elev.

+　9.84 B.S. by laser

796.15 H.I. of laser

−790.50 Finished elev.

5.65 Rod shot required

A level rod designed to be used with laser has a photocell that is sensitive to the laser beam. When the beam hits the rod, the photocell travels up or down until it aligns itself with the beam so that a narrow horizontal line indicates the rod reading with accuracy comparable to that of a self-leveling engineer's level. The laser beam itself cannot be read this accurately by eye.

8.6 EARTHWORK

Each construction project results in some change to the ground surface. Earth must be rearranged within the work area (*site*). Earth is excavated and hauled away from the site (*wasted*) or brought in from outside the site (*borrowed*). The rearranging, wasting, and borrowing are all included in the term *earthwork*. Earthwork is paid for by the cubic yard, and the volume must be calculated in cubic yards for cost estimates during planning, for preparation of bid quantities, and for determination of payments to the builder.

Volume Calculations

The volume is the difference between the original surface and the final surface whether the earthwork is excavation or embankment. Generally, the final surface is rather smooth throughout. It may consist of a level or nearly level area with steeply sloping sides, called *side slopes*, up or down to the original ground. Side slopes are measured by the ratio of vertical distance

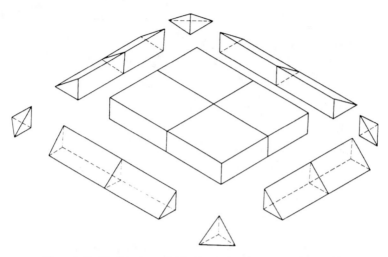

Figure 8.13   Earth volume divided into cubes, wedges, and pyramids

over horizontal distance, with a vertical component of one.   Typical side slopes are 1 on 1, 1 on 2, and 1 on 3.   An embankment of this shape is shown in Fig. 8.13.

Earthwork volume can best be determined by dividing the entire volume into geometric shapes.   Earthwork of a regular shape is easily divided into cubes, wedges, and pyramids as shown in Fig. 8.13.   Most earthwork has surfaces and boundaries that are more irregular, but any earth volume can be divided into cubes, wedges, and pyramids.

All these volumes equal the horizontal area multiplied by the average thickness.   The average thickness is always the average of the thicknesses at all corners.   Computing a volume consists of dividing the horizontal area into shapes for which it is easy to find the average thickness, determining their individual volumes, and totaling them.

Figure 8.14 shows typical earth volume calculations for a preliminary estimate (before construction).   The assumption is made that the original ground is level.   This enables the wedge and pyramid widths to be determined from their heights by use of the slope ratios.

The volume of a cube is length times width times average thickness (difference between original and final elevations) of the four corners.

The volume of a wedge is equal to the horizontal area multiplied by the average thickness of the four corners.   With a side slope of 1 on 2, the widths of the wedges are twice their height.   The horizontal area may be a rectangle but is usually a trapezoid.   The two corners, where final surface meets original surface, have no thickness.   Therefore, wedge volume equals horizontal area multiplied by the sum of the two vertical sides and divided by four.

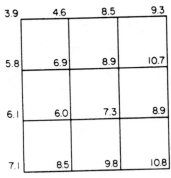

A sketch of an earth volume 300 ft wide by 300 ft long is shown with a 100 ft grid overlaid. Thickness of the earth is given at each grid point. Side slopes, starting at the edge of the grid, are 1:2.

To compute volume within the grid, the average of the thicknesses at the four corners of each square is assumed to be the average for the square, and is multiplied by the area of the square.

$$\frac{3.9 + 4.6 + 6.9 + 5.8}{4} = 5.3 \qquad \frac{4.6 + 8.5 + 8.9 + 6.9}{4} = 7.225 \qquad \frac{8.5 + 9.3 + 10.7 + 8.9}{4} = 9.35$$

$$\frac{5.8 + 6.9 + 6.0 + 6.1}{4} = 6.2 \qquad \frac{6.9 + 8.9 + 7.3 + 6.0}{4} = 7.275 \qquad \frac{8.9 + 10.7 + 8.9 + 7.3}{4} = 8.95$$

$$\frac{6.1 + 6.0 + 8.5 + 7.1}{4} = 6.925 \qquad \frac{6.0 + 7.3 + 9.8 + 8.5}{4} = 7.9 \qquad \frac{7.3 + 8.9 + 10.8 + 9.8}{4} = 9.2$$

$$5.3 + 6.2 + 6.925 + 7.225 + 7.275 + 7.9 + 9.35 + 8.95 + 9.2 = 68.325 \text{ ft}$$

$$68.325 \times 100 \times 100 \div 27 = 25,306 \text{ cu yd}$$

To compute volume of wedges, the average of the thicknesses at the four corners of each wedge is multiplied by the trapezoidal area of the wedge. The original ground is assumed to be level, so that the wedge thicknesses and widths have the side slope ratios of 1:2.

$$\frac{3.9 + 4.6}{4} \times \frac{7.8 + 9.2}{2} \times 100 = 1806 \qquad \frac{4.6 + 8.5}{4} \times \frac{9.2 + 17.0}{2} \times 100 = 4290 \qquad \frac{8.5 + 9.3}{4} \times \frac{17.0 + 18.6}{2} \times 100 = 7921$$

$$\frac{9.3 + 10.7}{4} \times \frac{18.6 + 21.4}{2} \times 100 = 10000 \qquad \frac{10.7 + 8.9}{4} \times \frac{21.4 + 17.8}{2} \times 100 = 9604 \qquad \frac{8.9 + 10.8}{4} \times \frac{17.8 + 21.6}{2} \times 100 = 9702$$

$$\frac{10.8 + 9.8}{4} \times \frac{21.6 + 19.6}{2} \times 100 = 10609 \qquad \frac{9.8 + 8.5}{4} \times \frac{19.6 + 17.0}{2} \times 100 = 8372 \qquad \frac{8.5 + 7.1}{4} \times \frac{17.0 + 14.2}{2} \times 100 = 6084$$

$$\frac{7.1 + 6.1}{4} \times \frac{14.2 + 12.2}{2} \times 100 = 4356 \qquad \frac{6.1 + 5.8}{4} \times \frac{12.2 + 11.6}{2} \times 100 = 3540 \qquad \frac{5.8 + 3.9}{4} \times \frac{11.6 + 7.8}{2} \times 100 = 2352$$

$$1806 + 4290 + 7921 + 10,000 + 9604 + 9702 + 10,609 + 8372 + 6084 + 4356 + 3540 + 2352 = 78,636 \text{ cu ft}$$

$$78,636 \div 27 = 2912 \text{ cu yd}$$

To compute volume of pyramids, the average of the thicknesses at the three corners of each pyramid is multiplied by the triangular area of the pyramid. The triangle dimensions are the same as the widths of the wedges.

$$\frac{3.9}{3} \times \frac{7.8 \times 7.8}{2} = 40 \qquad\qquad \frac{9.3}{3} \times \frac{18.6 \times 18.6}{2} = 536$$

$$\frac{7.1}{3} \times \frac{14.2 \times 14.2}{2} = 239 \qquad\qquad \frac{10.8}{3} \times \frac{21.6 \times 21.6}{2} = 840$$

$$40 + 536 + 840 + 239 = 1655 \text{ cu ft}$$

$$1655 \div 27 = 61 \text{ cu yd}$$

Figure 8.14 Earthwork volume calculations

The volume of one wedge at the upper left corner of the grid is computed here:

Horizontal area (trapezoid) = average width × length

$$= \frac{2 \times 3.9 + 2 \times 5.8}{2} \times 100 = 970 \text{ sq ft}$$

Average thickness $= \frac{3.9 + 5.8 + 0 + 0}{4} = 2.425 \text{ ft}$

Volume $= 970 \times 2.425 \times \frac{1}{27} = 87.1 \text{ cu yd}$

The volume of a pyramid is also equal to the horizontal area multiplied by the average thickness of the corners. Pyramids have three corners. The horizontal area is a triangle, and two of the three corners have no thickness. The volume of the pyramid at the upper left corner is computed here:

Horizontal area (triangle) $\frac{\text{length} \times \text{width}}{2}$

$$= \frac{(2 \times 3.9)(2 \times 3.9)}{2} = 30.4 \text{ sq ft}$$

Average thickness $= \frac{3.9 + 0 + 0}{3} = 1.3 \text{ ft}$

Volume $= 30.4 \text{ sq ft} \times 1.3 \text{ ft} \times \frac{1}{27} = 1.5 \text{ cu yd}$

Field Methods

Data for volume computation come from a field survey using a grid. Original ground elevations are determined at the grid points before earthwork takes place. A preliminary estimate of earth volume can then be made using proposed finished elevations and an assumption about ground elevations outside the grid where wedges and pyramids will be.

After earthwork is completed, final elevations of the finished surface are determined at the same grid points. Elevations are found in each case by running a level circuit with rod shots taken on the ground. The thicknesses used in volume computations are the differences between original elevations and final elevations.

The first step in laying out the grid is to space stakes accurately along a base line. The stakes serve as one line of the grid. The base line may be an edge of the grid or any other line of the grid. The base line and a similar line of stakes perpendicular to it are established with transit and tape. The rest of the grid is either established with transit and tape or by some other method.

Once the two perpendicular lines are established, the other grid points can be determined by the intersection of grid distances from two known points. This can be done with two steel or cloth tapes and requires a party of three people. A person holds zero at each of the two known points, and the third person marks the point where the grid dimensions on the two tapes coincide. The procedure is illustrated in Fig. 8.15.

The points within reach are set by taping from the base-line stakes. Additional points are set by taping from points previously set until all necessary points are set. The points farther from the base line are set with greater error. The errors may accumulate to an unacceptable value in setting up a large grid. If this happens, additional accurate base lines are needed.

Horizontal errors as large as a foot are often not significant because there is no significant difference in elevation within that distance. The effect on the total volume of a horizontal error this size is insignificant except for small areas.

The entire grid may be marked with stakes or with lath driven lightly into the ground. Extra marks should be set on the grid lines at the inner edges of side slopes and at other places where the finished surface will have significant slope changes. Extra marks should also be set at points of significant slope change on the original surface. All these points are later used as corners in dividing the total volume into geometric shapes. It is not

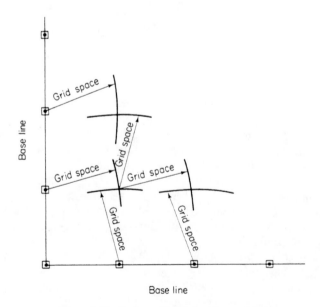

Figure 8.15 Setting grid points with two tapes

necessary to locate the outer edge of the side slopes when obtaining original elevations for volume calculations.

The field work should be performed in two stages in order to prevent confusion. The first step is to mark all points on the ground and sketch their locations in the field book. The second step is to run a level circuit from a B.M. with rod shots at the points. If the two steps are performed together, it is difficult to keep notes, and mistakes will most likely occur.

The grid spacing is selected to suit the roughness of the ground and the size of the project. The more irregular the ground is, the smaller the grid spacing must be to produce accurate results. The grid points should be close enough together so that the assumption that ground surface is straight from point to point does not cause significant error in the volume determination.

The grid points must be closer for small projects than for large ones in order to prevent accidental errors. Accidental errors tend to cancel each other when repeated many times over a large area but are likely to have a cumulative effect when there are only a few of them. Common grid spaces are 100, 50, and 25 ft.

The total extent of the grid must be large enough for the project. It must extend at least to the inner edges of the side slopes. Original and final elevations must be determined at all the grid points within the earthwork area and at the inner edges of side slopes. Elevations need not be determined at the edges of the earthwork because there is no thickness to the earth there. See Fig. 8.16.

The top of the finished fill is level with an elevation of 541.0. Thickness at the grid points and top of slope are computed using this elevation and the original elevations. The horizontal distances along grid lines from top to toe of slope must be measured in the field to compute volumes of wedges and pyramids accurately.

Original and final field notes are shown in Figs. 8.17 and 8.18. The necessary horizontal distances are shown with plusses as if the grid points were stations. If the locations of inner edges of side slopes are not known beforehand, they cannot be included in the original survey but are included in the final one. Volume computations are shown in Fig. 8.19 for some of the geometric shapes.

If the limits of earthwork are not known when original elevations are taken, the grid is made large enough to be certain that it includes the entire earthwork area. This may be the case when earth is borrowed and the quantity is measured at the *borrow pit* from where it is taken or when earth is wasted and measured at the place where it is dumped. Figure 8.20 shows a grid laid out over a waste area and the extent of the final waste embankment.

The waste embankment is graded to merge with the original ground. There are no well-defined side slopes and no rod shots at the upper edge of slope. The total volume still consists of cubes, wedges, and pyramids. Embankment that completely covers a grid square is a cube. That which covers

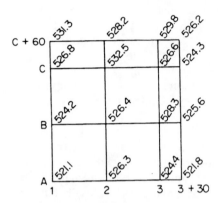

Grid and original elevations covering 260 ft
by 230 ft embankment area.

Side slopes are to be outside grid.

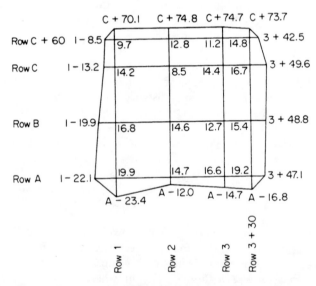

Finished embankment with height of fill at grid
points and grid locations at toe of slope.
Distances in negative direction are given with
minus signs.

Figure 8.16 Original grid and finished embankment

T.J.Olson Apartment Bldg. Original Elevations						page 56
Sta.	B.S.(+)	H.I.	F.S.(−)	Rod	Elev.	Date
BM3	9.11	532.79			523.68	See BM Book p.36 M.Toomey π
TP1	6.32	533.88	5.23		527.56	for description R. Jones $\diamond$
1A				12.8	521.1	F. Schayes ⊡
1B				9.7	524.2	Level 4913
1C				7.1	526.8	Cloth tape
1C + 60				2.6	531.3	Clear, Cool
2A				7.6	526.3	
2B				7.5	526.4	
2C				1.4	532.5	North
2C + 60				5.7	528.2	
3A				9.5	524.4	
3B				5.6	528.3	
3C				7.3	526.6	
3C + 60				4.1	529.8	
3 + 30A				12.1	521.8	
√ B				8.3	525.6	
√ C				9.6	524.3	
√ C + 60				7.7	526.2	
TP2	3.19	531.09	5.98		527.90	
BM 3			7.41		523.68	
	18.62		18.62			
		O.K				

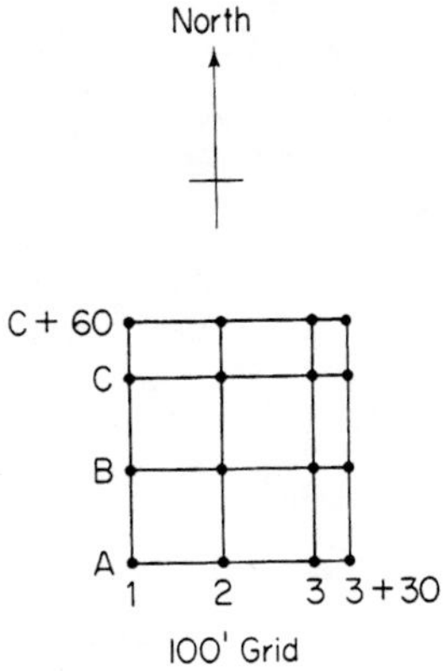

Figure 8.17   Field notes, original elevations

T.J.Olson Apartment Bldg. Final Elevations

Sta.	B.S.(+)	H.I.	F.S.(-)	Rod	Elev		Date
BM 4	9.81	545.53			535.72	See BM Book p.36	M.Toomey ⊼
1 – 22.1, A						Toe of slope	R.Jones ⟡
1 – 19.9, B						✓	F.Schayes ⊟
1 – 13.2, C						✓	Level 4913
1 – 8.5, C + 60						✓	Cloth tape
1, A – 23.4						✓	Warm, hazy
1, A				4.5	541.0	Top of slope	
1, B				4.5	541.0	✓	
1, C				4.5	541.0	✓	
1, C + 60				4.5	541.0	✓	
1, C + 70.1						Toe of slope	
2, A – 12.0						✓ ✓	
2, A				4.5	541.0	Top of slope	
2, B				4.5	541.0	✓	
2, C				4.5	541.0	✓	
2, C + 60				4.5	541.0	Top of slope	
2, C + 74.8						Toe of slope	
3, A – 14.7						✓ ✓	
3, A				4.5	541.0	Top of slope	
3, B				4.5	541.0	✓	
3, C				4.5	541.0	Top of slope	
3, C + 60				4.5	541.0	Top of slope	
3, C + 74.7						Toe of slope	
3+30, A – 16.8						✓	

Figure 8.18 Field notes, final elevations

228

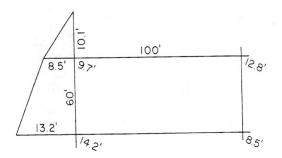

Cube

Horizontal area   = length × width

= 100 × 60 = 6000 sq ft

Average thickness = $\dfrac{9.7 + 12.8 + 14.2 + 8.5}{4}$ = 11.3 ft

Volume   = 6000 × 11.3 × $\dfrac{1}{27}$ = 2511 cu yd

Wedge

Horizontal area (trapezoid) = average width × length

= $\dfrac{8.5 + 13.2}{2}$ × 60 = 651 sq ft

Average thickness   = $\dfrac{9.7 + 14.2 + 0 + 0}{4}$ = 5.975 ft

Volume   = 651 × 5.975 × $\dfrac{1}{27}$ = 144.1 cu yd

Pyramid

Horizontal area (triangle) = $\dfrac{\text{length × width}}{2}$

= $\dfrac{10.1 × 8.5}{2}$ = 9.3 sq ft

Average thickness   = $\dfrac{9.7 + 0 + 0}{3}$ = 3.233 ft

Volume   = 9.3 × 3.233 × $\dfrac{1}{27}$ = 1.1 cu yd

Figure 8.19 Partial volume calculations from Figure 8.16

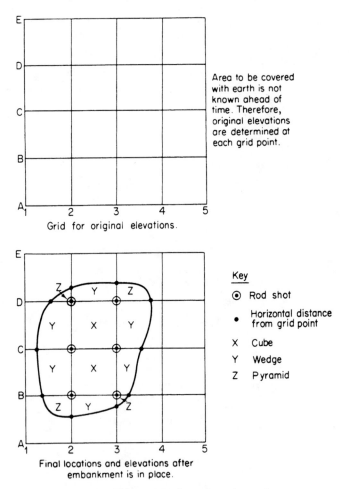

Grid for original elevations.

Area to be covered with earth is not known ahead of time. Therefore, original elevations are determined at each grid point.

Final locations and elevations after embankment is in place.

Key

⊙ Rod shot

• Horizontal distance from grid point

X Cube

Y Wedge

Z Pyramid

Figure 8.20 Field work to determine volume of waste

part of a grid square is a wedge or pyramid because it has no thickness at two corners. See Fig. 8.20. The placing of the original grid determines how much of the volume is in cubes and how much in wedges and pyramids.

Original elevations are determined at all grid points because it is not known which ones are needed. Final elevations are determined at all grid points within the fill area, and horizontal measurements are made from the edge of fill to the nearest grid point along grid lines.

Sufficient information is thus available to provide dimensions of all cubes, wedges, and pyramids needed to compute the total volume. Edges of the earth mass are considered to be straight lines from point to point on the grid lines.

Separating Cut from Fill

Earthwork often involves a gradual change from excavation to fill. To compute volumes of each accurately, the line separating them must be located. When depth of cut and height of fill are known at two adjacent grid points, the point at which cut changes to fill along the grid line can be found graphically. Original and final surfaces are considered to be straight. Straight lines representing a section view of the two surfaces form similar triangles with the vertical lines that represent cut and fill. See Fig. 8.21.

The point at which the two surfaces cross is the point of no cut or fill. Cut and fill must be drawn to the same vertical scale. The horizontal scale should be a much larger scale so that the horizontal distance appears short compared to the vertical distances. Lines connecting opposite ends of the cut and fill lines intersect at the transition point between cut and fill. If you try this using the same scale vertically and horizontally, it will be apparent that it cannot be done accurately using one scale.

The line separating cut and fill can be located across the entire grid using this method. See Fig. 8.22. Areas produced are trapezoids, triangles, or pentagons. All volumes are computed by multiplying the horizontal area by the average of all corner thicknesses. The pentagon areas can be computed by deducting the triangular area from the square area.

The grid covering the area where cut changes to fill is drawn to scale. Cuts are drawn to scale in one direction from their grid points, and fills are drawn from their grid points parallel and in the opposite direction. The ends are connected with a straight line that intersects the grid line at the point of change.

A plan view of the finished earthwork of Fig. 8.22 is shown in Fig. 8.23. The width of earthwork beyond the grid depends on the steepness of the side slopes. However, at the point separating cut from fill there is no width. Therefore the adjacent earth volumes are triangles in plan view with two

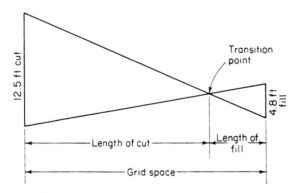

Figure 8.21 Separating cut and fill graphically by proportion

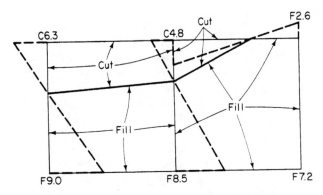

Figure 8.22 Separation of cut and fill within a grid

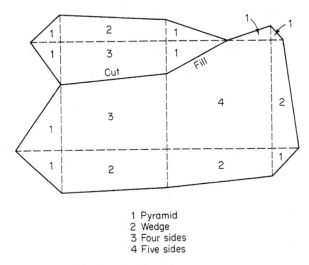

1 Pyramid
2 Wedge
3 Four sides
4 Five sides

Figure 8.23 Geometric volumes of Fig. 8.22

corners having no thickness. There are, therefore, a fill pyramid and an excavation pyramid adjacent to each transition from cut to fill.

The other sides have wedges at the side slopes, and all corners have pyramids. The cut-fill line divides the grid into two trapezoids, a triangle, and a five-sided figure. Earth volumes are all calculated by multiplying the area by the average corner height.

Slope Stakes

Before earthwork begins, the outer limits of the work must be marked with stakes because this is where the builder starts. These stakes are driven at the outer edges of the side slopes with their tops inclined away from the direction of earthwork and are called *slope stakes*.

Often the horizontal location and elevation of the inner edges of the side slope are known, and stakes must be set at the outer edges of the side slope. Figure 8.24 shows how the position of the slope stake varies with the shape of the original ground. The excavation is to have a level finished surface and side slopes of 1 on 2.

Stakes are set at the top of the slope so that the ratio of the vertical dimension of the entire finished slope to the horizontal dimension is 1 on 2. The builder then begins excavating at the outer limits defined by the stakes, proceeds inward and downward at a 1 on 2 slope, and reaches the toe of the slope at the correct vertical and horizontal location.

The vertical component of the slope is the difference between the elevation of the original ground at the stake and the elevation of the finished surface at the toe of the slope. The elevation of finished surface is known. The elevation of the original ground is found in the field. The horizontal distance from the inside edge of side slope to the stake is measured on a grid line with a cloth tape to the point of the rod reading. When the one spot is found where the difference between elevations and the taped distance give the correct side slope ratio, the stake is set. See Fig. 8.25.

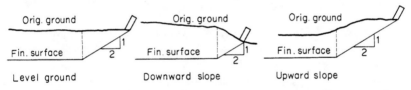

Figure 8.24 How horizontal length of side slope varies with slope of original ground

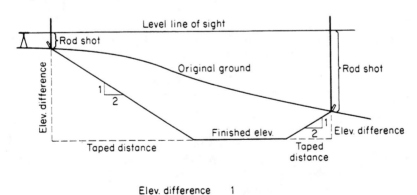

$$\frac{\text{Elev. difference}}{\text{Taped distance}} = \frac{1}{2}$$

Figure 8.25 Relationship between side slope and surveying measurements

Field work is performed by a party of three: an instrument person who uses a level or transit, a tape person who holds the zero end of the tape at the inside edge of the side slope, and a rod person who holds the other end of the tape and positions the rod at various locations until one is found where the tape reading at the rod is correct for the elevation difference. The necessary arithmetic may be done mentally or on scrap paper. The field notes show only the final results proving the stakes are correctly placed.

At the correct location, a stake is driven inclined from the vertical away from the direction of cut or fill. The perimeter stakes are the only guides for the builder to begin work. Any other stakes would be torn out by earthmoving operations. Field notes are shown in Fig. 8.26.

Any line that separates excavation from fill must also be marked for the builder. Such a line is a series of points where the elevation of natural ground is the same as the elevation of the finished surface. It is the one line where the elevation will not be changed. The rod reading down to the finished surface is computed, and the survey crew locates the points for stakes by moving the rod to various locations until the correct rod reading is found.

Laser

Laser can be very efficient for controlling earthwork projects, especially if large areas are to be finished level or to a constant slope. A battery-powered rotating laser is set up on a tripod to project its beam in a level plane or in a plane inclined at the desired angle. See Fig. 8.27. The laser has a range up to 1,000 ft.

A receiver is used that senses how far it is above or below the laser beam. The receiver is mounted on a mast attached to the blade of the earthmoving equipment. It must be above the cab so the laser beam reaches it from any direction. The receiver signals a mechanism that raises or lowers the blade almost instantaneously to match the receiver with the beam. The blade thus provides a smooth finished surface at a predetermined distance below the plane of the rotating laser beam.

The elevation of the laser beam need not be known. Finished grade is marked on a surveyor's stake. The blade of the equipment is adjusted by the operator to the finished grade, and the receiver is loosened and allowed to move up or down the mast to match the laser beam while the blade remains stationary. When the receiver lines itself up with the laser beam, receiver and blade are correctly related, and the receiver is clamped in place. The blade then follows the receiver to produce the desired finished surface as the equipment travels. See Fig. 8.28.

Bulldozers, scrapers, graders, and almost any other kind of equipment can be fitted with the laser controlling and operating system. Manipulation of the earthmoving portion of the equipment is completely taken over by the laser system. The operator need only steer and adjust speed.

B.D. Bundy
J. Carson { Cloth / Tape
C. Canon { Rod ₵ / Notes
Gurley level
clear, windy

Slope stakes for Berglund land reclamation

Sta.	B.S.(+)	H.I.	F.S.(–)	Rod	Elev.	Cut	Dist.
B.M. 3	9.29	647.71			638.42		
1				2.3	645.4	8.4	16.8'
2				3.3	644.4	7.4	14.8'
3				4.1	643.6	6.6	13.2'
4				1.7	646.0	9.0	18.0'
5				3.6	644.1	7.1	14.2'
6				6.9	640.8	3.8	7.6'
7				6.0	641.7	4.7	9.4'
8				7.8	639.9	2.9	5.8'
9				9.1	638.6	1.6	3.2'
10				8.3	639.4	2.4	4.8'
B.M. 3			9.29		638.42		

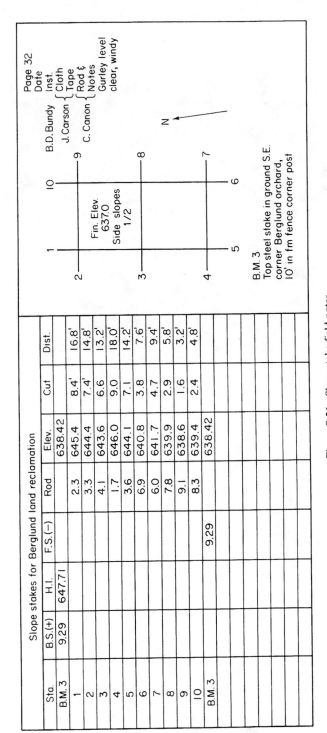

Fin. Elev. 637.0
Side slopes 1/2

N

B.M. 3
Top steel stake in ground S.E. corner Berglund orchard, 10' in fm fence corner post

Figure 8.26 Slope stake field notes

Figure 8.27 Rotary laser transmitter and self-aligning photocell mounted on a level rod (*Courtesy of Laserplane Corporation*)

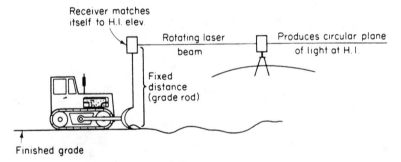

Figure 8.28 Automatic earthwork control by laser

PROBLEMS

1. Draw a layout sketch suitable for the field showing construction stakes with every dimension needed to set them by base line and offset method. Do not leave any addition or subtraction for the field.

   (a) Provide a stake at each corner with no offset. Provide two stakes at each corner with 6 ft offset and with 12 ft offset. Property lines are perpendicular. Calculate all possible diagonal check distances for each case.

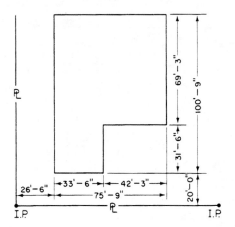

(b) Provide a stake at each corner with no offset. Provide two stakes at each corner with 8-ft offset and with 10-ft offset. Building is to be parallel to property line and 20 ft from it. Calculate all possible diagonal check distances for each case.

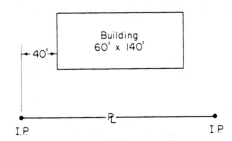

2. Draw sketches for each case and provide angles and distances from the instrument to each stake for staking the buildings in Problem 1.

3. Finish the following grade staking field notes:

Sta.	B.S.	H.I.	F.S.	Rod	Elev.	Fin Gr.	C or F
BM–1	10.69				185.43		
# 1				4.61		189.50	
# 2				10.72		189.50	
# 3				8.82		189.50	
# 4				6.21		189.50	
BM–1			10.69				

(a)

Sta.	B.S.	H.I.	F.S.	Rod	Elev.	Fin Gr	C or F
BM-1	5.96				596.59		
# 1				6.91		595.00	
# 2				3.22		595.00	
# 3				11.54		595.00	
TP-1	5.87		2.97				
# 4				9.43		596.50	
# 5				10.06		596.50	
TP-2	5.51		3.84				
# 6				12.36		596.50	
TP-3	3.71		9.03				
BM-1			5.20				

(b)

4. A contractor wants stake tops to be a whole number of ft above foundation forms. Top of form elevation is 144.00. H.I. is 160.23. A stake is driven, and a rod reading of 11.84 is read on the stake. The stake must be driven deeper until it is a whole number of ft above elevation 144.00. What are the final rod reading and cut or fill?

5. A stake is to be set with fill of 10.00 ft to the top of wall. Finished elevation of top of wall is 336.50, and the H.I. is 332.74. What rod reading is needed to set the stake at the proper elevation?

6. Design elevation of a footing is 483.30. A stake is set at elevation 484.11. What cut or fill should be marked on the stake? At what distance above and below the stake can a batter board be built to provide a cut or fill of a whole number of ft and what will cut or fill be at each of the two settings?

7. Finished grade is 153.00, a grade stake is at 157.96, and a grade rod of 6.00 ft is desired. How far above or below the grade stake should a batter board be built?

8. Original and final elevations are given for the 50-ft grid pattern shown. Compute the volume of earth removed. Side slopes are 1 on 3, and original ground can be assumed to be level.

Sta.	Original Elev.	Final Elev.
A1	225.6	224.6
A2	224.8	223.5
A3	225.6	222.3

A4	225.0	221.1
B1	226.9	225.2
B2	224.2	216.6
B3	223.1	215.5
B4	224.2	222.0
C1	226.0	226.0
C2	224.8	224.8
C3	223.6	223.6
C4	222.5	222.5

9. An embarkment is built to an elevation of 40.00 with a top width of 200 ft and length of 500 ft. Side slopes are 1:2. The 100-ft grid pattern is shown with the embankment superimposed. The original ground elevation could be interpolated at the toe of embankment slope, but such a refinement would make very little difference in the answer since the ground is nearly level.

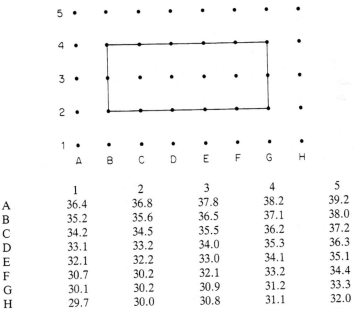

	1	2	3	4	5
A	36.4	36.8	37.8	38.2	39.2
B	35.2	35.6	36.5	37.1	38.0
C	34.2	34.5	35.5	36.2	37.2
D	33.1	33.2	34.0	35.3	36.3
E	32.1	32.2	33.0	34.1	35.1
F	30.7	30.2	32.1	33.2	34.4
G	30.1	30.2	30.9	31.2	33.3
H	29.7	30.0	30.8	31.1	32.0

10. Original ground elevations are given at the corners of a proposed 100-ft by 80-ft embankment for a building. The subgrade for the building is 100.00. Excavation will have slopes of 1:3, and fill will have slopes of 1:1. Compute volume of fill, volume of excavation, and volume of waste or borrow.

11. Cuts and fills are shown on 50-ft grids. Determine volume of excavation and fill. Side slopes are 1:4. Assume original ground level.

(a)

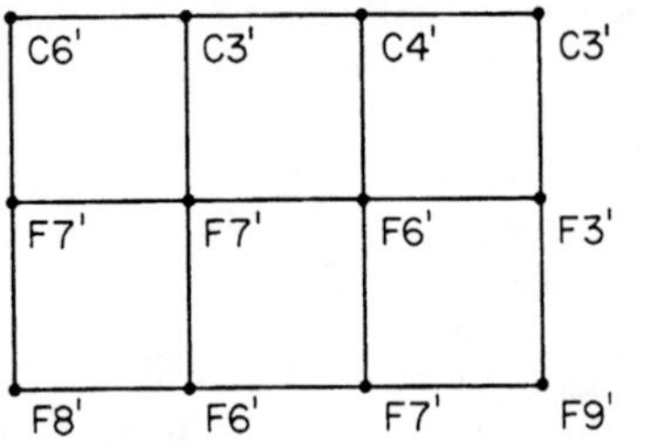

C6'	C3'	C4'	C3'
F7'	F7'	F6'	F3'
F8'	F6'	F7'	F9'

(b)

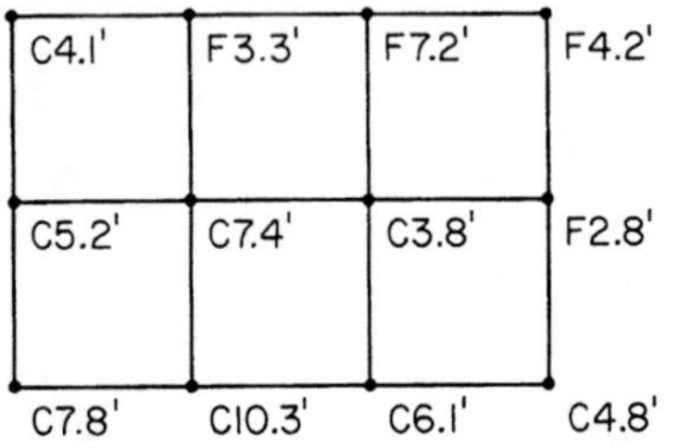

C4.1'	F3.3'	F7.2'	F4.2'
C5.2'	C7.4'	C3.8'	F2.8'
C7.8'	C10.3'	C6.1'	C4.8'

12. Cuts and fills are shown on 25-ft grids, and distances from grid to edge of finished earthwork are also shown. Determine volume of excavation and fill.

	13.2'	10.2'	7.1'	5.3'	
10.2'	C7.1	C6.4	C4.7'	C3.2'	6.0'
7.3'	C4.7'	C3.1'	F3.7'	F4.5'	6.8'
7.7'	F5.3'	F6.6'	F9.2'	F8.6'	12.4'
	8.9'	12.2'	15.6'	17.3'	

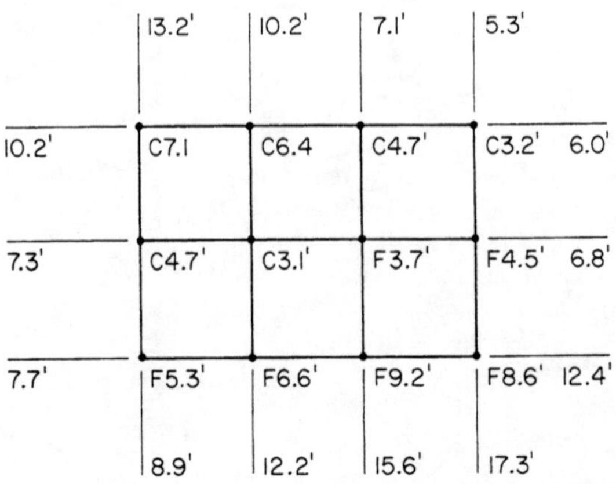

13. Convert the following lengths to ft and decimals of a ft.

$2\frac{1}{8}$ in.	$8\frac{3}{4}$ in.	$5\frac{1}{4}$ in.	$118\frac{9}{13}$ in.
$3\frac{1}{16}$ in.	$7\frac{7}{8}$ in.	$15\frac{12}{48}$ in.	$80\frac{14}{19}$ in.
$4\frac{1}{2}$ in.	$21\frac{11}{16}$ in.	$9\frac{3}{8}$ in.	$5\frac{6}{13}$ in.
$17\frac{7}{16}$ in.	$32\frac{5}{64}$ in.	$11\frac{7}{18}$ in.	$6\frac{12}{24}$ in.

14. Convert the following lengths to in. and fractions with the indicated denominators.

Nearest quarter	Nearest eighth	Nearest twentieth	Nearest eighteenth
1.31 ft	0.49 ft	0.88	0.10
0.79 ft	2.83	3.02	2.27
8.22 ft	3.39	5.14	3.92
5.93 ft	5.22	7.76	4.51

9

CONSTRUCTION SURVEYS DEALING WITH SLOPES

INSTRUCTIONAL OBJECTIVES

1. *Given a starting elevation and slope for a construction project, the student should be able:*
   a. To determine the elevation at any station.
   b. To prepare a grade sheet.
2. *Given cuts or fills at stakes, the student should be able to determine how far above or below stakes to construct batter boards for a grade rod of a given length.*
3. *Given stake elevations and cuts or fills at two stations and a rod shot on one stake, the student should be able to show mathematically how to align the transit so that the line of sight is parallel to finished grade and how to determine the grade rod.*
4. *Given an elevation and cut or fill at one stake and the slope, the student should be able to show mathematically how to align the transit so that the line of sight is parallel to finished grade and how to determine the grade rod.*
5. *Given base width, finished grade, side slope, and center-line stakes, the student should be able to determine locations for slope stakes with the assistance of an instrument person and a tape person. He or she should also be able to determine cut or fill at stakes and to keep field notes for slope staking.*
6. *Given cross sections drawn to scale or field data, the student should be*

*able to compute earth volume between two stations by the average end
area method and by using the prismoidal formula.*

Many construction projects are long and narrow with constantly changing
elevation and consist of repetitive construction for much of their length.
Examples are pipelines, highways, and tracks. Construction stakeout procedures for these projects are discussed in this chapter.

9.1 SLOPES

Slopes in civil engineering projects are designated by a percentage or decimal
that is equal to the tangent of the angle formed by the sloping line and a
horizontal line. The slope when designated this way is often called a *grade*.
The term *slope* is used instead in this book to prevent confusion with the
term *grade* meaning elevation. *Grade* is used throughout this book to mean
elevation. A slope of 1.15% or 0.0115 means that the sloping line changes
elevation 1.15 ft over a horizontal distance of 100 ft. Slope is thus a rate of
change in grade. A plus slope rises in a forward direction, and a minus slope
is downhill in a forward direction.

9.2 PIPELINES

When construction stakeout is considered, there are two categories of pipeline—pressure and gravity. Liquid or gas that fills a pipeline under pressure
flows upward as readily as downhill, and slope is of little importance. Water
and natural gas lines are of this type, and it is customary to construct them
at a certain depth below the surface without regard to the slope of the pipe.
Line is staked at an offset for this type of pipeline, and grade is measured
from the ground surface at the edge of the trench.
    Gravity pipelines are only partially full of liquid, and the liquid flows
from a higher elevation to a lower one. It flows only as far as the pipe
continues to slope downward. The steepness of the slope determines the
velocity at which the liquid flows and, therefore, the quantity that flows in a
given time. The slope is an important factor in the design and construction
of these pipelines. Storm drains and sanitary sewers are of this type, and
line and grade must be indicated for these pipes without regard to the grade
of the ground surface.

LINE AND GRADE

A plan and profile of a sanitary sewer are shown in Fig. 9.1. It is the
surveyor's task to set stakes indicating how to build it to proper line and

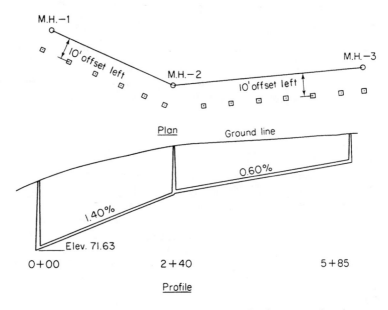

Figure 9.1 Plan and profile of sanitary sewer showing surveyor's stakes

slope. Stakes are shown arranged at 50-ft intervals to control the horizontal alignment of the sewer. An offset is needed to accommodate the top width of the trench. Note that stationing starts from the lower end of a gravity line.

In order for the surveyor to mark a cut on each stake, he or she must determine the grade of the sewer at the station of the stake. The pipe invert is the control point for grade. The invert is the low point of the inside circumference of the sewer. The liquid flowing in the pipe flows on this surface. Thus, it is a logical point of control.

The grade at any point of the sewer is determined by adding to the known grade of a lower point an increase in elevation determined by the horizontal distance from the lower point and the slope of the sewer. For example, if the grade at station $0+00$ is 71.63, the grade at station $0+50$ is 71.63 plus 50×0.014 or 72.33. The work should be tabulated and performed in an orderly way with suitable checks as shown on the *grade sheet* in Fig. 9.2.

The grade or elevation of the sewer is calculated at each station where a stake is to be set. When elevations of stake tops are known, cuts can be computed.

Description	Station	Slope	Invert Grade
MH−1	0+00		71.63
		.0140	.70
	0+50		72.33
		.0140	.70
	1+00		73.03
		.0140	.70
	1+50		73.73
		.0140	.70
	2+00		74.43
		.0140	.56
MH−2	2+40		74.99 out/75.09 in
		.0060	.06
	2+50		75.15
		.0060	.30
	3+00		75.45
		.0060	.30
	3+50		75.75
		.0060	.30
	4+00		76.05
		.0060	.30
	4+50		76.35
		.0060	.30
	5+00		76.65
		.0060	.30
	5+50		76.95
		.0060	.21
MH−3	5+85		77.16

Check

240' @ .0140 = 3.36'
345' @ .0060 = 2.07'
                5.43
      +   .10 M.H. drop
                5.53

71.63
+ 5.53
77.16

Figure 9.2   Grade sheet for sewer of Fig. 9.1

Construction Stakeout

Stakeout should be performed in two stages. First, stakes should be set at correct station and offset as described in Chapter 8. Then, a level circuit should be run with rod shots on all stakes. Stakes may be used as T.P.'s also, but there will be less likelihood of a mistake if a rod shot is recorded for each stake; and when a T.P. is read on a stake, a separate F.S. is recorded in addition to the rod shot for that stake.

Sample field notes are shown in Fig. 9.3. Cuts are computed in the field book. The station number, offset, and cut are then marked on each stake. Offset is marked on the side toward proposed construction, or it is marked right or left, meaning that the construction is right or left of the stake when one is looking forward.

Construction Methods

The traditional method of building a sewer to correct line and slope is to establish a string line at a vertical distance above the proposed sewer and parallel with it. The string line must therefore have the design slope of the sewer. The pipe is laid section by section starting at the lowest end with each section of pipe fitting into the previous one at the joint. The first piece of pipe is checked at both ends with a *grade rod* for proper distance below

STA	BS(+)	H.I.	FS(−)	Rod	Elev.	Fin Gr.	Cut		Date
	Baxter Ave. Sewer, Reed City								Page
BM−1	3.21	81.56			78.35				H. Hill inst.
0+00				4.28	77.28	71.63	5.65	MH−1	A. Bakalar
0+50				4.10	77.46	72.33	5.13		rod.
1+00				3.22	78.34	73.03	5.31		W. Higgins
TP−1	12.01	92.63	0.94		80.62				Chief
1+50				12.90	79.73	73.73	6.00		Wild transit
2+00				11.80	80.83	74.43	6.40		Wild level
2+40				10.85	81.78	74.99 out / 75.09 in	6.0 1 / 6.1 1	MH−2	Rod − 13
2+50				10.78	81.85	75.15	6.70		Tape − 11
3+00				9.71	82.92	75.45	7.47		clear, cool,
3+50				8.63	84.00	75.75	8.25		calm.
4+00				7.55	85.08	76.05	9.03		
4+50				6.51	86.12	76.35	9.77		
TP−2	5.72	91.95	6.40		86.23			MH−2	
5+00				5.82	86.13	76.65	9.48		
5+50				5.33	86.62	76.95	9.67		
5+85				5.36	86.59	77.16	9.43	MH−3	
TP−3	2.90	84.06	10.79		81.16				
BM−1			5.71		78.35				
	+23.84		−23.84						
	check								

MH−3

Sewer / Stakes

All offsets are 10' left of stakes

MH−1

BM − 1 See BM book p.3

Figure 9.3   Field notes for sewer stakeout (see Figs. 9.1 and 9.2)

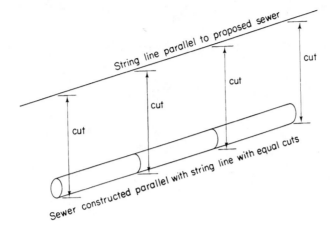

Figure 9.4   Pipe laid with string line as a guide

the string line, and its horizontal alignment is checked with a plumb bob hung from the string line.

The next piece of pipe is joined to the first and is laid so that the opposite end is the correct distance below the string line and on line. See Fig. 9.4 for illustration.

The string line is put into position by building a *batter board* at the correct height above each stake top to obtain a cut of predetermined length to the invert. The length is normally a whole number of ft, and a grade rod is prepared for this length. Each batter board is built over the trench with the top level and at the required elevation. A nail is driven into the top of the batter board at the correct offset to put it on line. A string line stretched from nail to nail is on line at the predetermined height above the sewer invert at all points. See Fig. 9.5 for illustration. See Fig. 9.6 for illustration of a grade rod and how it is used.

When a string line is used, two sections of string at the same line and slope should always be in place as a check against mistakes. They form one continuous straight line if the three batter boards and nails are correctly positioned.

A *manhole* is required at a change of slope or line in a sewer and at certain spacing when there is no change in slope or line. At the center of the manhole, a vertical drop may be needed to permit proper flow. In that case, two cuts are recorded on the construction stake, one for the outgoing sewer and one for the incoming sewer, and the string lines leading downstream and upstream start at different elevations. One-tenth of a ft is a typical drop for small-size sewers.

The string line can be replaced by a transit located on a platform over the center line of a manhole (or on the sewer center line opposite any stake).

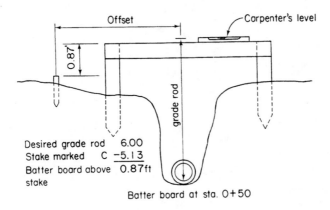

Desired grade rod   6.00
Stake marked   C   -5.13
Batter board above   0.87ft
stake

Batter board at sta. 0+50

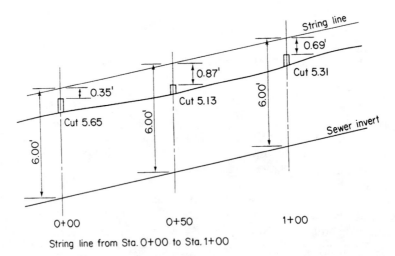

String line from Sta. 0+00 to Sta. 1+00

Figure 9.5 Batter boards and string line for sewer (see Fig. 9.3)

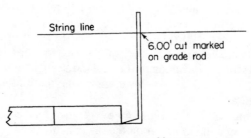

Figure 9.6 Grade rod in use

It is not practical to align the transit for a whole ft cut.   The grade rod must be marked to conform to the position of the transit.   Line can be taken from a plumb line held over the next manhole or over another point on line.   The point on line must be located by offset from the construction stake.

The line of sight can be adjusted to the correct slope by sighting the level rod at the correct reading as shown in Fig. 9.7, or a vertical angle can be calculated from the known slope and the transit set on line at that vertical angle by using a range pole or plumb bob string for line.   The level rod or range pole need not remain in place after the instrument is clamped.   The angle should be recorded when set and checked periodically during construction.

Slope is converted to a vertical angle as follows:

$$\text{tan of angle} = \text{slope}$$

$$\tan \alpha = 0.014$$

$$\alpha = 0°\ 48'$$

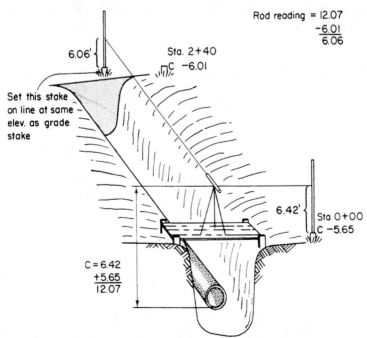

When transit sights 6.06 on new stake, the line of sight is on line and slope 12.07' above proposed invert line. Grade rod should be marked at 12.07'

Figure 9.7   Transit aligned to line and slope

The tan of 0° 48′ is 0.01396 when carried to five decimal places. Since the vertical vernier has a least count of one min, the transit cannot be aimed more accurately. The error in this case is 0.00004 multiplied by the horizontal distance, 0.01 ft at 240 ft. It could be as high as 0.03 ft at 240 ft due to the limited accuracy of the vertical angle. Errors of this size are not significant for ordinary sewer construction.

Use of Laser

Once the transit is aligned, the line of sight can be fixed by a laser beam directed through the transit as described in Chapter 8, and it can be read on the grade rod by the crew installing the pipe.

A laser designed specifically for the purpose is used extensively to control sewer construction. A laser is set up in the trench, usually at a manhole, so that the laser beam provides a center line to guide the pipe installers. See Fig. 9.8.

The trench can be dug with the laser beam used as a guide for line and approximate depth. Pipe is laid using a template that fits inside the pipe. The template has a translucent target at the center through which the light beam can be seen. The template is needed at both ends of the first piece of pipe to place it in position. Each piece after that is fitted to the joint of the previous piece, and the opposite end is aligned with the template and the laser beam. See Figs. 9.9 and 9.10 for illustration of the laser and template.

Using a template results in a sewer built with a straight center line rather than a straight invert, although the difference is negligible. Larger pipes are aligned with the target set at a specified short height above the invert for each piece of pipe.

Two stakes are set at each manhole to control the setting of the laser. The two stakes are 10 and 20 ft from the center of the manhole in line perpendicular to the sewer. The manhole center is established by holding a tape across the two stakes and 10 ft beyond the closer stake. The closer stake has the cut to the pipe invert written on it.

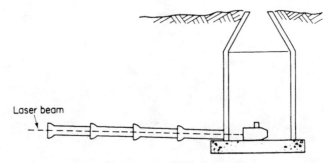

Figure 9.8   Laser positioned in manhole to define center line for pipelaying

Figure 9.9   Laser for construction of sewer lines (*Courtesy of Spectra-Physics*)

Figure 9.10   Template for aligning pipe with laser beam (*Courtesy of Spectra-Physics*)

In order to position the laser from the stake, the trench must be partially dug approximately to grade, using the offset and cut from the stake. The laser may be set up in a manhole or on the trench bottom before the manhole is built. It has a center of rotation similar to that of a transit. This center must be offset the correct distance from the stake and at a distance below the stake so that the sewer invert is at the correct cut. Then one point of the laser beam (at the center of the laser) will be on the design center line.

The correct offset distance is determined as described in Fig. 8.2. The correct elevation is determined as shown in Fig. 9.11. A predetermined rod shot is taken on the laser top, which is at a fixed distance above the laser beam. The laser must be adjusted in elevation until the correct rod reading is obtained. The fixed distance from top to laser beam, called the *laser constant*, is stamped on the laser or listed in the manufacturer's manual.

The laser beam is then adjusted to line. The trench must be extended about 20 ft beyond the device for this. A transit is set up on the manhole centered over the laser device. The transit telescope is aligned by reading the offset distance on a tape from the stake at the next manhole. The laser

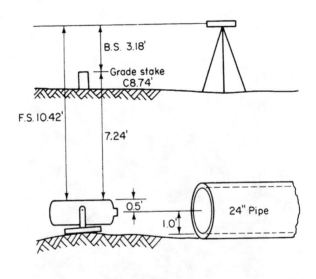

```
 8.74' cut to invert
-1.00' half pipe diameter
─────
 7.74' cut to laser beam
-0.50' fixed dist. top to beam
─────
 7.24' cut to top of laser
+3.18' B.S. on grade stake
─────
10.42' rod shot on top of laser
```

Figure 9.11 Determining rod shot to set up laser

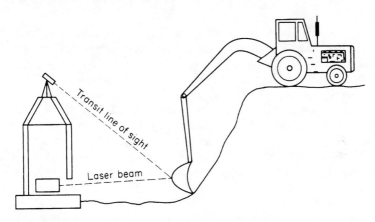

Figure 9.12   Putting the laser beam on line

beam is rotated horizontally until it matches the transit cross hairs on line on a smooth surface, such as the backhoe in Fig. 9.12.

If the manhole is not yet in place, the transit is set up over the stake and sighted on the next stake. The laser beam is aligned by aiming it at a plumb bob string suspended from a level tape at the offset distance from the transit line of sight.

The laser beam is then set to the design slope of the sewer. The beam is rotated in a vertical angle until the indicator shows that the design slope has been reached. The beam then defines the center line of the sewer as it should be built.

9.3 ROADWAYS AND TRACKS

Highways, streets, and tracks for vehicles must be built at design slopes. The shape of the ground precludes building them level, yet economy of vehicle operation dictates that slopes not be too steep. Excavating earth and building earth embankments are both expensive and are kept to a minimum when designing. Also, an effort is made to economize by matching embankment size with quantity of excavation. All these factors are involved in the decision to build at the design slope. Pavement construction is not highly accurate compared with buildings or even sewers. Nevertheless, stakes should be set and marked to one-hundredth of a ft, and precautions should be taken to avoid an accumulation of errors. Tracks must be more accurately controlled than pavement slope because the movement of the vehicles using tracks is completely controlled by the slopes and alignments of the tracks.

Surveyor's stakes are needed at 25-, 50- or 100-ft intervals, and in a few cases, the actual work can be guided by laser beam with stakes farther apart.

Grade sheet computations are the same as for sewer work. Stakes are set on the center line for highway pavement and at offsets of 2 ft to 4 ft outside the construction for streets and tracks.

For streets, the top of the curb is the reference grade, and stakes are driven by the paving crew at the correct offset and a string line stretched from stake to stake so that it duplicates the line and slope of the back of the proposed curb. A line of surveyor's stakes is often required for each curb because grade is not always the same on both sides of the street.

If the curb is to be of concrete, a long form is installed with its top edge duplicating the string line, and the concrete is placed into this form. If stone curb is to be installed, each piece is placed with its back edge touching the string line along its length. Usually, both curbs are built first, and pavement between curbs is built at the correct distance below the tops of curbs.

Track construction includes several steps. *Ballast*, consisting of crushed stone or similar material, is placed and compacted to an elevation so that wood or concrete ties can be placed on the ballast and rails attached to the ties with the top of rail approximately at correct grade.

Stakes for track construction are usually provided at finished grade. The rails are aligned by pushing long steel bars into the ground next to the rails and forcing the rails transversely; the rails are lowered or raised by removing or adding ballast under the ties until the rails are at line and grade as determined from the surveyor's stakes with a rule and carpenter's level. The rails are aligned between stakes by eye or with a string line stretched at the edge of the rail.

Tracks are also built by track-laying machines that lay rails and spike them in place at finished grade while being guided by a line at grade and at a predetermined offset. The line is of cord or wire stretched from one surveyor's stake to the next. The stakes may be required at 10-ft spacing for accurate alignment of high-speed tracks. Only one line of stakes is needed to control a pair of rails.

A variety of methods may be used to transfer line and grade from construction stakes for highway paving.

Bituminous concrete is placed by paving machines that place a continuous strip of pavement while following a line placed to define the edge of pavement or else at grade 1- or 2-ft off line. The machine follows the line with a sensor device that controls the paving to conform to the line. The line is ⌐ cord or wire stretched between the surveyor's stakes 10 ft apart. One control line is sufficient for pavements up to 30 ft wide. If bituminous curbs are built, they are constructed on top of the pavement edge after paving.

Portland cement concrete pavement is placed in forms similar to street paving but without curbs and requires one line of construction stakes at 50- or 100-ft spacing on straight sections and two lines at 25- or 50-ft spacing on curves. Center line grade is the reference grade for one line of stakes, and pavement edges are referenced when two lines are staked. Grade is transferred up to 20 or 30 ft by line level from construction stakes. Portland cement concrete is also placed by a method called *slip forming*, which is similar to bituminous concrete paving and is staked out in the same way.

9.4 EARTHWORK STAKEOUT

Before construction stakes are set for paving or laying track, the earth must usually be rearranged, sometimes to great depths in *cuts* or *excavations* or to great heights in *fills* or *embankments*. Stakes set to control the earthwork must be set at the extremities of the proposed excavation or embankment area.

The customary method is to stake the center line of the improvement at 50- or 100-ft intervals and at points where the earthwork final grade coincides with the existing grade. The designer's profile drawing shows where these points are. These points are the transition points between cut and fill and are important to the builder's operation. Stakes called *slope stakes* are set opposite the center-line stakes at the edge of the proposed embankment or excavation.

The finished sides of the embankment or excavation are called *side slopes*. These slopes are much steeper than the longitudinal center line slopes. They are designated by the tangent of the angle between the slope and a horizontal line and are expressed as a ratio. Typical side slopes are from 1 on 1 to 1 on 3. The vertical distance is always 1.

The horizontal distance from the center line to the edge of the earthwork, whether in cut or fill, depends on the width of the final surface, on the slope of the sides of the earthwork, and on the difference between elevation of the original ground at the limit of the earthwork and the final grade of the earthwork. The finished earthwork surface, whether in cut or fill, is called finished *base* because it is the base for pavement or tracks. See Fig. 9.13 for the relationships among these factors. Note that the total width of earthwork is related to the distance between the finished base and original ground at the earthwork limits, not under the finished base.

The distance from the center line to the edge of the earthwork is equal to one-half the width of the finished base plus the horizontal component of the side slope. The trick is to locate the point at which the side slope of the proposed earthwork will intersect the original ground. This is where the slope stake is driven. Fortunately, it does not have to be located with great accuracy and is measured only to the nearest one-tenth of a ft.

Stakeout requires two steps. Center-line stakes are set first using the preliminary survey traverse as a base for their location. The connecting traverse in Chapter 6 is an example of the type of preliminary traverse that is used to establish the line for the stakeout. A cross-section leveling circuit

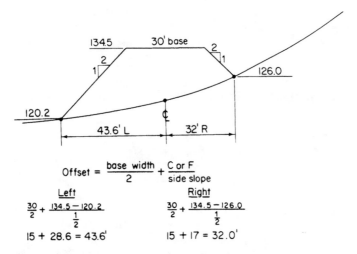

Figure 9.13   Relationships: base width, fill, side slopes, slope stake offsets

is then run to set slope stakes and also to obtain offsets and elevations needed to plot ground cross sections.

The design drawings show the relationship between the traverse and proposed center line. They also show finished grades at 50- or 100-ft intervals. Finished grade is top of rail or top of pavement, and top of earth base is a constant distance below that. This distance is shown on the track or pavement cross section that is part of the design drawings.

Center-line stakes will be lost because of earthmoving operations. The only practical place to mark cuts and fills is on stakes outside the embankment or excavation area. Slope stakes are marked with cut or fill computed from the ground adjacent to the stake. Cuts or fills for slope stakes are figured the same way as other cuts or fills except that they are measured to the tenth of a ft from the ground surface, not to the hundredth from the stake top.

It is convenient to compute the cuts and fills from rod readings without converting to elevations. With an H.I. determined from a B.M., the B.S. reading that would be read on a level rod if it could be held on the finished grade of the earthwork is computed. This figure is called the *grade rod.* Because the grade rod is the distance from H.I. to finished grade and the ground rod is the distance from H.I. to the existing grade, if both are below the H.I., the difference between them is the difference in elevation between existing surface and finished surface. This is either cut or fill. If grade rod is above the H.I., the difference between existing grade and finished grade is the sum of grade rod and ground rod. Ground rod is always below the H.I.

The grade rod is considered plus if the final grade is below the H.I. and minus if the final grade is above the H.I.; the ground rod is always considered minus. These signs are logical if the grade rod is considered a backsight and the ground rod a foresight. A foresight has a minus sign, and a backsight has a plus sign unless it is taken on a point above the H.I.

A simple method of computing cut or fill is to add ground rod and grade rod algebraically. If grade rod is plus, the sum of grade rod and ground rod may be either plus or minus depending on whether grade rod or ground rod is larger. A plus value indicates that finished grade is below existing grade and that the change in grade is a cut. A minus value indicates that finished grade is above existing grade and that the change in grade is a fill. If grade rod is minus, the sum of grade rod and ground rod is minus, and the change in grade is a fill. Computing the grade rod is illustrated in Fig. 9.14. Computing cut and fill is illustrated in Fig. 9.15.

The zero end of a tape is held over the center-line stake, the rod person walks at a right angle to the center line with the rod and other end of the tape to the point where it is judged that the embankment or excavation will meet the existing ground, and a rod shot is taken there. At the correct point,

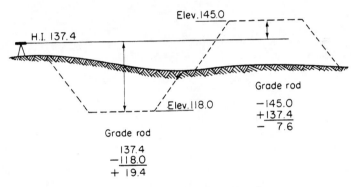

Figure 9.14   Computing grade rod

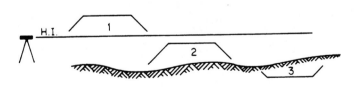

	1	2	3
Grade rod	− 3.4	+ 2.6	+ 13.7
Ground rod	− 8.2	− 8.2	− 8.2
Cut or fill	− 11.6 fill	− 5.6 fill	+ 5.5 cut

Figure 9.15   Computing cut and fill

the horizontal distance read on the tape will equal one-half the base width plus the cut or fill divided by the side slope. The relationship is illustrated in Fig. 9.16.

The rod person must compute mentally and adjust position until the rod is at the point where the horizontal distance and ground elevation satisfy the relationship expressed by the formula:

Distance = one-half the base width + (C or F) ÷ side slope

Mental arithmetic for the first trial and for two adjustments to locate one of the offsets in Fig. 9.13 is as follows:

Base width is 40 ft, and side slope is 1 on 2.

Try 35':

$$35' \neq 20 + (7.6 - 1.7)2$$

$$35' \neq 31.8'$$

Try 28':

$$28' \neq 20 + (7.6 - 3.2)2$$

$$28' \neq 28.8'$$

Try 29.2':

$$29.2' = 20 + (7.6 - 3.0)2$$

$$29.2' = 29.2'$$

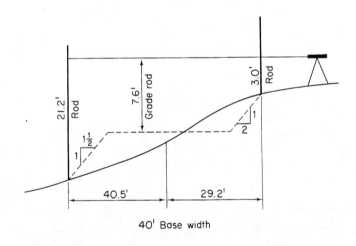

40' Base width

$$40.5 = 20 + (21.2 - 7.6)1\tfrac{1}{2}$$
$$40.5 = 40.4 \text{ O.K.}$$

$$29.2 = 20 + (7.6 - 3.0)2$$
$$29.2 = 29.2 \text{ O.K.}$$

Figure 9.16 Computing distance to edge of cut and fill

The mental calculations are actually easier with a little practice than they appear to be in print.   The rod person's performance is the key to a successful operation.   The party chief often handles this job.

Notes are usually started at the bottom of the page and continue up so that the notes and sketch coincide with the field locations while proceeding forward.   The note keeper is less likely to confuse right and left when using this procedure.   Figure 9.17 shows typical notes.   Rod shots are written over the line, and distance from the center line is written under the line.   Additional shots are taken at breaks in the ground surface as in the sample cross-section notes in Chapter 4.   It is understood that the farthest shot represents

Sta.	B.S.(+)	H.I.	F.S.(−)	elev.	Fin. grade	Grade rod	Left	℄	Right	Date
Morgan St. Expressway, Williamstown, Cross Sections.										p.53
			Base width 80' / side slopes 1:3				Level #38721 / Rod #5 / Cloth tape / Cool, breezy			𝛌 J.H. / ♦ A.H. / ▭ W.B. / Tape W.H.
BM−2			4.76	135.27			C8.2		C6.2	
3+00				128.30	+11.7		3.5 / 65.0	4.6	5.5 / 58.0	
2+50				127.80	+12.2		C9.1 / 3.1 / 67.0	5.0 / 20.1 5.1	C6.6 / 5.6 / 59.8	
2+00				127.30	+12.7		C10.5 / 2.2 / 71.5	4.0 / 21.0 4.6	C6.5 / 6.2 / 49.5	
TP−1	9.42	140.03	1.21	130.61						
1+50				126.80	+5.0		C3.4 / 1.6 / 50.0	3.8	F1.0 / 6.0 / 43.0	
1+00				126.30	+5.5		C5.1 / 0.4 / 55.0	4.6 8.0 / 37.2	F1.8 / 7.3 / 43.0	
0+50				125.80	+6.0		C4.5 / 1.5 / 53.5	5.3 8.8 / 38.0	F3.0 / 9.0 / 49.0	
0+00				125.30	+6.5		C5.1 / 1.4 / 55.0	6.9 / 10.4 7.5 8.7 / 36.2	F2.4 / 8.9 / 47.5	
BM−1	3.48	131.82		128.34				℄ Grove Ave.		

(Right margin: ℄ Morgan St.; 500' 0+00)

Note: Cut and fill are computed in the field and marked on the grade stakes.
Elevations are computed and original cross sections plotted in the office.

Figure 9.17   Field notes for grade stakes

the limit of earthwork. A slope stake is driven there on a slant to differentiate it from the center-line stakes, and it is marked with cut or fill and station. The notes provide the data necessary to plot a cross section of the original surface that is used to compute the quantity of earthwork.

9.5 EARTH VOLUME

The cross sections of original ground plotted to scale are known as *original cross sections*. These are kept until earthwork is complete. Field data are then obtained to plot *final cross sections* at the same stations. These are plotted with the original cross sections, and together they show the upper and lower boundaries of the earth volume that was placed or removed at that cross section. Thus, the cross-sectional area of the earthwork is plotted to scale at each station.

In most cases, the volume of earthwork between stations is a *prismoid* (nearly a prism) with two ends parallel and the sides defined by lines that are approximately straight. The volume between cross sections is approximately equal to the average of the two end areas multiplied by the distance between them. This approximation is called the *average end area method* and is accurate enough to be the most common way of determining volume of earthwork for payment to a builder who is being paid by the cubic yard.

The *prismoidal formula* gives more accurate results but requires a cross section midway between the two end areas. Thus, more office time is spent on calculations, and the added accuracy is usually not justified since field accuracy is not high and the price of earthwork is not high compared with other construction items. The prismoidal formula is:

$$V = \frac{(A_0 + 4M + A_1)}{6} \times L$$

where A_0 and A_1 are the two end areas, M is the area at the middle, and L is the total length. The size of the middle area is determined by averaging the lengths of all sides of the two end areas, no matter what their shape, as long as they have the same number of sides. The result is an area of similar shape. Its area is not the average of the two end areas. All data are in ft so that the answer is in cubic ft. To obtain cubic yards, the usual unit for earthwork, the answer is divided by 27.

The necessary areas may be determined in various ways. If the cross sections are rather simple, they can be divided into rectangles, trapezoids, and triangles, and the areas can be determined mathematically. The areas can be plotted on coordinate paper, the squares counted, and the total number of squares multiplied by the area of one square. The areas can be determined with a *planimeter*, which is a device for measuring irregular areas. The outline of the area is traced, and the planimeter indicates the area in square in. This area is then converted to square ft according to the scale of the cross section. Calculations are illustrated in Fig. 9.18.

The first and last volume sections of an embankment or excavation have one end with an area of zero at the locations where the earthwork meets original ground. Earthwork may begin or come to an end by gradually merging with the original ground, but often the end of embankment is the start of excavation or vice versa. In either situation, the earthwork coincides with the original ground at a line as illustrated in Fig. 9.19.

Special staking procedures are required. The line where finished grade coincides with original ground must be located. This line of transition does

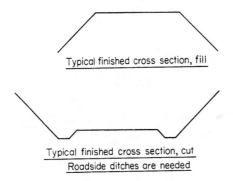

Typical finished cross section, fill

Typical finished cross section, cut
Roadside ditches are needed

If cross section areas are determined by planimeter it is necessary to plot final cross sections superimposed on original cross sections. It is helpful to do this no matter what method is used to determine areas. Either final cross sections are plotted from field leveling data or templates of the various specified final cross sections are prepared and the appropriate one is traced onto the original cross section at the correct distance above or below it.

Sta.	Area sq. in.	Area sq. ft.	Calculation	Volume, C.Y.
0+00	34.3	3430		
			$\frac{3430 + 4140}{2} \times \frac{50}{27}$	7010
0+50	41.4	4140		
			$\frac{4140 + 5650}{2} \times \frac{50}{27}$	9060
1+00	56.5	5650		
			$\frac{5650 + 4820}{2} \times \frac{50}{27}$	9700
1+50	48.2	4820		
			$\frac{4820 + 3970}{2} \times \frac{50}{27}$	8140
2+00	39.7	3970		
			Total	33,910 C.Y.

Figure 9.18   Determination of earth volume

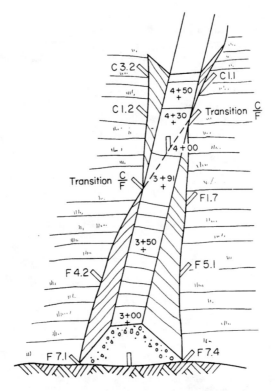

Figure 9.19 Earthwork showing transition from fill to cut

Sta.	Area		Calculation		Volume C.Y.	
	Cut	Fill	Cut	Fill	Cut	Fill
3+00		1260				
				$\frac{1260+1040}{2} \times \frac{50}{27}$		2130
3+50		1040				
				$\frac{1040+160}{2} \times \frac{41}{27}$		910
3+91 Transition.	0	160				
Pyramid	3+91‑4+30			$160 \times \frac{39}{3} \times \frac{1}{27}$		80
4+00	not	used				
Pyramid	3+91‑4+30		$140 \times \frac{39}{3} \times \frac{1}{27}$		70	
4+30 Transition	140	0				
			$\frac{140+360}{2} \times \frac{20}{27}$		190	
4+50	360					

Figure 9.20 Earth volume at transition between cut and fill (see Figure 9.19)

not occur at a station nor is it perpendicular to the axis of the earthwork. Its center is staked as part of the center-line stakeout. Its ends are located at an offset on either side of the center line of one-half the base width. All 3 points are located by successive trials with a level rod until the rod shot is the same as the grade rod. At these points, the final base grade coincides with the grade of the existing ground. Slope stakes are set at the outer points, and together with the center-line stake they define the transition line.

The volume of an end section can be determined by treating it as a wedge or pyramid, or a combination of the two, whichever most nearly approximates its shape. A wedge and a pyramid have one end with zero area. The volume of a wedge equals half the one end area multiplied by the length. The volume of a pyramid equals one-third of the one end area multiplied by the length. See Fig. 9.20 for illustration.

PROBLEMS

1. A line slopes uphill at 3.1% from station 0 + 00 at elevation 123.57. What is the elevation of the line at station 3 + 62?

2. A line slopes downhill at 2.7% from station 7 + 50 at elevation 2340.17. What is the elevation of the line at station 9 + 23?

3. Station 14 + 31.62 has an elevation of 42.16, and station 17 + 18.29 has an elevation of 49.73. What is the slope?

4. Station 0 − 86.14 has an elevation of 596.42, and station 2 + 17.86 has an elevation of 604.91. What is the slope?

5. What is the horizontal distance for a rise of 4 ft at a slope of 3.74%?

6. What is the horizontal distance for a rise of 1.79 ft at a slope of 0.0076?

7. Prepare a grade sheet at 50-ft intervals for a sewer line with a slope of 1.2% from station 0 + 00 to station 1 + 40 and 1.6% from station 1 + 40 to station 2 + 00. Station 0 + 00 has an elevation of 321.06.

8. Prepare a grade sheet at 50-ft intervals for a gravity pipeline from station 0 + 00 with elevation 119.24 to station 2 + 71 with elevation 121.05.

9. A stake is marked C−2′−8½″. How far above or below the stake should a batter board be built for a 5-ft grade rod?

10. A stake is marked C−7′−5″. How far above or below the stake should a batter board be built for a 6-ft grade rod?

11. A laser with a laser constant of 0.59 is to be set for the center line of a 15-in. pipe from a stake marked C−6.32 ft. A backsight of 3.04 is read on the stake. What rod reading is needed?

12. A laser with a laser constant of 0.50 is to be set 6 in. above the invert of a 30-in. pipe from a stake marked C−5.93. A backsight of 4.52 is read on the stake. What rod reading is needed?

13. A laser with a laser constant of 0.65 is to be set 8 in. below the inside top of a 36-in. pipe from a stake marked C−8.17 ft. A backsight of 3.72 is read on the stake. What rod reading is needed?

14. A pipeline is to be constructed at a constant slope. A transit over station 0 + 00 is 5.19 ft above a stake marked C–6.46. A stake at 2 + 00 is marked C–7.93. In order to align the transit line of sight parallel to the proposed pipeline, a level rod is held on the stake at station 2 + 00. What will the rod reading be when the transit is properly aligned?

15. In order to set the line of sight parallel to a pipeline with a slope of 3.3%, what vertical angle should be used.

16. Find the volume of earth fill in cubic yards between stations 2 + 00 and 3 + 00 by average end area method.

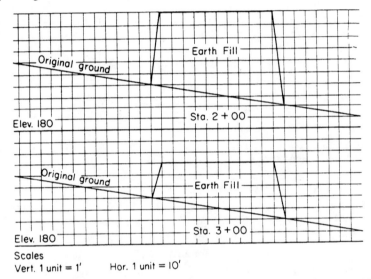

17. A pipeline is to be constructed with a slope of 2%. A transit is set up 4.72 ft above a stake marked C–9.13. What verticle angle should be set into the transit to align it parallel to the pipeline and what will the grade rod be when using the transit line of sight?

18. Find the volume of earth fill in cubic yards by average end area method between stations 113 and 114 if the embankment has a 30-ft base width and side slopes of 1 on 1½. Cross-section grade stake notes are given. See field notes in Fig. 9.17. Assume original ground has constant slope.

Sta.	L		R	grade rod
113	F6.2	F3.3	F1.8	+3.0
	9.2		4.8	
	24.3		17.7	
114	F7.8	F6.1	F3.4	+5.6
	13.4		9.0	
	26.7		20.1	

10

CONSTRUCTION CURVES

INSTRUCTIONAL OBJECTIVES

1. *Given the angle of intersection between two streets, pavement width, curb radius, and offset distance, the student should be able to determine the necessary angles and distances to set stakes at the centers of the curb arcs and on the radii to the P.C. and P.T.*

2. *Given the radius, angle of intersection, desired spacing of stakes on the curve, and station of P.I., the student should be able to determine deflection angles and distances for staking a circular curve either with stakes at equal spaces or with stakes at specified stations. Distances should be calculated for taping from the P.C. and for taping between adjacent stakes.*

3. *Given the slopes of the two tangents, the station and elevation of the PVI, and length of curve, the student should be able to determine elevations on a vertical curve at designated stations.*

Curves are often required in construction. The simplest curve used is an arc of a circle, and its most frequent use is in pavement construction where a curve is preferable to an angular change of direction. A curve is a necessity for safety on high-speed highways and is also used for changes in direction on low-speed streets because of its more pleasing appearance. A curve is designed for the speed at which it will be used and must, therefore, be constructed accurately. Vehicles at high speeds and vehicles riding on rails at any speed require transition curves so that they can gradually ease from straight-line travel to a circular curve and from the curve to the new straight-line direction. Only circular curves are covered in this book.

10.1 CIRCULAR CURVE GEOMETRY

The center line of a vehicular route is designed with bearings and distances between angle points. A change in direction is measured by deflection angle designated *I* and is called the *angle of intersection*. When dividing a tract of land into streets and building lots, instead of the center line, the boundaries of the streets, called *right-of-way lines*, are designed with bearings, distances, and angle points. Arcs of circular curves are placed at the angle points as illustrated in Fig. 10.1. Each curve is tangent to the two straight lines. The straight-line segments between curves are called *tangents*. When proceeding forward, the point at which a curve starts is a *point of curvature* (P.C.), and the point at which the next tangent starts is a *point of tangency* (P.T.).

Because the curve is part of a circle, radii at the P.C. and P.T. are perpendicular to the tangents and intersect at the center of the circle. Construction of these two radii illustrates some relationships shown in Fig. 10.2.

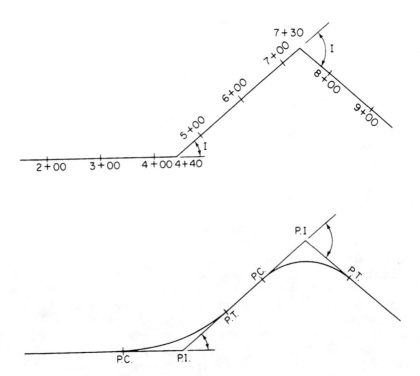

Figure 10.1 Route with curves

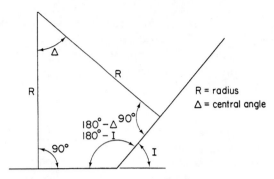

a. Relationship's showing Δ and I are equal.

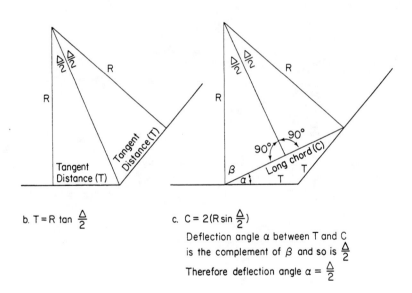

b. $T = R \tan \dfrac{\Delta}{2}$

c. $C = 2(R \sin \dfrac{\Delta}{2})$

Deflection angle α between T and C
is the complement of β and so is $\dfrac{\Delta}{2}$

Therefore deflection angle $\alpha = \dfrac{\Delta}{2}$

Figure 10.2   Circular curve relationships

10.2 CIRCULAR CURVE STAKEOUT

The radius is selected by the designer, and other relationships are determined from it so that the curve can be staked out.   The station of the point of intersection (P.I.) and the angle I are also fixed by the designer.   The rest of this chapter deals with street and highway pavement. However, the computations and stakeout procedures for circular curves are useful for staking right-of-way lines on curves, and the principles apply to railroad track curves, although the method used for them is different.

Street Curb

An example of a circular curve on a vehicular route is the curved curb, called a *curb return* or *radius curb*, at the intersection of two streets. The curb return is built on a circular arc of short radius to facilitate traffic movement around the corner. The radius of the curb depends on the speed and volume of traffic. A longer radius provides easier traffic movement but is more costly; therefore it is not used unless volume and speed of traffic justify the cost.

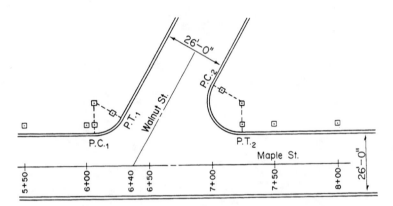

Requirements:
  Place stakes at 50ft intervals P.C. and P.T. with 5ft offsets and at center of curves for Maple St. curbs.

Procedure:
  1. Set up on offset line and set stakes up to P.C.$_1$
  2. Set up on P.C.$_1$ stake, back sight on offset line, turn $90°$ and set center stake at distance R − offset, turn to deflection angle and set P.T.$_1$ stake at chord distance (based on R − offset), turn $180°$ and set P.T.$_2$ stake.
  3. Set up on P.T.$_2$ stake, backsight on offset line and set stakes similarly to step 2.

Calculations:
  Given: Station at intersection of Maple $\mathcal{C}$ and Walnut $\mathcal{C}$.
  Find: Station of P.C.$_1$
  Method: Distance back from $\mathcal{C}$ intersection to P.C.$_1$ is "T" of a curve of radius equal to the curb radius plus half the street width. See following example.

Figure 10.3 Stakeout for radius curb

The designer of the street intersection selects a radius length for the curb returns. The method of stakeout and the required computations are the surveyor's responsibility. The builder usually requires offset stakes at 25- or 50-ft intervals for curbs of both streets plus an additional stake at each end of the curve. Another stake is set at the center of the circle so that the builder can swing a radius from this stake with a tape to guide construction of the radius curb. Finished grade is commonly a straight slope from P.C. to P.T. and is determined by the builder. See Fig. 10.3 for illustration.

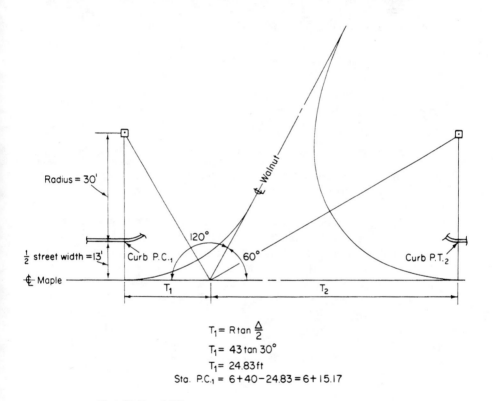

$$T_1 = R \tan \frac{\Delta}{2}$$
$$T_1 = 43 \tan 30°$$
$$T_1 = 24.83 \, \text{ft}$$
$$\text{Sta. P.C.}_1 = 6+40-24.83 = 6+15.17$$

Find: Station of P.T.$_2$
Method: Distance ahead from ℄ intersection to P.T.$_2$ is "T" of a curve with the same radius and a central angle which is the complement of the previous central angle.

$$T_2 = R \tan \frac{\Delta}{2}$$
$$T_2 = 43 \tan 60°$$
$$T = 74.48 \, \text{ft}$$
$$\text{Sta. P.T.}_2 = 6+40+74.48 = 7+14.48$$

Figure 10.3 (Cont.)

Highway Pavement

A survey party staking out highway pavement usually proceeds forward along the center-line setting stakes at 50- or 100-ft intervals and sets a stake at the P.C. The station of the P.C. is determined by subtracting the tangent distance (T) from the station of the P.I.

With the transit at the P.C. and with a backsight on line to the rear, the telescope can be plunged and the P.I. staked. Then, the deflection angle $\frac{\Delta}{2}$ can be laid off, and the P.T. can be located on line at the *long chord* distance (C). The transit can then be set up on the P.T., and a backsight can be taken on the P.I. Plunging the telescope aligns the transit on the next tangent.

The station of the P.T. is determined by adding the length of the curve (L) to the station of the P.C. Length of curve is determined by proportion. The curve is a part of a complete circle, and its length is proportional to its central angle. A complete circle has a central angle of 360° and a length of $2\pi R$. Therefore, the length of a circular curve is $\frac{\Delta}{360} \times 2\pi R$. Stationing on circular curves of railroad tracks is determined by laying off 100-ft chords. The highway and street practice of stationing by curve length is covered in this chapter.

Stakes are set on a curve by setting the transit at the P.C. and positioning stakes by deflection angle and distance from the P.C. In order to set stakes at intermediate points, the curve may be considered to be divided by the stakes into a number of arcs. Each arc from P.C. to stake has a central angle that determines the deflection angle and chord distance to set that stake. Formulas for locating the P.T. as given in Fig. 10.2c apply to the whole curve or any part of the curve.

For example, the partial curve to the midpoint of a full curve has a central angle one-half the size of the central angle of the full curve. The deflection angle is therefore one-half the deflection angle for the full curve or $\frac{\Delta}{4}$, and the length of the chord to that point is $2\left(R \sin \frac{\Delta}{4} \right)$. See Fig. 10.4 for illustration.

Sample calculations are shown in Fig. 10.5 for a case in which stakes are desired on the curve at spacing no greater than 25 ft. The length of curve is determined and divided into the minimum number of equal parts necessary to make the spacing less than 25 ft. The chord from the transit at the P.C. to each stake is computed in Fig. 10.5. All stakes can thus be set with one end of the tape held at the P.C.

The chord from any stake to an adjacent stake is equal to the chord from the P.C. to stake #1 because the curve lengths between stakes are equal. The curve can thus be staked out by taping a distance equal to the first chord

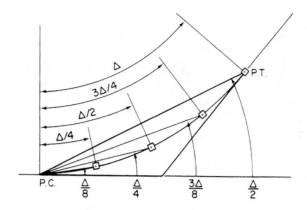

Figure 10.4 Deflection angles to intermediate points on a curve

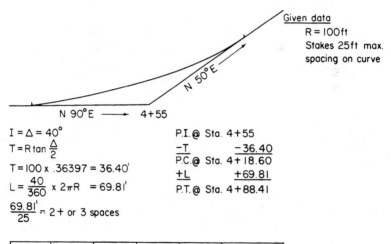

Figure 10.5 Computations for curve stakeout—equal short chords

length from each stake to the succeeding stake.   Angles are still turned from the P.C.

The P.T. must be accurately located because it is the point from which the next tangent starts.   It may be located by the long chord from the P.C., by a succession of short chords from the P.C., or by setting up the transit at the P.I. and measuring from the P.I.   The method requiring fewest tape measurements is the most accurate, but obstacles may sometimes prevent using that method.

A circular curve by its construction is symmetrical about a line connecting its center with the P.I. Therefore, the curve in Fig. 10.4 or 10.5 could be staked out from either the P.C. or P.T. with the same angles and distances. To put the transit on line in the direction of the forward tangent, it can be set up on the P.T., backsighted on the P.C., the deflection angle $\frac{\Delta}{2}$ turned, and the scope plunged to the forward tangent. Therefore, it is not necessary to set the P.I. in order to stake the forward tangent. The forward tangent is staked at the first station beyond the P.T., and then stakes are set at regular intervals on the tangent.

Deflection angles and chords can be computed to set stakes from any stake on the curve. The transit can be set up over any stake, and a B.S. can be taken on any other stake to set additional stakes. See Fig. 10.6 for illustration. The deflection angle from P.C. to 1 is turned to the left to put the transit on line tangent to the curve, the scope is plunged, the deflection angle from 1 to 2 is laid off to the left, and the stake is set at the subchord distance. The entire angle can be laid off in one step either before or after plunging instead of turning the deflection angles separately.

In most cases, the curve that is to be staked out is designed on a slope. The stakes must be marked with cuts and fills and must therefore be located at points where the finished grade is known. It is customary to compute finished grades at 25- or 50-ft intervals on a curve and to set a stake at each of these points.

If the curve in Fig. 10.5 is to have stakes set at 25-ft intervals, the first stake beyond the P.C. is at station 4 + 25. The tangent distance, length of curve, and P.C. station are computed in the same way as in Fig. 10.5. Necessary calculations for setting stakes at 25-ft intervals are shown in Fig. 10.7. The central angle of the subchord from the P.C. to station 4 + 25 is proportional to the length of curve that subtends it. This applies to the central angle of any chord. Central angles are computed by proportion, and chords are computed from the angles.

It is usually advantageous to turn angles from the P.C. and to tape from stake to stake instead of taping all chords from the P.C. The subchords necessary to do this can be calculated as follows:

$$C = 2R \sin \frac{\Delta}{2}$$

From station 4 + 25 to station 4 + 50, $\Delta = 17°59' - 3°40'$ (see Fig. 10.7):

$$\Delta = 14°19' \quad \text{and} \quad \frac{\Delta}{2} = 7°09'30''$$

$$C = 200 \sin \quad 7°09'30'' = 24.92 \text{ ft}$$

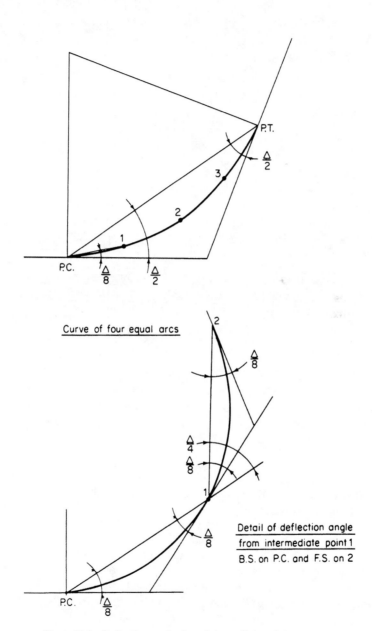

Figure 10.6   Deflection angles from intermediate point on a curve

Given: $I = \Delta = 40°$
        $T\quad = 36.40'$
        $L\quad = 69.81'$
       P.I. sta. $= 4+55$
       P.C. sta. $= 4+18.60$
       P.T. sta. $= 4+88.41$

Curve length from sta $4 + 18.60$ to $4 + 25 = 6.40$

Central angles

P.C. $-$ sta. $4+25$ $\dfrac{6.40}{69.81} \times 40° = 3° - 40'$

P.C. $-$ sta. $4+50$ $\dfrac{6.40+25}{69.81} \times 40° = 17° - 59'$

P.C. $-$ sta. $4+75$ $\dfrac{6.40+50}{69.81} \times 40° = 32° - 18'$

P.C. $-$ P.T. $= 40°$

Stake	Δ	$\Delta/2$	sin	2R	$C = 2R \sin \Delta/2$
4+25	3°−40′	1°−50′	.03199	200	6.40′
4+50	17°−59′	8°−59−30″	.15629	200	31.26′
4+75	32°−18′	16°−09′	.27829	200	55.66′
4+88.41	40°	20°	.34202	200	68.40′

Figure 10.7 Calculation of subchords

C from station $4 + 50$ to station $4 + 75$ is the same.
From station $4 + 75$ to P.T., $\Delta = 40° - 32°18'$ (see Fig. 10.7):

$$\Delta = 7°42' \quad \text{and} \quad \frac{\Delta}{2} = 3°51'$$

$$C\ 200 \sin 3°51' = 13.43 \text{ ft}$$

From these calculations and Fig. 10.7, deflection angles and chord lengths can be obtained between any two stakes on the curve. The deflection angle is the same from either end of any chord. With the transit at any stake and with a backsight on any other stake, turning the deflection angle for that chord puts the transit on line on the tangent to the curve. The scope can then be plunged, and the deflection angle for the new stake can be laid off.

This can be done in one step by backsighting the appropriate stake, turning an angle equal to the sum of the two deflection angles, and plunging the scope. It is then on line to set the new stake. See Fig. 10.8 for illustration.

The total deflection angle to be turned is one-half the central angle between B.S. and F.S. no matter what point the instrument is on and no matter how many points there are between B.S. and F.S. It is also the

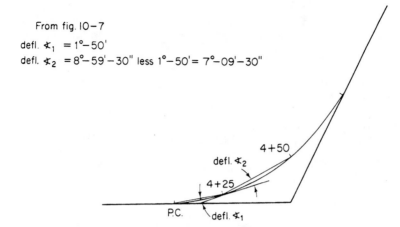

From fig. 10-7

defl. $\measuredangle_1$ = 1°-50'

defl. $\measuredangle_2$ = 8°-59'-30" less 1°-50'= 7°-09'-30"

To set a stake at 4 + 50 with the instrument at 4 + 25, backsight P.C., turn 8° 59' 30" (1° 50' plus 7°09' 30") to left, plunge scope and set stake on line at the subchord distance.

Rule: With instrument at any point on the curve, the sum of deflection angles to set a point with another point as a B.S. is one half the central angle between the B.S. point and the F.S. point.

Figure 10.8   Deflection angle from one intermediate point to another

difference between the deflection angle from P.C. to B.S. and the deflection angle from P.C. to F.S.

Field notes arranged so that the transit can be set up at any stake are shown in Fig. 10.9.   Notes should be set up before going into the field.   They provide information so that the curve can be staked even if it is impossible to sight all points from the P.C.   The instrument can then be moved to a convenient point to continue the stakeout.

The radius of the curve of stakes is not necessarily the design radius. The design radius is normally to the center line of pavement or the right-of-

P.C.4+18.60	defl. $\measuredangle$	subchord
	1°- 50'	6.40'
+ 25	1°- 50'	6.40'
	7°-09'-30"	24.92'
+ 50	8°-59'-30"	31.26'
	7°-09'-30"	24.92'
+ 75	16°-09'	55.66'
	3°-51'	13.43'
P.T. 4+88.41	20°-00'	68.40'

Figure 10.9   Field note arrangement, deflection angles, and subchords

To set offset stakes for a curve

1. Determine deflection angles on the design curve. Deflection angles are the same for all curves having a common Δ. Therefore deflection angles can be calculated on the design curve. It is convenient to do so because the design length has already been determined for stationing and the length for any other radius would have to be calculated. Using only the design curve helps eliminate mistakes caused by working with several curves.

2. Determine short chord lengths to set stakes for a curve of the desired radius.

Given: The curve of Fig. 10–7 as the center line of a 24-ft pavement.
Required: Stakeout on both sides at stations and 25-ft intervals.

From Fig. 10 – 7			Stakes at inside edge		Stakes at outside edge	
sta	Δ/2	sin	2R	c= 2R sin Δ/2	2R	c= 2R sin Δ/2
P.C. 4 + 18.60						
4 + 25	1°–50'	.03199	170 ft	5.44	230 ft	7.36
4 + 50	8°–59'–30"	.15629	170 ft	26.57	230 ft	35.95
4 + 75	16°–09'	.27829	170 ft	47.31	230 ft	64.01
P.T. 4 + 88.41	20°	.34202	170 ft	58.14	230 ft	78.66

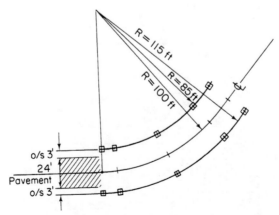

Figure 10.10 Stakeout of curve with a different radius

way line, but stakes may be set at the edge of pavement or offset from the edge of pavement. Calculations for stakeout are similar to those in Figs. 10.5 and 10.7 except that the radius of the line of stakes is used. See Fig. 10.10 for illustration.

10.3 VERTICAL CURVE

The designer of a vehicle route chooses the most advantageous slopes according to the ground surface. The design consists of a series of straight slopes connected to each other at points along the route.

Transition from one straight slope to the next is eased by a curve in a vertical plane similar to the curve between tangents in a horizontal plane. The vertical curve is a parabola with formula $y = kx^2$. It departs from one straight line at a rate that increases as the square of the horizontal distance along the straight line and returns to the next straight line at the same, but decreasing rate. Thus, it provides a smooth change in direction for vehicles, which improves passenger comfort and also provides increased sight distance for the driver. See Fig. 10.11 for illustration.

Stationing is measured in a horizontal direction as usual, and offsets to the curve from the straight lines are computed in a vertical direction. The offsets added to or subtracted from the elevations on the straight lines give the finished grades. Elevations are needed every 25 or 50 ft for stakeout.

The point at which the curve begins is the *point of vertical curvature* (PVC); the point of intersection of the two straight lines is the *point of vertical intersection* (PVI); the point at which the curve ends is the *point of vertical tangency* (PVT). The two straight lines are called the *back tangent* and the *forward tangent*.

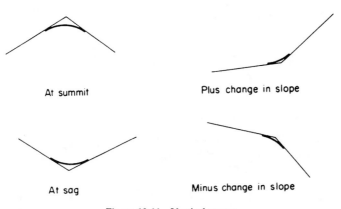

Figure 10.11   Vertical curves

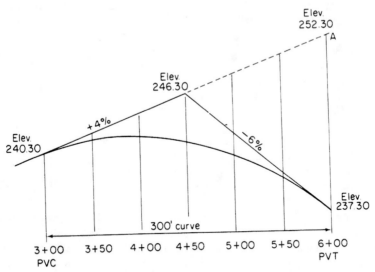

1. Distance from A to PVT is $150(4\% + 6\%) = 15$ ft
2. Number of spaces is $\frac{300}{50} = 6$
3. Vertical offsets vary directly as the square of the horizontal distance from PVC
4. If each 50 ft length is considered one unit, then offsets are to be computed at 1,2,3,4, and 5 units and 15 ft is the offset at 6 units.
5. The proportions used for determining offsets are

$$\frac{\phi_1}{1^2} = \frac{15}{6^2} \quad \text{or} \quad \phi_1 = \frac{15}{36} \times 1$$

$$\frac{\phi}{2^2} = \frac{15}{6^2} \quad \text{or} \quad \phi_2 = \frac{15}{36} \times 4 \quad \text{etc.}$$

Sta.	Back tan Elev.	Offset factor	ϕ	Elev.
3+00	240.30	0		
3+50	2.00 242.30	$\frac{1}{36} \times 15$	.42	241.88
4+00	2.00 244.30	$\frac{4}{36} \times 15$	1.67	242.63
4+50	2.00 246.30	$\frac{9}{36} \times 15$	3.75	242.55
5+00	2.00 248.30	$\frac{16}{36} \times 15$	6.66	241.64
5+50	2.00 250.30	$\frac{25}{36} \times 15$	10.42	239.88
6+00	2.00 252.30	$\frac{36}{36} \times 15$	15	237.30

Figure 10.12 Elevations for vertical curve stakeout—first method

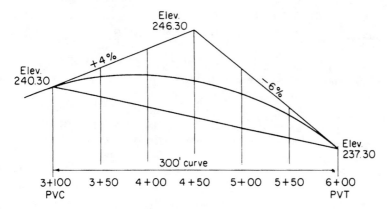

1. Elevation of a chord at the centerline through PVI is the average of PVC
   and PVT or $\dfrac{240.30 + 237.30}{2} = 238.80$

2. The vertical curve elevation at the centerline is halfway between chord
   and PVI or $\dfrac{238.80 + 246.30}{2} = 242.55$

3. The offset from PVI to curve is $246.30 - 242.55 = 3.75$

4. Offsets at all stations are proportional to the square of the station's distance from
   PVC or PVT and are calculated as fractions of the offset at PVI

Sta.	Tan. elev.	Distance from PVC or PVT	Offset factor	Offset	Elev.
3 + 00	240.30	0	0	0	240.30
3 + 50	+2.00 242.30	50	$\frac{1}{9}$	.42	241.88
4 + 00	+2.00 244.30	100	$\frac{4}{9}$	1.67	242.63
4 + 50	+2.00 246.30	150	1	3.75	242.55
5 + 00	−3.00 243.30	100	$\frac{4}{9}$	1.67	241.63
5 + 50	−3.00 240.30	50	$\frac{1}{9}$	.42	239.88
6 + 00	−3.00 237.30	100	0	0	237.30

Figure 10.13 Elevations for vertical curve stakeout—second method

Finished grades at the points to be staked are computed as follows:

1. Compute elevations on back tangent and back tangent extended at points needed for stakeout.
2. Compute the vertical distance from point A to the PVT. The distance can be determined by multiplying the rate of divergence between the two slopes by the horizontal length from PVI to PVT.
3. Compute offsets from the back tangent and back tangent extended at points needed for stakeout. These offsets vary according to the relationship $y = kx^2$ with x measured horizontally forward from the PVC and y measured in a vertical direction from the back tangent and back tangent extended. The offsets can be computed by proportions, each offset being proportional to the square of its horizontal distance from the PVC.
4. Determine elevations at the points using the offset and the elevation of the back tangent and the back tangent extended. See Fig. 10.12 for illustration.

The vertical curve may also be considered to be symmetrical about a center line through the PVI, and offsets computed for stations on both sides of the center line according to their distances from the center line. The center-line offset is determined, and other offsets are computed by using the rule that the offsets vary in proportion to the square of the distance from the PVC and PVT. See Fig. 10.13 for illustration.

PROBLEMS

1. Two streets intersect as shown here. Each has 30-ft pavement width, and the curves at the intersection have a radius of 50 ft. Determine stations of P.C. and P.T. on Proctor St. and of P.T. and P.C. on Hill St.

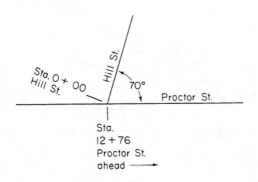

2. Two streets intersect as shown here.   Each has 36-ft pavement width, and the curves at the intersection have a radius of 50 ft.   Determine stations of P.C. and P.T. on Lincoln St. and of P.T. and P.C. on Ogden Ave.

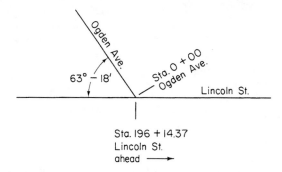

Sta. 196 + 14.37
Lincoln St.
ahead ⟶

3. Find deflection angles and distances to P.T. and to middle of circular curve from P.C. for a curve with radius of 500 ft and angle of intersection of 36°.

4. Find deflection angles and distances to quarter points and P.T. from P.C. for a curve with R = 300 ft and I = 25°.

5. A curve of 300-ft radius and 46° angle of intersection is to be staked out.   The P.I. is at station 93 + 50.   Find stations of P.C. and P.T.   Determine deflection angles and subchords for stakeout at 50-ft intervals.

6. A curve of 100-ft radius and 40° angle of intersection is to be staked out.   The P.I. is at station 4 + 55.   Find stations of P.C. and P.T.   Determine deflection angles and subchords for stakes at equal spacing not to exceed 25 ft between stakes.

7. A curve of 220-ft radius and 48° angle of intersection is to be staked out.   P.C. is at station 3 + 24.16.   Set up field notes for stakeout at 25-ft intervals.   Determine deflection angle and subchord to stakeout a point at station 4 + 09.64.

8. A curve of 250-ft radius and 29° angle of intersection is to be staked out.   P.T. is at station 13 + 17.96.   Set up field notes for stakeout at 20-ft intervals plus a point at station 12 + 51.17.

9. A curve of 160-ft radius and 38° angle of intersection is to be staked out with offsets of 1 ft from a pavement width of 30 ft.   P.I. is at station 11 + 32.43.   Set up field notes for stakeout at 10-ft intervals.

10. Calculate the vertical distance from A to PVT for the following vertical curves:

Curve length	Back tan slope	Forward tan slope
100'	+2.7%	−8.2%
250'	+4.68%	+9.34%
350'	+5.2%	+2.2%
480'	−4.8%	+6.4%
150'	−6.3%	−2.8%
220'	−7.23%	−10.52%

11. Using data from problem 10, calculate elevation of the points indicated, one for each curve of problem 10.

PVC elevation	Distance from PVC
902.45	46'
870.63	103'
842.21	126.47'
993.54	397.43'
682.26	113.62'
941.20	175.28'

12. A street has a change in slope at station 16 + 50 from +1.3% to +4.8%. The PVI at 16 + 50 is at elevation 117.36. Determine elevations at 50-ft intervals for a 200-ft vertical curve.

13. A street has a change in slope at station 37 + 00 from −7.0% to −2.3%. The PVI at station 37 + 00 is at elevation 846.35. Determine elevations at 50-ft intervals for a 400-ft vertical curve.

14. A highway has a change in slope from −1.6% to +2.1% at station 3 + 50. The PVI at station 3 + 50 is at elevation 79.28. Determine elevations at full stations for a 500-ft vertical curve.

Appendix

REFERENCE TABLES

TABLE I   Temperature Corrections for Steel Tapes per 100-Ft. Length

Temp. °F.	Correction	Temp. °F.	Correction	Temp. °F.	Correction
0	.043860	34	.021930	68	0
1	.043215	35	.021285	69	.000645
2	.042570	36	.020640	70	.001290
3	.041925	37	.019995	71	.001935
4	.041280	38	.019350	72	.002580
5	.040635	39	.018705	73	.003225
6	.039990	40	.018060	74	.003870
7	.039345	41	.017415	75	.004515
8	.038700	42	.016770	76	.005160
9	.038055	43	.016125	77	.005805
10	.037410	44	.015480	78	.006450
11	.036765	45	.014835	79	.007095
12	.036120	46	.014190	80	.007740
13	.035475	47	.013545	81	.008385
14	.034830	48	.012900	82	.009030
15	.034185	49	.012255	83	.009675
16	.033540	50	.011610	84	.010320
17	.032895	51	.010965	85	.010965
18	.032250	52	.010320	86	.011610
19	.031605	53	.009675	87	.012255
20	.030960	54	.009030	88	.012900
21	.030315	55	.008385	89	.013545
22	.029670	56	.007740	90	.014190
23	.029025	57	.007095	91	.014835
24	.028380	58	.006450	92	.015480
25	.027735	59	.005805	93	.016125
26	.027090	60	.005160	94	.016770
27	.026445	61	.004515	95	.017415
28	.025800	62	.003870	96	.018060
29	.025155	63	.003225	97	.018705
30	.024510	64	.002580	98	.019350
31	.023865	65	.001935	99	.019995
32	.023220	66	.001290	100	.020640
33	.022575	67	.000645		

Corrections are based on a coefficient of expansion of 0.00000645.

When correcting a distance measured between two points:
    Above 68° F.—add correction
    Below 68° F.—subtract correction

When preparing to set a point at a predetermined distance:
    Above 68° F.—subtract correction
    Below 68° F.—add correction

TABLE II Slope Corrections—Slope Angle Given (Subtract Correction per 100 Ft. of Slope Distance)

Slope Angle	Corr.	Slope Angle	Corr.	Slope Angle	Corr.	Slope Angle	Corr.
0°00′	.00	3°35′	.20	5°06′	.40	6°16′	.60
0°34′	.00	3°39′	.20	5°09′	.40	6°18′	.60
0°35′	.01	3°40′	.21	5°10′	.41	6°19′	.61
0°59′	.01	3°45′	.21	5°13′	.41	6°21′	.61
1°00′	.02	3°46′	.22	5°14′	.42	6°22′	.62
1°16′	.02	3°50′	.22	5°17′	.42	6°24′	.62
1°17′	.03	3°51′	.23	5°18′	.43	6°25′	.63
1°31′	.03	3°55′	.23	5°20′	.43	6°27′	.63
1°32′	.04	3°56′	.24	5°21′	.44	6°28′	.64
1°42′	.04	4°00′	.24	5°24′	.44	6°30′	.64
1°43′	.05	4°01′	.25	5°25′	.45	6°31′	.65
1°53′	.05	4°05′	.25	5°28′	.45	6°33′	.65
1°54′	.06	4°06′	.26	5°29′	.46	6°34′	.66
2°03′	.06	4°10′	.26	5°31′	.46	6°36′	.66
2°04′	.07	4°11′	.27	5°32′	.47	6°37′	.67
2°12′	.07	4°14′	.27	5°35′	.47	6°39′	.67
2°13′	.08	4°15′	.28	5°36′	.48	6°40′	.68
2°21′	.08	4°19′	.28	5°38′	.48	6°42′	.68
2°22′	.09	4°20′	.29	5°39′	.49	6°43′	.69
2°29′	.09	4°24′	.29	5°42′	.49	6°45′	.69
2°30′	.10	4°25′	.30	5°43′	.50	6°46′	.70
2°37′	.10	4°28′	.30	5°45′	.50	6°48′	.70
2°38′	.11	4°29′	.31	5°46′	.51	6°49′	.71
2°44′	.11	4°32′	.31	5°48′	.51	6°51′	.71
2°45′	.12	4°33′	.32	5°49′	.52	6°52′	.72
2°51′	.12	4°37′	.32	5°52′	.52	6°54′	.72
2°52′	.13	4°38′	.33	5°53′	.53	6°55′	.73
2°58′	.13	4°41′	.33	5°55′	.53	6°57′	.73
2°59′	.14	4°42′	.34	5°56′	.54	6°58′	.74
3°05′	.14	4°45′	.34	5°58′	.54	6°59′	.74
3°06′	.15	4°46′	.35	5°59′	.55	7°00′	.75
3°11′	.15	4°49′	.35	6°02′	.55	7°02′	.75
3°12′	.16	4°50′	.36	6°03′	.56	7°03′	.76
3°17′	.16	4°53′	.36	6°05′	.56	7°05′	.76
3°18′	.17	4°54′	.37	6°06′	.57	7°06′	.77
3°23′	.17	4°57′	.37	6°08′	.57	7°08′	.77
3°24′	.18	4°58′	.38	6°09′	.58	7°09′	.78
3°29′	.18	5°01′	.38	6°11′	.58	7°11′	.78
3°30′	.19	5°02′	.39	6°12′	.59	7°12′	.79
3°34′	.19	5°05′	.39	6°15′	.59	7°13′	.79

TABLE II cont.

Slope Angle	Corr.	Slope Angle	Corr.	Slope Angle	Corr.	Slope Angle	Corr.
7°14′	.80	8°02′	.98	8°46′	1.17	9°26′	1.35
7°16′	.80	8°03′	.99	8°47′	1.17	9°27′	1.36
7°17′	.81	8°05′	.99	8°48′	1.18	9°28′	1.36
7°19′	.81	8°06′	1.00	8°49′	1.18	9°29′	1.37
7°20′	.82	8°07′	1.00	8°50′	1.19	9°30′	1.37
7°21′	.82	8°08′	1.01	8°51′	1.19	9°31′	1.38
7°22′	.83	8°10′	1.01	8°52′	1.20	9°32′	1.38
7°24′	.83	8°11′	1.02	8°54′	1.20	9°33′	1.39
7°25′	.84	8°12′	1.02	8°55′	1.21	9°34′	1.39
7°27′	.84	8°13′	1.03	8°56′	1.21	9°35′	1.40
7°28′	.85	8°15′	1.03	8°57′	1.22	9°36′	1.40
7°29′	.85	8°16′	1.04	8°58′	1.22	9°37′	1.41
7°30′	.86	8°17′	1.04	8°59′	1.23	9°38′	1.41
7°32′	.86	8°18′	1.05	9°00′	1.23	9°39′	1.42
7°33′	.87	8°19′	1.05	9°01′	1.24	9°40′	1.42
7°35′	.87	8°20′	1.06	9°03′	1.24	9°41′	1.43
7°36′	.88	8°22′	1.06	9°04′	1.25	9°42′	1.43
7°37′	.88	8°23′	1.07	9°05′	1.25	9°43′	1.44
7°38′	.89	8°24′	1.07	9°06′	1.26	9°45′	1.44
7°40′	.89	8°25′	1.08	9°07′	1.26	9°46′	1.45
7°41′	.90	8°26′	1.08	9°08′	1.27	9°47′	1.45
7°42′	.90	8°27′	1.09	9°09′	1.27	9°48′	1.46
7°43′	.91	8°29′	1.09	9°10′	1.28	9°49′	1.46
7°45′	.91	8°30′	1.10	9°11′	1.28	9°50′	1.47
7°46′	.92	8°31′	1.10	9°12′	1.29	9°51′	1.47
7°47′	.92	8°32′	1.11	9°13′	1.29	9°52′	1.48
7°48′	.93	8°33′	1.11	9°14′	1.30	9°53′	1.48
7°50′	.93	8°34′	1.12	9°15′	1.30	9°54′	1.49
7°51′	.94	8°36′	1.12	9°16′	1.31	9°55′	1.49
7°52′	.94	8°37′	1.13	9°18′	1.31	9°56′	1.50
7°53′	.95	8°38′	1.13	9°19′	1.32	9°57′	1.50
7°55′	.95	8°39′	1.14	9°20′	1.32	9°58′	1.51
7°56′	.96	8°40′	1.14	9°21′	1.33	9°59′	1.51
7°57′	.96	8°41′	1.15	9°22′	1.33	10°00′	1.52
7°58′	.97	8°42′	1.15	9°23′	1.34		
8°00′	.97	8°43′	1.16	9°24′	1.34		
8°01′	.98	8°45′	1.16	9°25′	1.35		

Multiply correction by slope distance/100 and subtract the result from the slope distance.

Example: Find horizontal distance for 230.50 ft. measured on a slope of 7°36′.

Answer: correction $= .88 \times \dfrac{230.50}{100} = 2.03$ ft.

horizontal distance $= 230.50 - 2.03 = 228.47$ ft.

TABLE III Stadia Reduction

Stadia reduction involves determining H, V, and Elevation from the stadia intercept and the vertical angle as read and recorded in the field. The table contains horizontal distances and differences in elevation for a stadia intercept of 1.00 and vertical angles from 0° to 16°. Each value in the table must be multiplied by the stadia intercept to obtain the appropriate distance and difference in elevation. The values thus determined are H and V as shown in Figures 7-4 and 7-5. H is the horizontal distance and V is used to determine elevation.

Minutes	0°		1°		2°		3°	
	Hor. dist.	Diff. elev.	Hor. dist.	Diff. elev.	Hor. dist.	Diff. elev.	Hor. dist.	Diff. elev.
0.........	100.00	0.00	99.97	1.74	99.88	3.49	99.73	5.23
2.........	100.00	0.06	99.97	1.80	99.87	3.55	99.72	5.28
4.........	100.00	0.12	99.97	1.86	99.87	3.60	99.71	5.34
6.........	100.00	0.17	99.96	1.92	99.87	3.66	99.71	5.40
8.........	100.00	0.23	99.96	1.98	99.86	3.72	99.70	5.46
10.........	100.00	0.29	99.96	2.04	99.86	3.78	99.69	5.52
12.........	100.00	0.35	99.96	2.09	99.85	3.84	99.69	5.57
14.........	100.00	0.41	99.95	2.15	99.85	3.90	99.68	5.63
16.........	100.00	0.47	99.95	2.21	99.84	3.95	99.68	5.69
18.........	100.00	0.52	99.95	2.27	99.84	4.01	99.67	5.75
20.........	100.00	0.58	99.95	2.33	99.83	4.07	99.66	5.80
22.........	100.00	0.64	99.94	2.38	99.83	4.13	99.66	5.86
24.........	100.00	0.70	99.94	2.44	99.82	4.18	99.65	5.92
26.........	99.99	0.76	99.94	2.50	99.82	4.24	99.64	5.98
28.........	99.99	0.81	99.93	2.56	99.81	4.30	99.63	6.04
30.........	99.99	0.87	99.93	2.62	99.81	4.36	99.63	6.09
32.........	99.99	0.93	99.93	2.67	99.80	4.42	99.62	6.15
34.........	99.99	0.99	99.93	2.73	99.80	4.48	99.62	6.21
36.........	99.99	1.05	99.92	2.79	99.79	4.53	99.61	6.27
38.........	99.99	1.11	99.92	2.85	99.79	4.59	99.60	6.33
40.........	99.99	1.16	99.92	2.91	99.78	4.65	99.59	6.38
42.........	99.99	1.22	99.91	2.97	99.78	4.71	99.59	6.44
44.........	99.98	1.28	99.91	3.02	99.77	4.76	99.58	6.50
46.........	99.98	1.34	99.90	3.08	99.77	4.82	99.57	6.56
48.........	99.98	1.40	99.90	3.14	99.76	4.88	99.56	6.61
50.........	99.98	1.45	99.90	3.20	99.76	4.94	99.56	6.67
52.........	99.98	1.51	99.89	3.26	99.75	4.99	99.55	6.73
54.........	99.98	1.57	99.89	3.31	99.74	5.05	99.54	6.78
56.........	99.97	1.63	99.89	3.37	99.74	5.11	99.53	6.84
58.........	99.97	1.69	99.88	3.43	99.73	5.17	99.52	6.90
60.........	99.97	1.74	99.88	3.49	99.73	5.23	99.51	6.96

TABLE III cont.

Stadia Reduction

Minutes	4°		5°		6°		7°	
	Hor. dist.	Diff. elev.	Hor. dist.	Diff. elev.	Hor. dist.	Diff. elev.	Hor. dist.	Diff. elev.
0.........	99.51	6.96	99.24	8.68	98.91	10.40	98.51	12.10
2.........	99.51	7.02	99.23	8.74	98.90	10.45	98.50	12.15
4.........	99.50	7.07	99.22	8.80	98.88	10.51	98.48	12.21
6.........	99.49	7.13	99.21	8.85	98.87	10.57	98.47	12.26
8.........	99.48	7.19	99.20	8.91	98.86	10.62	98.46	12.32
10.........	99.47	7.25	99.19	8.97	98.85	10.68	98.44	12.38
12.........	99.46	7.30	99.18	9.03	98.83	10.74	98.43	12.43
14.........	99.46	7.36	99.17	9.08	98.82	10.79	98.41	12.49
16.........	99.45	7.42	99.16	9.14	98.81	10.85	98.40	12.55
18.........	99.44	7.48	99.15	9.20	98.80	10.91	98.39	12.60
20.........	99.43	7.53	99.14	9.25	98.78	10.96	98.37	12.66
22.........	99.42	7.59	99.13	9.31	98.77	11.02	98.36	12.72
24.........	99.41	7.65	99.11	9.37	98.76	11.08	98.34	12.77
26.........	99.40	7.71	99.10	9.43	98.74	11.13	98.33	12.83
28.........	99.39	7.76	99.09	9.48	98.73	11.19	98.31	12.88
30.........	99.38	7.82	99.08	9.54	98.72	11.25	98.29	12.94
32.........	99.38	7.88	99.07	9.60	98.71	11.30	98.28	13.00
34.........	99.37	7.94	99.06	9.65	98.69	11.36	98.27	13.05
36.........	99.36	7.99	99.05	9.71	98.68	11.42	98.25	13.11
38.........	99.35	8.05	99.04	9.77	98.67	11.47	98.24	13.17
40.........	99.34	8.11	99.03	9.83	98.65	11.53	98.22	13.22
42.........	99.33	8.17	99.01	9.88	98.64	11.59	98.20	13.28
44.........	99.32	8.22	99.00	9.94	98.63	11.64	98.19	13.33
46.........	99.31	8.28	98.99	10.00	98.61	11.70	98.17	13.39
48.........	99.30	8.34	98.98	10.05	98.60	11.76	98.16	13.45
50.........	99.29	8.40	98.97	10.11	98.58	11.81	98.14	13.50
52.........	99.28	8.45	98.96	10.17	98.57	11.87	98.13	13.56
54.........	99.27	8.51	98.94	10.22	98.56	11.93	98.11	13.61
56.........	99.26	8.57	98.93	10.28	98.54	11.98	98.10	13.67
58.........	99.25	8.63	98.92	10.34	98.53	12.04	98.08	13.73
60.........	99.24	8.68	98.91	10.40	98.51	12.10	98.06	13.78

TABLE III   cont.

Stadia Reduction

Minutes	8°		9°		10°		11°	
	Hor. dist.	Diff. elev.	Hor. dist.	Diff. elev.	Hor. dist.	Diff. elev.	Hor. dist.	Diff. elev.
0.........	98.06	13.78	97.55	15.45	96.98	17.10	96.36	18.73
2.........	98.05	13.84	97.53	15.51	96.96	17.16	96.34	18.78
4.........	98.03	13.89	97.52	15.56	96.94	17.21	96.32	18.84
6.........	98.01	13.95	97.50	15.62	96.92	17.26	96.29	18.89
8.........	98.00	14.01	97.48	15.67	96.90	17.32	96.27	18.95
10.........	97.98	14.06	97.46	15.73	96.88	17.37	96.25	19.00
12.........	97.97	14.12	97.44	15.78	96.86	17.43	96.23	19.05
14.........	97.95	14.17	97.43	15.84	96.84	17.48	96.21	19.11
16.........	97.93	14.23	97.41	15.89	96.82	17.54	96.18	19.16
18.........	97.92	14.28	97.39	15.95	96.80	17.59	96.16	19.21
20.........	97.90	14.34	97.37	16.00	96.78	17.65	96.14	19.27
22.........	97.88	14.40	97.35	16.06	96.76	17.70	96.12	19.32
24.........	97.87	14.45	97.33	16.11	96.74	17.76	96.09	19.38
26.........	97.85	14.51	97.31	16.17	96.72	17.81	96.07	19.43
28.........	97.83	14.56	97.29	16.22	96.70	17.86	96.05	19.48
30.........	97.82	14.62	97.28	16.28	96.68	17.92	96.03	19.54
32.........	97.80	14.67	97.26	16.33	96.66	17.97	96.00	19.59
34.........	97.78	14.73	97.24	16.39	96.64	18.03	95.98	19.64
36.........	97.76	14.79	97.22	16.44	96.62	18.08	95.96	19.70
38.........	97.75	14.84	97.20	16.50	96.60	18.14	95.93	19.75
40.........	97.73	14.90	97.18	16.55	96.57	18.19	95.91	19.80
42.........	97.71	14.95	97.16	16.61	96.55	18.24	95.89	19.86
44.........	97.69	15.01	97.14	16.66	96.53	18.30	95.86	19.91
46.........	97.68	15.06	97.12	16.72	96.51	18.35	95.84	19.96
48.........	97.66	15.12	97.10	16.77	96.49	18.41	95.82	20.02
50.........	97.64	15.17	97.08	16.83	96.47	18.46	95.79	20.07
52.........	97.62	15.23	97.06	16.88	96.45	18.51	95.77	20.12
54.........	97.61	15.28	97.04	16.94	96.42	18.57	95.75	20.18
56.........	97.59	15.34	97.02	16.99	96.40	18.62	95.72	20.23
58.........	97.57	15.40	97.00	17.05	96.38	18.68	95.70	20.28
60.........	97.55	15.45	96.98	17.10	96.36	18.73	95.68	20.34

TABLE III cont.

Stadia Reduction

Minutes	12°		13°		14°		15°	
	Hor. dist.	Diff. elev.	Hor. dist.	Diff. elev.	Hor. dist.	Diff. elev.	Hor. dist.	Diff. elev.
0.........	95.68	20.34	94.94	21.92	94.15	23.47	93.30	25.00
2.........	95.65	20.39	94.91	21.97	94.12	23.52	93.27	25.05
4.........	95.63	20.44	94.89	22.02	94.09	23.58	93.24	25.10
6.........	95.61	20.50	94.86	22.08	94.07	23.63	93.21	25.15
8.........	95.58	20.55	94.84	22.13	94.04	23.68	93.18	25.20
10.........	95.56	20.60	94.81	22.18	94.01	23.73	93.16	25.25
12.........	95.53	20.66	94.79	22.23	93.98	23.78	93.13	25.30
14.........	95.51	20.71	94.76	22.28	93.95	23.83	93.10	25.35
16.........	95.49	20.76	94.73	22.34	93.93	23.88	93.07	25.40
18.........	95.46	20.81	94.71	22.39	93.90	23.93	93.04	25.45
20.........	95.44	20.87	94.68	22.44	93.87	23.99	93.01	25.50
22.........	95.41	20.92	94.66	22.49	93.84	24.04	92.98	25.55
24.........	95.39	20.97	94.63	22.54	93.81	24.09	92.95	25.60
26.........	95.36	21.03	94.60	22.60	93.79	24.14	92.92	25.65
28.........	95.34	21.08	94.58	22.65	93.76	24.19	92.89	25.70
30.........	95.32	21.13	94.55	22.70	93.73	24.24	92.86	25.75
32.........	95.29	21.18	94.52	22.75	93.70	24.29	92.83	25.80
34.........	95.27	21.24	94.50	22.80	93.67	24.34	92.80	25.85
36.........	95.24	21.29	94.47	22.85	93.65	24.39	92.77	25.90
38.........	95.22	21.34	94.44	22.91	93.62	24.44	92.74	25.95
40.........	95.19	21.39	94.42	22.96	93.59	24.49	92.71	26.00
42.........	95.17	21.45	94.39	23.01	93.56	24.55	92.68	26.05
44.........	95.14	21.50	94.36	23.06	93.53	24.60	92.65	26.10
46.........	95.12	21.55	94.34	23.11	93.50	24.65	92.62	26.15
48.........	95.09	21.60	94.31	23.16	93.47	24.70	92.59	26.20
50.........	95.07	21.66	94.28	23.22	93.45	24.75	92.56	26.25
52.........	95.04	21.71	94.26	23.27	93.42	24.80	92.53	26.30
54.........	95.02	21.76	94.23	23.32	93.39	24.85	92.49	26.35
56.........	94.99	21.81	94.20	23.37	93.36	24.90	92.46	26.40
58.........	94.97	21.87	94.17	23.42	93.33	24.95	92.43	26.45
60.........	94.94	21.92	94.15	23.47	93.90	25.00	92.40	26.50

TABLE IV   Conversion from Hundredths of a Foot to Inches and Fractions

Ft	In.	Ft	In.	Ft	In.	Ft	In.
.01	$\frac{1}{8}$	.26	$3\frac{1}{8}$	.51	$6\frac{1}{8}$	.76	$9\frac{1}{8}$
.02	$\frac{1}{4}$	.27	$\frac{1}{4}$	.52	$\frac{1}{4}$	.77	$\frac{1}{4}$
.03	$\frac{3}{8}$	.28	$\frac{3}{8}$	.53	$\frac{3}{8}$	.78	$\frac{3}{8}$
.04	$\frac{1}{2}$	.29	$\frac{1}{2}$	.54	$\frac{1}{2}$	.79	$\frac{1}{2}$
.05	$\frac{5}{8}$	.30	$\frac{5}{8}$	.55	$\frac{5}{8}$	.80	$\frac{5}{8}$
.06	$\frac{3}{4}$	.31	$\frac{3}{4}$	.56	$\frac{3}{4}$	.81	$\frac{3}{4}$
.07	$\frac{7}{8}$	.32	$\frac{7}{8}$	.57	$\frac{7}{8}$	.82	$\frac{7}{8}$
.08	1	.33	4	.58	7	.83	10
.09	$\frac{1}{8}$	.34	$\frac{1}{8}$	.59	$\frac{1}{8}$	.84	$\frac{1}{8}$
.10	$\frac{1}{4}$	.35	$\frac{1}{4}$	.60	$\frac{1}{4}$	.85	$\frac{1}{4}$
.11	$\frac{3}{8}$	.36	$\frac{3}{8}$	.61	$\frac{3}{8}$	.86	$\frac{3}{8}$
.12	$\frac{1}{2}$	.37	$\frac{1}{2}$	.62	$\frac{1}{2}$	.87	$\frac{1}{2}$
.13	$\frac{1}{2}$	.38	$\frac{1}{2}$	.63	$\frac{1}{2}$	.88	$\frac{1}{2}$
.14	$\frac{5}{8}$	.39	$\frac{5}{8}$	.64	$\frac{5}{8}$	.89	$\frac{5}{8}$
.15	$\frac{3}{4}$	.40	$\frac{3}{4}$	.65	$\frac{3}{4}$	.90	$\frac{3}{4}$
.16	$\frac{7}{8}$	.41	$\frac{7}{8}$	.66	$\frac{7}{8}$	.91	$\frac{7}{8}$
.17	2	.42	5	.67	8	.92	11
.18	$\frac{1}{8}$	.43	$\frac{1}{8}$	.68	$\frac{1}{8}$	.93	$\frac{1}{8}$
.19	$\frac{1}{4}$	.44	$\frac{1}{4}$	.69	$\frac{1}{4}$	.94	$\frac{1}{4}$
.20	$\frac{3}{8}$	.45	$\frac{3}{8}$	.70	$\frac{3}{8}$	.95	$\frac{3}{8}$
.21	$\frac{1}{2}$	.46	$\frac{1}{2}$	.71	$\frac{1}{2}$	.96	$\frac{1}{2}$
.22	$\frac{5}{8}$	.47	$\frac{5}{8}$	.72	$\frac{5}{8}$	.97	$\frac{5}{8}$
.23	$\frac{3}{4}$	.48	$\frac{3}{4}$	.73	$\frac{3}{4}$	.98	$\frac{3}{4}$
.24	$\frac{7}{8}$	.49	$\frac{7}{8}$	.74	$\frac{7}{8}$	.99	$\frac{7}{8}$
.25	3	.50	6	.75	9	1.00	12

TABLE V   Lengths of Circular Arcs for Radius of 1.0

Sec.	Length	Min.	Length.	Deg.	Length.	Deg.	Length.
1	.0000048	1	.0002909	1	.0174533	61	1.0646508
2	.0000097	2	.0005818	2	.0349066	62	1.0821041
3	.0000145	3	.0008727	3	.0523599	63	1.0995574
4	.0000194	4	.0011636	4	.0698132	64	1.1170107
5	.0000242	5	.0014544	5	.0872665	65	1.1344640
6	.0000291	6	.0017453	6	.1047198	66	1.1519173
7	.0000339	7	.0020362	7	.1221730	67	1.1693706
8	.0000388	8	.0023271	8	.1396263	68	1.1868239
9	.0000436	9	.0026180	9	.1570796	69	1.2042772
10	.0000485	10	.0029089	10	.1745329	70	1.2217305
11	.0000533	11	.0031998	11	.1919862	71	1.2391838
12	.0000582	12	.0034907	12	.2094395	72	1.2566371
13	.0000630	13	.0037815	13	.2268928	73	1.2740904
14	.0000679	14	.0040724	14	.2443461	74	1.2915436
15	.0000727	15	.0043633	15	.2617994	75	1.3089969
16	.0000776	16	.0046542	16	.2792527	76	1.3264502
17	.0000824	17	.0049451	17	.2967060	77	1.3439035
18	.0000873	18	.0052360	18	.3141593	78	1.3613568
19	.0000921	19	.0055269	19	.3316126	79	1.3788101
20	.0000970	20	.0058178	20	.3490659	80	1.3962634
21	.0001018	21	.0061087	21	.3665191	81	1.4137167
22	.0001067	22	.0063995	22	.3839724	82	1.4311700
23	.0001115	23	.0066904	23	.4014257	83	1.4486233
24	.0001164	24	.0069813	24	.4188790	84	1.4660766
25	.0001212	25	.0072722	25	.4363323	85	1.4835299
26	.0001261	26	.0075631	26	.4537856	86	1.5009832
27	.0001309	27	.0078540	27	.4712389	87	1.5184364
28	.0001357	28	.0081449	28	.4886922	88	1.5358897
29	.0001406	29	.0084358	29	.5061455	89	1.5533430
30	.0001454	30	.0087266	30	.5235988	90	1.5707963
31	.0001503	31	.0090175	31	.5410521	91	1.5882496
32	.0001551	32	.0093084	32	.5585054	92	1.6057029
33	.0001600	33	.0095993	33	.5759587	93	1.6231562
34	.0001648	34	.0098902	34	.5934119	94	1.6406095
35	.0001697	35	.0101811	35	.6108652	95	1.6580628
36	.0001745	36	.0104720	36	.6283185	96	1.6755161
37	.0001794	37	.0107629	37	.6457718	97	1.6929694
38	.0001842	38	.0110538	38	.6632251	98	1.7104227
39	.0001891	39	.0113446	39	.6806784	99	1.7278760
40	.0001939	40	.0116355	40	.6981317	100	1.7453293
41	.0001988	41	.0119264	41	.7155850	101	1.7627825
42	.0002036	42	.0122173	42	.7330383	102	1.7802358
43	.0002085	43	.0125082	43	.7504916	103	1.7976891
44	.0002133	44	.0127991	44	.7679449	104	1.8151424
45	.0002182	45	.0130900	45	.7853982	105	1.8325957
46	.0002230	46	.0133809	46	.8028515	106	1.8500490
47	.0002279	47	.0136717	47	.8203047	107	1.8675023
48	.0002327	48	.0139626	48	.8377580	108	1.8849556
49	.0002376	49	.0142535	49	.8552113	109	1.9024089
50	.0002424	50	.0145444	50	.8726646	110	1.9198622
51	.0002473	51	.0148353	51	.8901179	111	1.9373155
52	.0002521	52	.0151262	52	.9075712	112	1.9547688
53	.0002570	53	.0154171	53	.9250245	113	1.9722221
54	.0002618	54	.0157080	54	.9424778	114	1.9896753
55	.0002666	55	.0159989	55	.9599311	115	2.0071286
56	.0002715	56	.0162897	56	.9773844	116	2.0245819
57	.0002763	57	.0165806	57	.9948377	117	2.0420352
58	.0002812	58	.0168715	58	1.0122910	118	2.0594885
59	.0002860	59	.0171624	59	1.0297443	119	2.0769418
60	.0002909	60	.0174533	60	1.0471976	120	2.0943951

Add values for degrees, minutes, and seconds of the central angle, and multiply the total by the radius.

Example:

Find L for a circular curve with $\Delta = 66°18'24''$ and R = 400 ft.

Answer: 1.1519173
.0052360
.0001164

1.1572697 × 400 = 462.91 ft.

INDEX

A

Accidental errors, 23, 24, 225
Accuracy, 23
Accuracy standards, 27
Alidade, 100
American type transit, 99, 134
Anchor bolts, 217
Angle:
  average, 123
  clockwise, 97
  counterclockwise, 97
  deflection, 96
  field check, 154
  of intersection, 266
  left, 96
  right, 96
  vertical, 97
  zenith, 97
Architect's drawings, 205
Arithmetic check, 75
As built drawings, 3
Average angle, 123

Average end area, 260
A vernier, 100
Azimuth, defined, 7

B

Back bearing, defined, 12
Backsight, angles, 112
Backsight, angles, defined, 96
Backsight, leveling, defined, 67
Back tangent, 277
Ballast, 254
Base, 255
Base plate, 69
Batter board, 215, 247
Bearing, 110, 148
Bearing, defined, 7
Bench mark, 211
Bench mark, defined, 6, 66

M

N

O

P

Q

R

S